Eat Right, Balance Hormones

Pippa Campbell is an experienced functional hormone nutritionist, weight loss practitioner, certified nutrigenomics practitioner and qualified naturopath. She is a certified metabolic balance coach, registered with the Institute of Functional Medicine and Association of Naturopathic Practitioners. She has over 15 years' experience specialising in female health and weight loss. She is the author of the bestselling book, *Eat Right, Lose Weight*.

PIPPA CAMPBELL

Eat Right, Balance Hormones

Simple strategies and delicious food for healthy hormones

Lagom

First published in the UK by Lagom
An imprint of Bonnier Books UK
4th Floor, Victoria House
Bloomsbury Square
London WC1B 4DA

Owned by Bonnier Books
Sveavägen 56, Stockholm, Sweden

Trade Paperback – 9781785121432
Ebook – 9781785121449
Audio – 9781785123009

All rights reserved. No part of the publication may be reproduced, stored in a retrieval system, transmitted or circulated in any form or by any means, electronic, mechanical, photocopying, recording or otherwise, without prior permission in writing of the publisher.

A CIP catalogue of this book is available from the British Library.

Designed by Envy Design Ltd
Printed and bound by Clays Ltd, Elcograf S.p.A.
1 3 5 7 9 10 8 6 4 2

Copyright © Pippa Campbell, 2024

Pippa Campbell has asserted her moral right to be identified as the author of this Work in accordance with the Copyright, Designs and Patents Act 1988.

MIX
Paper | Supporting responsible forestry
FSC® C018072

Every reasonable effort has been made to trace copyright holders of material reproduced in this book, but if any have been inadvertently overlooked the publishers would be glad to hear from them.

Lagom is an imprint of Bonnier Books UK
www.bonnierbooks.co.uk

The information in this book is not a substitute for medical advice. If you know or suspect you have a health condition, it is recommended that you seek medical advice from your GP before embarking on any dietary change. All efforts have been made to ensure the accuracy of the information contained in this book as of the date of publication. The author and publisher shall have no liability or for any loss, damage or injury incurred, or alleged to have incurred, directly or indirectly, by the information or suggestions contained in this book.

To all the women I know, and those I don't

CONTENTS

Prologue	ix
Introduction	1
PART ONE: WHAT'S HAPPENING TO ME?	**13**
Chapter 1: Solving the Hormone Puzzle	15
Chapter 2: The Six Keys to Hormone Health	35
PART TWO: THE PCM HORMONE BALANCE PLAN	**45**
Chapter 3: The Food Framework	47
Chapter 4: Healthy Hormone Habits	65
PART THREE: SOLVING YOUR SYMPTOMS	**87**
Chapter 5: Adrenal Dysfunction	97
Chapter 6: Progesterone Drop	117
Chapter 7: Oestrogen Dominance	135
Chapter 8: Oestrogen Deficiency	153
Chapter 9: Androgen Dominance	171

Chapter 10: Androgen Deficiency	183
Chapter 11: Low Thyroid Function	197
Chapter 12: Blood Sugar Dysregulation	215
PART FOUR: THE PCM HORMONE BALANCE RECIPES	**235**
Breakfast	237
Lunch	251
Dinner	266
Side dishes	293
Sauces and dressings	301
Cakes and puddings	303
Teas	316
Endnotes	319
Index	341
Acknowledgements	355

PROLOGUE

I blamed my first perimenopause symptoms – feeling a little more tired and a lot less resilient to stress – on a heavy workload. It was during lockdown and there were so many women asking to have clinic consultations that I found myself on video calls for 12 hours a day, most days. But I just didn't feel like myself any more.

A few months later, I started to wake up a couple of times each night. One day, I realised that my nipples were sore, in a similar way to the let-down feeling when you start breastfeeding. I caught myself being snappier with my husband James and my two (then) teenaged children. And I noticed I was feeling anxious, even when I was supposed to be relaxing in the evenings. I started having heart palpitations too.

Having helped hundreds of women in their thirties, forties and fifties, I soon connected the dots of my symptoms. I thought, *Oh I'm 48, I know what's going on! It's the perimenopause.* When I looked back, I realised that the fatigue and stress symptoms must have been the beginning of my hormones changing.

My training as a functional nutritionist taught me that what we eat is crucial not only to how we feel but also to our hormones. I'm qualified in naturopathy, which, like functional medicine, has helped me to see hormones, mind and body as a joined-up system. I'm trained in genetic testing (nutrigenomics) and in analysing hormone tests, which we use together in clinic to get a full picture of how a woman makes, uses and eliminates her hormones. Having looked at hundreds of tests, I've learnt that we inherit hormonal patterns, how our genetics determine our hormones, but that food and lifestyle have a huge impact on how those patterns play out, how we feel and the symptoms we develop.

When I realised the likely cause of my symptoms, I did a month-long cycle-mapping hormone test with a company called DUTCH. You pee on blotting paper each day and send them off for analysis, and the report gives you a total picture of the ups and downs of your hormones. This confirmed that I was in the early stages of perimenopause. The picture was becoming clearer: by this time, my cycle had gone down from 26 days to 24 or 25. The test showed that was ovulating early, on day 10 instead of my usual day 14. (Ovulating earlier and a shorter cycle are classic signs of perimenopause.) I had also begun to get PMS symptoms, just like the ones I'd had in my twenties.

I knew what I had to do to feel better – I had to go back to basics. My diet was good but I began to be more consistent in what I was eating. I tweaked my supplements too. I became very strict about stopping emails and being offline from 8pm, started meditating and doing breathwork.

In the space of just a month I felt different – and I've continued to feel better. But I'm always keeping an eye on my symptoms because until menopause, women's hormones continue to change. I know I can't get back the hormone levels of my twenties, so my aim is to have the best hormones for my age, which is what my DUTCH test now shows. Best of all, I feel like myself again, with a sharp brain and the energy to tackle life.

I know that how I feel now is down to how I eat, exercise and look after myself. I'm currently not on HRT because, so far, the natural route is working for me (I will take HRT if I need it). But I've seen that whether a woman takes HRT or not, she still needs to support her body with good food and habits during this transition.

At the same time as working on my own hormones, I've continued to research the nutrition and lifestyle habits that can help my clients in midlife too. Because I love to cook, I've created delicious dishes that help support hormones. Together with my team, I've consulted with thousands of women aged 35 to 60, most of whom feel at the mercy of their hormones. We have tried and tested many things to find what works – you'll see some clients' stories dotted through these pages. Now I've put everything I've learnt in this book, making it a one-stop hormone-balance bible.

I know that some of you are barely coping right now. I have heard from hundreds of women who aren't sleeping, who can't think, who feel at the end of their tether, who don't feel like themselves any more. Please be assured that the years leading up to menopause do not have to be marred by symptoms. This book explains all the things you can do to get back to being yourself again. And that if you're not yet at this stage, some small changes now will make sure this transition is a smooth one.

If you look after yourself with good food and habits, you can spend these years feeling energetic and clear-headed, able to work and be a good parent, daughter and/or partner, pain-free so you can exercise, feeling positive so you can have good relationships and just get on with living. If you're one of the millions of midlife women in the world, whatever stage you're at, this book is for you.

Much love,

Pippa

INTRODUCTION

When you were in your early twenties, did you imagine that life could be this complicated? So many of the women who I see in clinic are at the peak of their career while navigating life admin and carrying the emotional and practical load of children and the household. For women in midlife, every day can feel like one of those obstacle courses on a TV show, a never-ending round of challenges: child taking exams! Parent needing more care! Going for promotion at work!

Clients often tell me that they were coping with the juggle – but then, suddenly, in their late thirties or during their forties, they weren't. The hormonal changes of the perimenopause can be the last straw in a busy life, the thing that wipes women out.

In your twenties and thirties, you may have got away with not looking after yourself: going to bed late, not doing enough exercise, fuelled by carbs, coffee and maybe wine too. Now, suddenly, you find that you are in bed by 9pm but that you're still tired; that eating sugar gives you an energy slump; a glass of wine has you waking up at 3am and more than two coffees leaves you jangling. You feel bloated, you've got headaches and maybe your eczema or acne has come back too.

It can feel as if your brain power, energy and/or sex drive have just disappeared. What makes this more complicated is that very often, women don't associate these symptoms with hormone changes – at least, not at first. They may think they are too young – but if you consider that the average age of menopause is 51, and that hormone changes happen in the 10 to 15 years prior to that, for some women these changes will start as early as 35 (though for most it's from the age of 40).

Women also often blame their symptoms on stress, as I did at first, or on other life challenges. This is totally understandable, as a lot of the earliest symptoms of perimenopause, even before periods change, are so non-specific.

Feeling tired? You may assume you've been overdoing it.

Not sleeping? You blame work stress.

Losing your temper? Children are at a tricky age.

Getting bad PMS symptoms? It happens.

Irritable or even ragey with your family or colleagues? Well, they're so ANNOYING!

Putting on weight or not being able to lose weight? You're still post baby or you haven't got time to exercise or you're too hungry to eat less.

Because it's so common to have babies in our late thirties and early forties now, it may be hard to differentiate between feeling exhausted from lack of sleep or running around during your baby's toddler years from hormonal shifts.

THE MANY AND VARIED SYMPTOMS OF PERIMENOPAUSE AND MENOPAUSE

Breast pain and tenderness
Breast swelling
Heart palpitations
Increased blood pressure
Increased LDL cholesterol
Hot flushes
Night sweats
Dry skin
Itching
Thinning skin
Acne
Face and body hair
Hair thinning
Weight gain
Fat around the middle
Visceral fat
Headaches
Noise sensitivity
Hearing changes
Tinnitus
Dry eyes
Dry or burning mouth
Joint soreness, stiffness or swelling
Restless legs
Dizziness
Insomnia
Anxiety
Panic attacks
Poor memory
Difficulty concentrating

Low mood
Mood swings
Irritability
Rage
Loss of confidence
Brain fog
Feeling 'flat'
Overwhelm
Loss of sex drive
Shorter or longer menstruation
Shorter or longer cycles
Irregular cycles
Not ovulating
Bleeding between periods
Clotting
Heavy bleeds and flooding
Painful periods
PMS
Bone weakness (osteopenia and osteoporosis)
Fatigue
Poor digestion
Acid reflux
Bloating
Vaginal dryness
Vaginal atrophy (drying and thinning of the vaginal walls)
Needing to pee more frequently
Needing to pee urgently
UTIs

Women can often assume their psychological symptoms are down to them not trying hard enough to keep it together or to focus. They blame themselves for not getting things done. When I tell women that their symptoms are down to hormones, they're often surprised and relieved. It's reassuring to discover that you're not imagining things or losing your grip on reality, that there is a concrete and biological cause for how you're feeling.

Welcome to the peri grey zone

While a lot of GPs are better educated than ever about perimenopause, not all of them are. Even the most clued up often don't know that women get symptoms even before their periods change. A lot of clients come to clinic having already seen their GP about their symptoms. Often, either the issue of perimenopause hasn't come up or they've been told that they're not in perimenopause when they are.

This happened to me. I made an appointment with my gynaecologist before I had any cycle changes. I knew that my symptoms – anxiety, heart palpitations, having to get up a couple of times a night, breast pain – were down to perimenopause. Despite that, she told me that I couldn't possibly be in perimenopause because I was having regular periods.

I've given this time before your cycle changes a name: the peri grey zone. It's a grey zone because it can be unclear whether your symptoms are due to perimenopause or lifestyle factors and stressors. But it's also a grey zone because you just don't feel right.

This can be a confusing time. For example, people don't know that heart palpitations, a common symptom, can be down to the drop in progesterone that's one of the first changes of perimenopause. Clients have told me that they've gone to their GP terrified they were having a heart attack. The GP has sent them to be tested for heart problems, the results have come back negative, so the GP has told them that the palpitations must be down to stress. (N.B. If you have heart palpitations, do get them checked out.)

Even once symptoms become more obviously perimenopausal – for example, when your periods change or you're getting hot flushes – often women don't get a diagnosis easily. Plus, a lot of GPs are still wary of giving women HRT, despite evidence of its safety for most women (see page 25 for more on this).

Even when women start HRT, often they discover that it isn't a magic pill that makes all symptoms disappear. As this book explains, the perimenopause is about so much more than the two hormones – oestrogen and progesterone – that usually make up an HRT prescription. It's bigger than this: a fundamental shift in the way your body works. That means it requires a fundamental and holistic shift in the way you treat your body too, and that is the purpose of the Pippa Campbell Method (PCM).

The PCM is about finding the root cause or causes of your symptoms. We do this by looking at your diet and lifestyle as well as your constitution. We consider how you breathe and your emotional state, ask about your exercise and how you feel physically. We look at what you do to relax, your daily routine and how much time you spend in nature. We can also do tests, including DNA, DUTCH hormone, blood and/or stool tests, although symptoms are our first guide.

For example, three clients might have constipation, but they each have a different emotional constitution. One might be anxious, one might have past trauma that hasn't been dealt with and one might be a perfectionist with an overly strict diet. Each requires a different approach. Or we may find that a client keeps getting ill – but that the root cause isn't that their immune system isn't functioning properly, it's that their stress system has gone wrong.

We go into both mind and body because if the body is hardware, the mind is the software that runs it. If somebody is very negative, helping them to change their mindset is part of the process. That's why, as explained in chapter four of this book, we aim to get your mind on board this perimenopause journey, too. We empower our clients by giving them practical things to do, not just by giving them advice – which is why this book is full of tools you can adopt, one by one. Ultimately, it's up to you to do the work.

Eat Right, Balance Hormones explains the root causes of the symptoms that women experience from the very beginning of midlife changes all the way through to menopause and beyond. Hormone levels are, of course, key to this but so are all the body systems that are affected, from the gut and liver to blood sugar balance.

There are lots of elements that have built up to the holistic way we treat women for hormonal symptoms in clinic. When I started my own clinic, I realised that most women have some kind of hormonal imbalance. I have massive empathy for women whose hormones are out of balance, not least because of my experience of my own hormonal havoc in my twenties and then during my perimenopause. Having helped myself, I have a deep belief that I can help other women too.

At the beginning of the pandemic, I suddenly became booked up with women aged 35-plus who had hormone-related symptoms but who couldn't get help from their GPs. I felt their frustration; even before the pandemic, there simply wasn't useful information available on how food and lifestyle affect hormones. I saw how, given the right guidance, women could be empowered to solve their own symptoms.

In clinic, I used DUTCH tests to find out what was going on for each woman, and the results were fascinating. I ran so many tests that I was analysing them on a daily basis! Doing that many DUTCH tests, I began to see patterns of symptoms in the results, each one corresponding to a typical hormonal imbalance. These have become the chapters in this book. So many of the women who joined the

Female Food Club – our online membership programme – were perimenopausal. I realised that I could help these women without hormone testing, simply by using their symptoms as a guide.

I threw myself into learning more about hormones – going to functional medicine symposiums, doing courses, questioning experts, reading books. Now, we have treated thousands of clients with hormonal issues. Each week, my practitioners and I still spend a few hours discussing women's results.

The PCM includes a whole range of tools to help you feel better – food of course, but also exercise, sleep, relaxation and, if you'd like some extra help, supplements. Chapter three – 'The Food Framework' – explains how to eat, including my key eating guidelines: the '5 Foundations'. Nutrition is key because food is one of the most powerful tools you have to heal your body. Chapter four – 'Healthy Hormone Habits' – covers lifestyle habits you can adopt or refine to benefit your hormones, including how to exercise, relax and get better sleep.

The perimenopausal years are a time when you can lose a significant amount of muscle. You'll see that in chapter three, I advise you to eat enough protein at every meal, which gives you the building blocks for making muscle. Plus, in chapter four, I recommend you do regular strength training, ideally with weights.

The plan isn't about losing weight, even though a lot of clients come to me at this time of life wanting to lose weight. Instead, this is a way of eating that helps your hormones to get back into balance, which helps you to feel full and energetic, giving you the energy to exercise. If you're looking to lose weight, you'll find that, over time and with consistency, this will happen, alongside a reduction in other perimenopausal symptoms. (If you'd like specific advice on weight loss, see my previous book, *Eat Right, Lose Weight*.)

We can't replicate the tests we do in clinic in a book, but there are some patterns of symptoms that indicate different hormonal imbalances. As you'll discover in part two, your symptoms are in fact a very good pointer to your imbalances and so can help you personalise specific eating and lifestyle changes, prioritising the ones that will help you the most. To show you how this process works in real life, there are some of our lovely clients' stories dotted throughout the book.

By following the advice in this book, you can not only reduce perimenopausal symptoms but improve your overall health too during this pivotal point in your life. It's a great opportunity to support your body so that you can reduce the risk of negative health conditions post-menopause, such as cardiovascular disease, bone loss and osteoporosis. Think of it as the instruction manual to completing the puzzle of midlife hormones – one you can keep returning to as your hormones evolve. And if you do the right things now, you'll ensure a healthier and happier 'third act'.

If you treat yourself with care, feeding yourself the right food, you can make this perimenopausal ride so much smoother. I've seen this happen time and again in clinic – it's so heartening when women can regain their full power, feeling happy and healthy, positive and confident, fit and energetic. I can't wait for you to start feeling those changes, too.

How to use this book

PART ONE – WHAT'S HAPPENING TO ME?

If you're someone who likes to understand what's going on in your body before making any changes, read this book from the beginning. Chapter one explains what happens to hormones during perimenopause. Chapter two looks at the body systems that you'll be working on while doing the plan.

PART TWO – THE PCM HORMONE BALANCE PLAN

Chapters three and four are the nuts and bolts of the plan: what to eat and what to do to feel better. Think of the Food Framework (chapter three) and the Healthy Hormone Habits (chapter four) as your instructions to help bring hormones into balance.

It's best to approach any changes in a slow and steady way, not all at once. The more methodically you adopt any new habits, the more likely they are to stick. I advocate that you follow the plan 80 per cent of the time because an 80:20 approach makes it more sustainable. The plan isn't about calorie counting or deprivation, but about a new way of life that responds to your body's needs.

If you want to start making changes while you're reading, start with the 5 Foundations (page 48). I've seen these powerful, science-based rules transform women's symptoms, even on their own. If you ever lose your way and get confused about what you should or shouldn't be doing, just keep coming back to my 5 Foundations.

> ### YOUR HORMONE JOURNAL
>
> *It will help to track your symptoms in a hormone journal, so you can see how you progress through the weeks. You can also use a menstrual cycle tracking app, such as Flo, Spot On or Cycles.*
>
> *If you're still having a cycle, the first day of your period is day one. Each day, write down how you feel and what you did. This will help to show you if the changes you are making are having an impact. You might already know you get PMS, for example, but this will reveal any new symptoms, as well as track how your PMS is improving over time as you change your diet and lifestyle. Over a longer period of time, tracking will also tell*

you if your cycle is getting shorter, which tends to happen mid-perimenopause, or if you've missed a period, which happens as you get closer to the menopause itself. If your cycle is very irregular, start on any day. Write the following details daily:
Day of your cycle (if you have a cycle):

How you slept: ....

Mood and energy levels: ....

Any other symptoms: ....

....

Morning routine: (if you have one) ....

....

Food: ....

Exercise: ....

....

Meditation: ....

Other activities: ....

....

Evening routine: (if you have one) ....

....

PART THREE – SOLVING YOUR SYMPTOMS

We each experience the lead up to the menopause and beyond differently, due to our unique combination of genes, diet and lifestyle. This is the part of the book that will help you to personalise your plan to treat your specific symptoms.

This section starts with a list of symptoms. You should tick all that apply to you. Each group of symptoms corresponds to a hormonal imbalance that is common during perimenopause, outlined in the chapters that follow. Most women find that more than one chapter applies to them – and that's normal because at midlife, hormones can become imbalanced in different ways, and levels can change from week to week and month to month too. The chapters in this part of the book will show you how to treat the symptoms of a particular hormone imbalance. If you recognise you follow the pattern of symptoms of a particular hormone imbalance (you have at least three or more of the symptoms listed) – work through that chapter and combine the specific advice there with the general advice in chapters three and four.

The instruction in these chapters allows you to personalise your plan. So, for example, the main plan suggests you eat at least one portion of cruciferous veg (broccoli, cauliflower, kale, etc.) a day. However, if you tick the boxes that apply to oestrogen dominance, you will be encouraged in the chapter on this imbalance to eat at least two portions a day. Another example is strength training. Chapter four explains why everyone needs to do it. But your personalised chapters may also provide extra evidence as to why it should be a particular focus in light of your hormonal imbalance. I've included suggestions for supplements in each chapter, which are optional. I've formulated a range of my own supplements according to the needs I've come across most often in clinic, and I've included recommendations for these in the relevant sections. However, if I haven't suggested a brand and you want to find one, I recommend some in the 'Pippa Loves' section on pippacampbellhealth.com.

If you're short of time, start with the advice in chapter three (the eating plan) and chapter four (the lifestyle plan).

PART FOUR – THE PCM HORMONE BALANCE RECIPES

This section of the book contains 60 hormone-friendly recipes you can try. All the recipes suit all hormone imbalances, so you can mix and match.

From what I've seen in clinic, most women who follow the PCM start to feel better within the first few weeks. They feel less bloated, more energetic, sleep better and their moods are less changeable too. It can take a few cycles for the more concrete symptoms to change, such as how heavy or painful your periods are (that said, on page 31 you can read Nicky's story. She has noticed her cycle changes each month according to what she's eating).

After two to three months, women generally say their periods are lighter, they are getting less PMS, their mood is noticeably better and their brain feels less foggy. If they had weight to lose, they have generally lost around 5 to 7lb by this point.

The longer your body has been out of balance hormonally, the longer it will take to feel better. If you were eating a lot of sugar, additives and processed foods, and drinking a lot of alcohol and coffee, you're likely to feel tired and experience some cravings in the first week. But you can get through this – and once you do, the positive energy you'll start to feel will make all the changes worthwhile.

By the end of three months, you'll know it's worth eating and living according to the PCM. You'll know the foods and supplements that are helpful to keep you on track. And you'll have found the recipes that you like and that work for your life and your hormones.

Part 1

What's Happening to Me?

In this section, you'll learn how key hormones change during perimenopause. And you'll see how these changes can have knock-on effects all over your body and in your brain, causing the various symptoms that you may be experiencing. You'll see that your brain and various body systems are not separate but interlinked. Knowing this will help you understand why rebalancing your hormones works best when you use the holistic approach in this book, which includes diet but also stress management, exercise and sleep.

CHAPTER 1

Solving the Hormone Puzzle

Do you remember the first time you tried to do a Rubik's cube? You probably managed to work out how to make all the squares of one side, say the red side, the same colour. But then each time you tried to complete a second side, say green, you'd unmake the red side. Your hormones are like that too: change one and it affects the others.

Hormones are chemicals that act like messengers in your body's internal communications system. Their job is to keep relaying information from the brain to organs and other parts of the body and back again, with the aim of bringing your body into balance. That is, until the perimenopause, when things go a bit haywire. Perimenopause is the transitional phase leading up to menopause, which can span from four to 15 years. It's when the ovaries – the factory that has been in charge of producing most oestrogen and progesterone – start to go offline. This stage has been called a second puberty because just like during puberty, oestrogen is fluctuating in an erratic way.

This is why perimenopause symptoms demand understanding, guidance and a touch of innovation. It isn't as simple as replacing oestrogen and progesterone with HRT because your symptoms are often not a direct result of a lack of these hormones. They're usually due to a cascade of reactions in your hormonal system, and then, as you'll see in chapter two, in your gut, liver and stress system too. And the changes that take place in these body systems often affect your hormones again too.

On top of this, hormones have a variety of different jobs, fitting into receptors all over your brain and body. So while oestrogen and progesterone control your monthly cycle, they also have other roles. This is another reason why perimenopause symptoms aren't always obvious (like a change in periods) but are often harder to pin down, such as sleeping less, waking more or waking up feeling less rested. Or you may find you can't concentrate or that your PMS is getting worse. You can find yourself overtaken by rushes of anger or sadness. You may feel lethargic and 'meh'. Your joints may ache a little more – or a lot. You may find that no matter what you eat, you keep gaining weight.

That's why it's so useful to look at your perimenopause through the lens of functional medicine. Conventional medicine tends to treat each hormone and each body system as separate, but functional medicine looks at how they interact and influence one another. It gives a 360-degree approach to treating your symptoms.

This chapter is a rundown of how sex hormones interact and explains how they change during the perimenopause. This understanding is invaluable because knowledge is power: it allows you to take control over your body.

The sister hormones: oestrogen and progesterone

Let's start with two key players in the female cycle: oestrogen and progesterone. In the fertile years they act like sisters, working together to shape your cycle so that you ovulate, grow a womb lining for any potential pregnancy and shed that lining ready for the next ovulation. This incredible up and down of hormones starts at puberty and goes on through the fertile years.

Below, you'll see a 'typical' cycle of someone in their fertile years. This shows how oestrogen peaks at ovulation, then progesterone comes in during the second (luteal) half of the cycle.

HOW OESTROGEN AND PROGESTERONE WORK TOGETHER OVER THE COURSE OF A MENSTRUAL CYCLE

— *Oestrogen*
— *Progesterone*

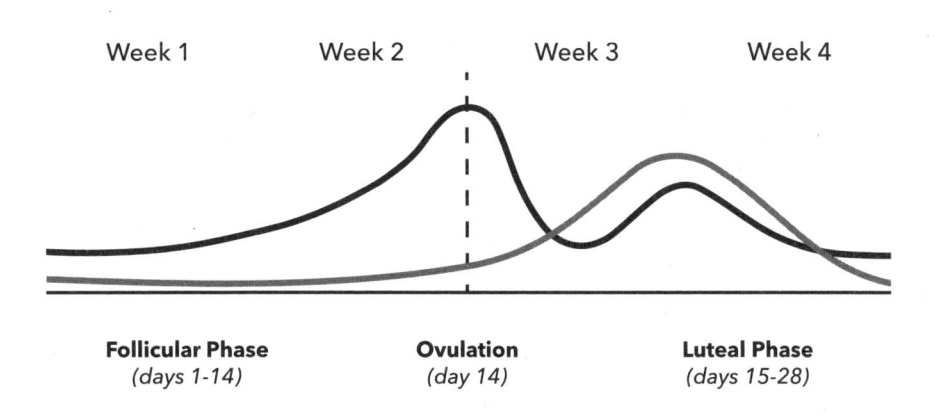

Week 1 Week 2 Week 3 Week 4

Follicular Phase **Ovulation** **Luteal Phase**
(days 1-14) *(day 14)* *(days 15-28)*

As your egg supply runs lower, your hormones start moving to the next phase of life, where oestrogen and progesterone aren't running the show. But in the meantime, they can fluctuate wildly. Overleaf is one example of what a cycle can look like when hormones change – although yours may look different. In fact, this is a picture of my cycle in perimenopause, before I started working on my hormones. It shows my oestrogen getting very high. As you'll discover, there are multiple ways the hormones that drive your cycle can change over this time.

HOW THE MONTHLY RHYTHM OF OESTROGEN AND PROGESTERONE CAN CHANGE DURING PERIMENOPAUSE

— Pippa's Oestrogen
— Pippa's Progesterone

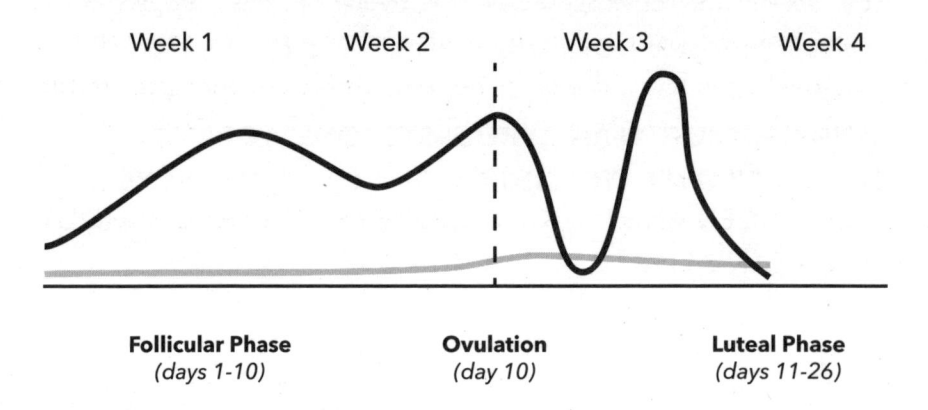

| Week 1 | Week 2 | Week 3 | Week 4 |

Follicular Phase (days 1-10)   **Ovulation** (day 10)   **Luteal Phase** (days 11-26)

Though oestrogen and progesterone will fluctuate throughout the perimenopause, the general trend is downwards, towards the lower levels that are typical of a woman's late fifties and beyond (unless you take HRT).

GOING DOWN (AND UP): PROGESTERONE AND OESTROGEN

The first hormone to change is progesterone. As your egg store in your ovaries runs lower, you begin to skip ovulation during some cycles. And if you don't ovulate, you don't make the levels of progesterone that you'd usually have during the second half of your cycle.

Some women don't notice much difference at first. Or the changes can be so subtle that it's not until you look back months or years later that you think, *Oh yes, I was a bit more anxious or bloated in the second half of my cycle*, or, *My sleep/PMS did get a little worse*.

If you are stressed, it's likely that you'll feel your symptoms more or they will be more obvious. That's because, as you'll see in chapter two, stress has a negative impact on your hormones, in particular on progesterone. But by managing your stress and supporting your body with food and possibly the right supplements, you can reduce negative symptoms.

The change in oestrogen during perimenopause can be a bit more dramatic, as it tends to go up and down more erratically. In fact, oestrogen levels can be higher than they were during the fertile years, as this graph shows.

OESTROGEN AND PROGESTERONE LEVELS THROUGHOUT A WOMAN'S LIFE

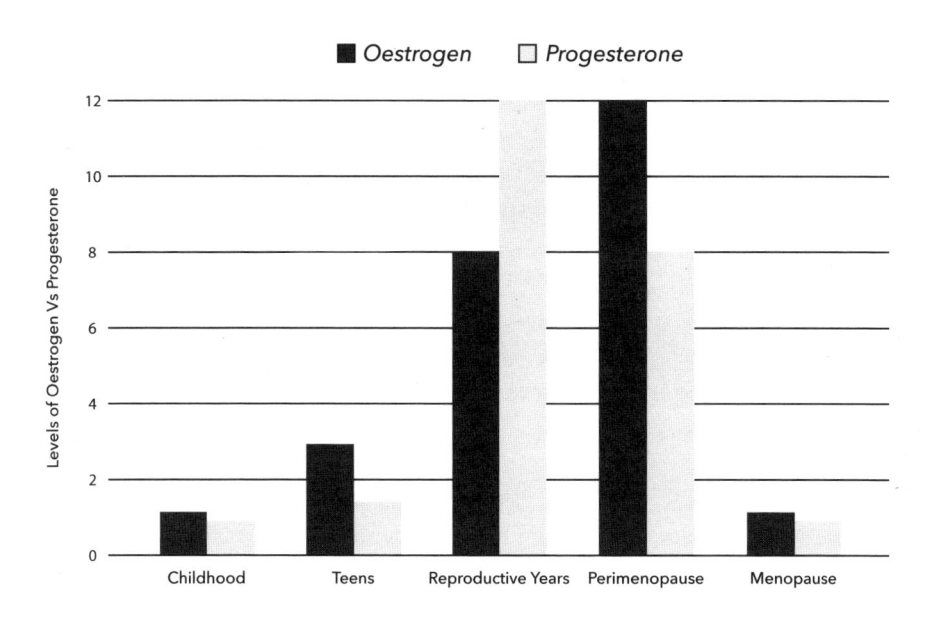

One of progesterone's jobs is to balance out the effects of oestrogen. And so if your progesterone levels are low, you can get symptoms of high oestrogen, such as breast tenderness, headaches and PMS. If you're someone who tended to have higher oestrogen levels during your fertile years (for example you may have been diagnosed with fibroids), this oestrogen imbalance can get worse during perimenopause (see chapter seven for more on the symptoms of high oestrogen).

This is important to note as many women assume that their perimenopause symptoms must be due to low oestrogen, when in fact they are down to having relatively high oestrogen. This is for two reasons:

1. Progesterone usually starts to decline first, in the early years of perimenopause, which throws out the crucial oestrogen–progesterone balance, leading to a condition called oestrogen dominance.
2. Oestrogen can increase dramatically in early perimenopause. We see this a lot on women's DUTCH hormone tests. It's as if their body is saying 'last chance to make a baby!' The brain tells the ovaries to ramp up egg production, then the ovaries produce more oestrogen and release multiple eggs. This is why pregnancies in perimenopause can result in twins.

Then, later in perimenopause and post-menopause, if you don't detoxify your used-up oestrogen properly, you can have symptoms caused by oestrogen dominance, *even when your oestrogen is low.*

But remember – your cycles will keep changing. As you get deeper into perimenopause, you'll have more and more cycles when you don't ovulate, so your progesterone levels will go down. Your oestrogen levels may go up and down during perimenopause but, over time, the general trend is downwards. Eventually, as you get closer to menopause (a year after your last period), you're more likely to experience the symptoms of low oestrogen, such as hot flushes.

The missing link: Testosterone

The third hormone that's key for your cycle is testosterone, one of the androgen hormones. The word comes from the Greek word for male, but women need these hormones too. As you'll see from the graph on page 17, in a fertile cycle, testosterone peaks mid-cycle around ovulation, possibly to help make you more interested in sex. During perimenopause, you can get symptoms of high testosterone as your hormones go out of balance. If you were diagnosed with PCOS when you were younger, you already tend to have higher than average testosterone, and this can become more pronounced in perimenopause.

Or you may have low testosterone levels. The symptom people most associate with this is low libido. Like all hormones, though, testosterone has a lot of jobs, such as maintaining bones and muscle, and fuelling energy and motivation too. Women often describe feeling 'meh' when testosterone is low (see chapter ten).

Just as oestrogen and progesterone balance each other, your levels of testosterone and oestrogen affect each other too: oestrogen, the quintessential female hormone, is made from testosterone, the ultimate male hormone. When I tell clients this fact, it often blows their minds! The raw ingredient for all your sex hormones is cholesterol, which is made in your liver. Using protein, fat and other nutrients, your clever body turns cholesterol into a hormone called pregnenolone, which is why some people call it the 'grandmother hormone' (see diagram overleaf). On the right, you'll see this can become DHEA, or the 'mother hormone', which turns into testosterone. And finally, testosterone can turn into oestrogen.

HOW HORMONES ARE MADE, STARTING WITH THE RAW INGREDIENT CHOLESTEROL

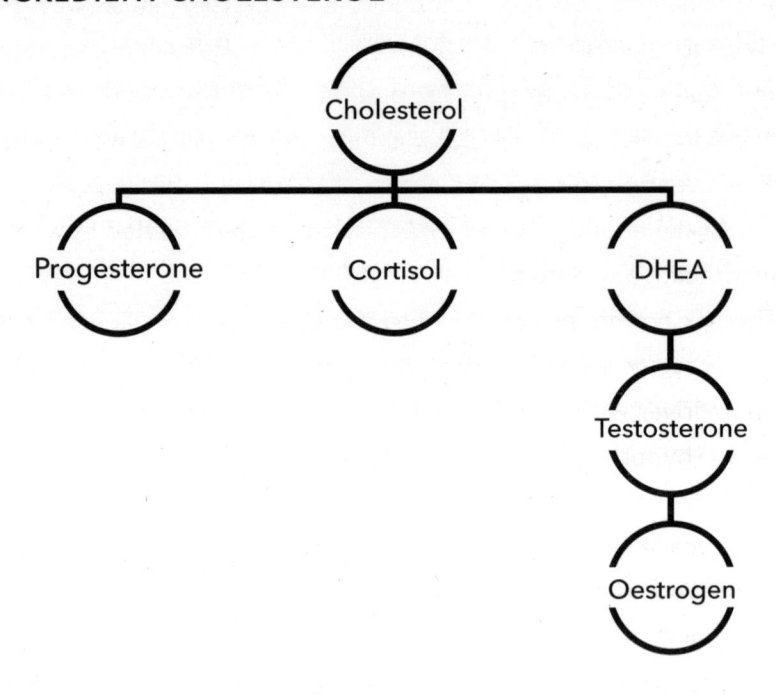

```
                    Cholesterol
                         |
        ┌────────────────┼────────────────┐
  Progesterone        Cortisol          DHEA
                                          |
                                     Testosterone
                                          |
                                      Oestrogen
```

On the left, you'll see that pregnenolone can also become progesterone or the stress hormone cortisol. So, in other words, the raw materials for the stress hormone cortisol are the same raw materials you need to make progesterone. That's one reason why if you're often or always stressed, it can have such a major effect on your cycle and on perimenopause symptoms too. For example, one study showed that midlife women going though stressful life events have 21 per cent more hot flushes. As you'll read in chapter five, your body is always going to prioritise making a stress hormone such as cortisol over sex hormones such as progesterone because survival is more important than fertility. So you can see why looking after your stress system is the key to having fewer symptoms in perimenopause.

As the ovaries' hormone-making factory winds down, your adrenals – small glands just above your kidneys – are supposed to take over the production of sex hormones. The type of oestrogen you tend to make changes now too, although it acts in a very similar way. Your fertile oestrogen is mainly E2 (estradiol), while the kind your adrenals make is mainly E1 (estriol).

The adrenals don't make the level of sex hormones women have in their twenties. But women who aren't stressed, in my experience, tend to make enough and so are less likely to be troubled by a lot of perimenopause symptoms.

The sex hormones are linked to the stress system via a brain-to-body messaging system. When you encounter something stressful – a lion, a driver with road rage, an angry boss – the part of the brain called the hypothalamus sends a message via the pituitary gland to tell your adrenals that it's time to make stress hormones. This messaging system is called the hypothalamic-pituitary-adrenal axis, or HPA axis for short. And the messaging system that tells your ovaries to make sex hormones takes a similar brain route; it's called the hypothalamic-pituitary-ovarian (HPO) axis. When you're stressed a lot, the HPA axis can become dysregulated (for more, see chapter five). And in order for the HPO axis to work well, we need the HPA axis to work well too. Especially as the HPA axis becomes even more important over the course of the perimenopause, as production of sex hormones moves from the ovaries to the adrenals.

As you'll see in part three, there are more key hormones that are affected by midlife changes in sex hormones, too. For example, when your levels of progesterone go down, it can make it more likely that you'll have low thyroid function, and your thyroid function drives the speed of your metabolism (more on this in chapter 11). Also, lower levels of oestrogen drive a shift in how you respond to insulin, the hormone in charge of blood sugar regulation and fat storage. This shift makes it easier for you to put on weight, particularly around your midsection.

Is HRT the answer?

Wouldn't it be lovely if you could just take HRT and all your symptoms would disappear? We live in an instant culture where we expect solutions on demand. We are encouraged to see the world as akin to a huge vending machine, from which we can expect everything to be available now – clothes and make-up, takeaways, even dates. Often, clients are disappointed to find that there isn't a magic bullet that will get rid of perimenopause symptoms.

What I've seen in clinic is that HRT can work brilliantly for some women but others find it doesn't suit them. Or, more often, it doesn't address *all* their symptoms. Clients say: 'Taking HRT helped with my hot flushes but I'm still putting on weight' or 'I'm sleeping better on HRT but it hasn't stopped me getting headaches'. Some feel better on HRT for a few months but then their symptoms return or they get new ones.

As I'm not a medical doctor, I don't advise clients on HRT. That's a conversation to have with your GP or gynaecologist (see box on page 25). But I've seen how it often takes trial and error to get the dosage right, as well as to identify the right form of HRT, whether it's patches or creams, pills or pessaries. (This is why it's important to have regular check-ups and reviews of your HRT.) Some women don't want to take HRT or aren't able to due to health conditions.

It's not surprising that HRT doesn't always work. As you've learnt in this chapter, there's so much more going on than just a drop in oestrogen and progesterone, so simply topping up the levels of those hormones with HRT isn't going to address every issue.

In the next chapter, we'll look more closely at how hormones affect so many of your body systems, including your liver and your gut, your adrenals which control stress, your blood sugar balance and your metabolism. The advice that follows will help you to look at your body in a holistic way, so you can begin to get these body systems and your hormones back into balance and, by doing so, treat your symptoms. The aim is to *replenish* all your hormones to the best level they can be for your age and stage, rather than replacing them.

> ### PERIMENOPAUSE: WHAT CAN YOUR GP OFFER?
>
> **By Ms Hina Pathak Sra, consultant obstetrician and gynaecologist**
>
> #### How does HRT work?
>
> *Current NICE (National Institute for Health and Care Excellence) guidelines say: if you have vasomotor symptoms (for example, hot flushes) and period changes, you are over 45 and have no contra indications, you are in perimenopause. In perimenopause, symptoms are due to fluctuations in hormones and/or low levels of progesterone and oestrogen. By giving you a steady level of hormones, HRT prevents some symptoms and can reduce others.*
>
> #### Is HRT safe?
>
> *HRT has been shown to cut the increased risk of heart disease and osteoporosis in postmenopausal women. In the 2010s, there was a breast cancer scare involving HRT, which is why a lot of GPs are still reluctant to prescribe it. The studies on which this scare was based have since been discredited. There is a slightly higher cancer risk if you takeoestrogen and progesterone HRT. Out of 1,000 women, 23 will get breast cancer. Within the group of women who take HRT, there will be four extra cases – i.e. the risk is*

27 in 1,000. It's important to note that being obese doubles the risk of breast cancer, while drinking more than two units of alcohol a day increases the risk more than being on HRT does. Most women can take HRT even if they have a family history of breast cancer.

What will I be offered?

NICE guidelines for HRT say that women should be given oestrogen and progesterone together from the beginning of treatment (or oestrogen only if the woman has had a total hysterectomy – removal of both the uterus and cervix). Oestrogen encourages the build-up of the lining of the womb, which can lead to uterine cancer. The progesterone is added to HRT to prevent the lining of the womb from becoming thicker. It can be given as tablets or as the Mirena coil.

There are 'body identical' forms of both hormones, which means they are exactly the same as the hormones in your body. The body identical version of progesterone is Utrogestan tablets. Oestrogen can be given via the skin, as a patch (Estradot, Evorel), spray (Lenzetto) or gel (Oestrogel, Sandrena).

For vulvovaginal symptoms such as vaginal atrophy (dryness), superficial dyspareunia (painful intercourse), urinary incontinence (leakage of urine), you can be prescribed topical vaginal oestrogen (Estriol, Vagifem) plus water-based lubricants.

Most health professionals prescribe HRT specific to the patient's needs. In the NHS, this is usually based on their symptoms. Private doctors may also use blood tests, which are not recommended by NICE for most women.

Does HRT include testosterone?

Testosterone is not prescribed as part of HRT on the NHS. NICE guidelines state that testosterone can be prescribed for loss of libido after other treatments have been tried. It is prescribed 'off label' in the UK, since there are no preparations licensed for women in the UK. (See page 187 for more.) It is prescribed by private doctors to women who have low levels of testosterone in blood tests and also symptoms of deficiency, such as low libido, fatigue and muscle loss.

Are there other treatments?

When HRT isn't recommended due to medical history or if you prefer not to take it, there are other alternative medications or herbal remedies available for specific symptoms, too. Check with your doctor before you try any herbal remedies, as herbs can interact with certain medications. There are also other treatments (such as laser treatments) available privately for vaginal symptoms such as vaginal dryness and urinary incontinence.

SHOULD I HAVE MY HORMONES TESTED?

By Dr Klaudia Raczko, a functional medicine doctor who specialises in hormones

You are unlikely to be offered a blood test to find out if you are in perimenopause by your GP, as current NICE guidelines say that women over the age of 45 can be prescribed HRT on symptoms alone. And menopause is diagnosed based on the date of your last period rather than a blood test.

What you need to be aware of is that blood tests only give you a snapshot of what's going on, and that during this time of your life (perimenopause), hormone levels may change throughout the month and even month to month. Therefore, testing hormone levels may be challenging, due to those fluctuations.

At the same time, in an ideal world, we would base our decisions on both symptoms and some objective evidence such as a blood test (and ideally a DUTCH test) to see if the woman's experience is reflected in her physiology. I like to have a baseline hormone level prior to starting HRT as it makes it easier to monitor the response to hormonal replacement long term, and some hormones do not fluctuate significantly (e.g. testosterone). Sometimes, you can also have some unexpected findings. In addition, a lot of women are learning more about peri and menopause and they want to know what is happening in their body.

It is worth having your hormones tested if:

1. *You've tried HRT and you're not responding to it as expected. Some women don't absorb oestrogen very well, so that even when they are on HRT, their levels may be*

> *still low. On the other hand, some women may have a significant increase in their oestrogen level even with relatively low doses. Always monitor your symptoms and make note of any changes, good or bad.*
> 2. *You want to know if your HRT regime is doing its job. For example, if oestrogen is reaching a level that protects your bones.*
> 3. *You want a baseline before you introduce any changes (including lifestyle changes). However, an improvement in your symptoms will also indicate that what you are doing is working!*

What hormone tests can I have?

DUTCH TEST

'DUTCH' stands for 'dried urine test for comprehensive hormones'. You pee on a series of little blotting papers that, once dried, are sent off to be tested. The DUTCH test looks at levels of key hormones including oestrogen, cortisol, progesterone, melatonin and testosterone. But it also looks at hormone metabolites, showing if and how the body is using the hormones, which is what counts.

The DUTCH Complete test is done over the course of 24 hours and is suitable for women on HRT or who don't have a cycle. The DUTCH Cycle Mapping test lasts a month and is suitable for women who have a cycle and aren't on HRT. (It's also the right test if you've had a partial hysterectomy or you have a hormonal IUD such as the Mirena coil.)

DNA TEST

This test looks at the genes which influence your hormonal patterns. It gives your genetic predisposition or blueprint, which influences how well you make and eliminate hormones and how sensitive you are to them. It reveals certain variations or mutations, usually called SNPs, that affect how genes are 'expressed' – i.e. what happens in the body.

But while genes have an influence, they are not the whole story. Your genetic inheritance is affected by what you eat and your lifestyle. This is called epigenetics – the epi part of the word literally means over and above genetics.

BLOOD TEST

Often, clients will have done hormone blood tests with their doctor before they come to us. A blood test is a snapshot of your hormones on that particular day, so it's sometimes not as useful as it could be. If you have a regular cycle, it's best to get a blood test between days 19 and 22 of your cycle; this will give the most useful reading of your progesterone levels.

Nicky's story

I started following Pippa on Instagram around a year ago, when I was 41. I was looking for help because I had terrible PMS symptoms. The unbearable one was sore boobs. The pain would start at ovulation, then continue into the first few days of my period. I'm a 32E and my boobs were so sensitive that they'd hurt in the shower, when my kids cuddled me, even when I turned over in bed.

I went to see my GP because I was seriously considering having a breast reduction, hoping that would stop the pain. It wasn't clear whether the operation would help, so it didn't seem a good idea go through such a big procedure and an anaesthetic too. The GP suggested taking evening primrose oil so I tried it, but it didn't work.

I thought I'd just have to put up with the pain. My mood was low and I was getting a lot of premenstrual rage. My husband and kids were getting the brunt of that and I thought, *Something needs to give.*

That's when I found Pippa. I decided to follow the way of eating she explained on her Instagram. I'm fit and a yoga teacher and I didn't need to lose weight, but I thought it might help maybe take my boobs down a size. We've never eaten much processed food at home as I've always cooked from scratch, but we weren't eating as many vegetables as Pippa suggested. Some meals I'd have no veg – for example, I'd often grab a quick cheese sandwich for lunch. So I started adding in more whole foods and lots more vegetables. I decided to trial excluding dairy and wheat because Pippa explained in her book, *Eat Right, Lose Weight*, that they are the foods that cause the most issues. She advised cutting them out for 30 days. After that, when I reintroduced them (separately) it would become clear if they suited me or not.

In just a few weeks, I noticed a massive improvement in my symptoms. That month, I didn't get sore boobs until a few days before my period, which was shorter and lighter. And I felt less bloated too. The next month, we went on holiday to France, and I decided I couldn't not eat bread and Camembert. Lo and behold, before my next period, my boobs were horrendously sore, my period was heavy and I was full of rage too.

After that, I got back on track with Pippa's way of eating. I stopped snacking between meals too. Again, I had almost no pain until a couple of days before my period and my boobs were definitely smaller. I was more patient too.

Then it was half term and, when I was out with the children, I started eating a few snacks again, like chocolate. Again, that month the sore boobs were back!

I contacted Pippa and told her about my experience, following her method. I said I felt a little like a one-woman experiment! She suggested my symptoms could be due to oestrogen dominance – that is, high oestrogen relative to progesterone.

I decided to get really serious about helping my symptoms. I began to eat a raw carrot every day because, as Pippa explained, the fibre is really good for carrying used up oestrogen out of the body. It's important to go to the loo every day, too. I used to go each morning but it was a loose bowel movement. In fact, I wasn't emptying fully. Once I introduced more veg and fibre-filled foods, including a kiwi fruit every day, plus drinking more water, I finally realised what a healthy poop should be like!

I do have months when I'm less strict about food, but I mostly stick to the plan. Every time I eat sugary foods and snacks, I feel more bloated and my gut motility isn't as good. If I eat even three cubes of chocolate, I'll get a headache straight away. If I eat bread, my tummy bloats. As much as I love dairy and wheat, I now know they're not for me.

My usual breakfast is coconut yoghurt with kiwi, banana and/or some other fruit. For lunch I have a good portion of protein – chicken or fish – with rocket, tomatoes and other raw veg. Pippa's most helpful advice is to have four different vegetables each day; before, I was having the same vegetables all the time. For dinner, we often have a slow-cook casserole with lentils and chickpeas, plus meat or fish. I always make sure that the first couple of mouthfuls of food I eat are protein and that helps me not need to snack. When I eat more mindfully, I notice when my portion sizes are getting too big, as well.

Besides my boobs feeling a lot better and my periods being easier, the other main change that I've noticed is in my energy levels. I do a lot of exercise – I teach one to three classes a day, train with light weights and swim too. But whereas before I'd be exhausted-tired – floppy with fatigue and need to crawl into bed – now I'm good-tired.

CHAPTER 2

The Six Keys to Hormone Health

Why is it that some women seem to sail through the perimenopause years but others are floored by multiple symptoms? Some of it may be down the way your hormones change, as described in the previous chapter, and your sensitivity to those changes. But the causes of your symptoms run deeper than changes in oestrogen and progesterone.

One of the things I hear a lot from clients is that they've been told by doctors that how they are feeling is 'normal' for their age. Or their symptoms have been written off as something to put up with. Often, the doctor hasn't joined up the dots to see that the woman's varied symptoms are due to hormonal changes interacting with some key body systems. The principle of functional medicine is to look at the roots of an issue and the bigger picture too, and that's what we'll do in this chapter. These key body systems are:

1. The gut and digestion
2. The liver and the detox system

3. Blood sugar balance
4. Stress and adrenal function
5. Building muscles and bone
6. Manufacturing hormones and brain chemicals

Knowing how your hormones affect these body systems will not only make it clear why you may not have the same perimenopausal symptoms as other women (more on this in part three of the book) but, more than that, you'll be able to see why changing your food and lifestyle is powerful when it comes to minimising and solving symptoms. This chapter also describes how the Pippa Campbell Method can target these systems, helping you build resilience to hormonal changes.

1. Support your gut

Let's start from the bottom up (excuse the pun!). The main way you eliminate toxins – and this includes hormones after they have been used – is via stools. For this to happen, you need to be pooping regularly, which means one to three times a day. Otherwise, you can end up reabsorbing the used-up old hormones.

Moving further up into the lower intestine, your gut bacteria has a whole range of jobs, including as the first line of defence of your immune system, digesting proteins and fibre, making vitamins B and K, and extracting other nutrients from food too. But it's also key for hormone balance. The healthiest microbiome is a diverse one but there's evidence that during perimenopause, your community of microbes undergoes a shift in the wrong direction – a reduction in diversity. This causes an increase in inflammation, which can lead to 'leaky gut', when food particles travel straight into the bloodstream and cause immune reactions and inflammation.

The estrobolome is part of the microbiome that – when it's working well – regulates oestrogen levels in the body. It helps break down used-up oestrogen to be eliminated. But it also can reactivate old oestrogen to turn it back into circulation as active oestrogen. The PCM hormone balance plan helps to feed the good bugs and support the diversity of your microbiome, including a well-functioning estrobolome, because it encourages you to eat plenty of prebiotic, gut-friendly foods, including fibre-packed vegetables, whole grains, beans and pulses, plus probiotic, fermented foods (see page 57) as well as phytoestrogen foods (such as flaxseeds, see page 159). There's also evidence that eating as described in the Food Framework (which we'll cover in chapter three) helps in making anti-inflammatory compounds. And all the fibre you'll be eating will help keep you regular, too!

2. Love your liver

Everything that we eat, breathe, touch, smell and make in our bodies – including used up hormones – needs to be detoxified. As the main organ of detoxification, the liver is a busy organ. But the word 'detox' has a bad reputation. People assume it means a juice diet or extreme fasting or not eating. What I mean by detox in this context is giving the liver the support it needs. This allows it to efficiently process used-up hormones, including oestrogen, testosterone, progesterone and the stress hormone cortisol. The plan includes ways to take the pressure off your liver, which is taxed by processed foods, high-sugar foods, alcohol and caffeine. It encourages you to reduce your intake of these.

Another one of the liver's 500 jobs is to process environmental toxins. A lot of these are endocrine disruptors – i.e. they mimic our hormones – fitting into hormone receptors so your own hormones can't. Xenoestrogens in plastic such as bisphenol A (BPA), for example, fit into your oestrogen receptors. We can't stop our exposure to environmental chemicals, but chapter four explains some key ways to reduce it.

HOW YOUR BODY ELIMINATES USED-UP HORMONES (AND OTHER TOXINS)

This table shows the stages that used-up hormones go through in order to be eliminated. It uses the example of oestrogen, but testosterone takes a similar route (as does alcohol), while progesterone detoxification starts at phase two.

Phase 1 (in the liver):	First, used-up oestrogen is changed into a compound that's toxic to the body. You need some specific nutrients for this phase, including B vitamins, amino acids (from protein) and flavonoids (from plants). In clinic, we often find that people have a fast phase 1 but then a slow phase 2 when it comes to alcohol; this is a recipe for a hangover, as it leaves the toxic compounds hanging around.
Phase 2 (in the liver):	In this phase, the toxic compound is turned from a fat-soluble compound to a safer, water-soluble one that's ready to be excreted. First, the substance is methylated – for this, you need nutrients including specific amino acids. It's then carried out of the liver in bile salts. These are made by the liver then stored in the gall bladder, ready to be released when you eat. They're also important for fat digestion. If you have high levels of oestrogen (naturally, from taking HRT and/or xenoestrogens from the environment), your bile salts can become sticky and sludgy and unable to carry out all the toxins

Phase 2 (in the liver):	from the liver, including that used-up excess oestrogen. High oestrogen is why women are more likely to develop gall bladder problems, including gallstones in midlife, especially when taking HRT. Because bile salts help fat digestion, there are some clues you're either not making enough bile salts or your gall bladder isn't releasing them: you feel nauseous after eating a fatty meal and/or you have stools that are pale and float. Having an underactive thyroid makes it more likely you'll have poor bile flow too. Bitter foods (see page 55) help you make and release bile.
Phase 3 (in the gut):	For phase 3, you need the right balance of gut bacteria. Some gut bugs (part of the estrobolome, see page 39) produce an enzyme called beta-glucuronidase. This enzyme can reactivate the inactive forms of oestrogen and send them around the body again – so you don't want too little or too much of it.
Elimination (via stools):	This is why it's important to make sure you poop regularly. If you don't, used-up oestrogen (and other toxins) can be reabsorbed while in the colon.

To support your liver and gut, the Food Framework includes all the nutrients your body needs to effectively carry out the steps above. For example, one key food type you'll eat every day is cruciferous vegetables: broccoli, cabbage, sprouts and so on (see page 54 for a full list). You'll also be making sure you get enough B vitamins, sufficient protein (see page 50) and plenty of flavonoids – natural chemicals that give fruits and vegetables their colour. As I've mentioned in the box, eating bitter foods, such as bitter leaves, chicory and artichokes, will help keep bile salts flowing and support the gall bladder.

3. Balance blood sugar

Midlife hormone changes can put your blood sugar on an out-of-control rollercoaster, which can be intensified by changes in the microbiome, stress and poor sleep. Some women have symptoms of low blood sugar, so that if you don't eat for a few hours, you feel hungry, anxious, hangry or faint. Some tend towards high blood sugar, which can shift your metabolism so you're more likely to put on weight, especially around your middle.

If your blood sugar isn't working as well as it used to, you will notice that your usual breakfast of toast or cereal leaves you tired and/or hungry soon after eating. That's because sugary foods, foods made from white carbs such as cornflakes and beige foods generally spike blood sugar, which will then drop. If you keep eating foods that spike blood sugar, eventually your blood sugar control can become faulty, a condition called insulin resistance, which is one step closer to type 2 diabetes.

The plan tackles midlife blood sugar issues on two fronts. Firstly, the carbs you'll be eating will be low glycaemic, i.e. they help keep blood sugar spikes to a minimum. You'll also see that the recipes I've included in the final part of the book combine fibre-rich and wholefoods with protein and some healthy fat. This slows the transit of glucose from the food into the blood, flattening blood sugar spikes (more on page 51). The second part of the plan concerns exercise because muscles that move regularly are better at storing excess blood sugar and more sensitive to insulin.

4. Manage your stress

I've seen multiple times how working on stress management can be a game changer when it comes to reducing perimenopause symptoms.

As you read in chapter one, the stress hormone system is intimately connected with the sex hormone system. Both types of hormones are made from similar ingredients, their communication systems are linked via the same brain areas, plus you make both in the adrenals, too. In addition, as your ovaries start to produce less oestrogen and testosterone, your adrenals are supposed to take over as the hormone manufacturer. But if your adrenals are getting signals that you are stressed, they will prioritise making stress hormones instead. This is why, apart from getting your nutrition right, the most important change you can make is to work on reducing your stress levels.

Almost all the clients we see in clinic are stressed and/or anxious and overwhelmed. When this is the case, sometimes we don't suggest any food changes during the first session. In order to have the capacity to make big changes in the way you eat, you need to be able to manage your stress. I might ask clients to start a calming bedtime routine with herbal tea (see page 71) and/or to do some breath exercises throughout the day (see chapter four).

One client was so overwhelmed by having too many things to do that she'd end up sitting at her computer and getting nothing done! I spent the first consultation talking through her daily routine, giving her a schedule that included food shopping and meal prep, but also walking the dogs, answering emails and meditation. It helped her to get in the right place to make bigger changes. The lesson? If you're stressed, start the plan as slowly as you need to, prioritising the stress reduction ideas in chapter four.

5. Build muscle

Most of us need to move more, not only to improve our cardiovascular function but to build our muscles and to support our bone health too. After the age of 35, it really is use it or lose it when it comes to muscles. Unless we actively build muscles, we will lose muscle mass each year. People aged under 40 can have 17 to 41 per cent more muscle strength than people over 40.

It may feel hard to get up and at it: lower oestrogen can bring achy joints and revive that old back, neck or knee problem that you thought was under control. If you're coming back to exercise after a break, the advice in chapter four will help you start slow and steady, building up to the NHS guidelines, which is 150 minutes of moderate intensity cardio or 75 minutes of vigorous cardio per week. If you're already an exerciser, you'll learn that varying your exercise is best, including strength work. Lifting weights and bodyweight exercises come out on top for building both muscles and bones, plus you need to add mobility and balance work, as this is key for longevity. The good news is that you don't have to find hours to do your sessions; breaking it down into small sessions throughout the day is just as good.

6. Make hormones and brain chemicals

You know that the right food is important for supporting the gut and liver to do its work of processing hormones. But the Food Framework is also designed to supply all the important raw ingredients to make your hormones and neurotransmitters – brain chemicals that affect your mood, such as serotonin and dopamine. Because eating good food really does affect how you feel. One study showed that people who eat more brightly coloured yellow/orange/red vegetables, beans and pulses, and cruciferous vegetables tend to feel less stressed.

As hormones and neurotransmitters are made from amino acids, you need to ensure you eat protein at every meal. As we age, our requirement for protein goes up, and a lot of women find that upping their protein makes a huge difference to how they feel, reducing their hunger level and boosting their energy, as well as supporting muscle growth. It's hard to eat enough of the right amino acids if you're vegetarian or vegan; read the section on protein in chapter three for advice on how to do this. You also need good fats to make hormones, found in oily fish, avocado, seeds and nuts (see page 64).

In the next chapter, you'll find out how to make sure you're getting all the right nutrients for your body to make and to metabolise hormones too, as well as support your gut and liver function.

> ### *EASY WIN: INSTANT MEAL*
>
> *1 bag rocket leaves (rocket is in the cruciferous family) or 1 portion broccoli, steamed*
>
> *1 piece poached salmon, 1 chicken breast or 1 packet of tofu*
>
> *Mix together and dress with extra virgin olive oil, lemon juice and/or apple cider vinegar, salt and pepper. (You could also add Dijon mustard and some chopped herbs if you like.)*

Part 2

The PCM Hormone Balance Plan

The next two chapters are the bedrock of the Hormone Balance Plan. Thousands of women, including me, have now followed the Pippa Campbell Method to help with hormonal symptoms. Over the 15 years I've been practising as a nutritionist, I have refined it down to the core guidelines in these two chapters. This isn't a diet or an eating plan, but suggestions and practical tools for eating and living that will allow you to take back control of your symptoms, mood and overall health.

The truth is, as you pass through perimenopause, you do have to work harder at being healthy, but by following the advice in these chapters, each day you can choose health and vitality by keeping your blood sugar even, feeding your microbiome and supporting your metabolism and your stress system. If you can follow the food framework just 80 per cent of the time, you will experience an easier per-imenopause. It's about consistency in looking after yourself, whether you're taking HRT or not, as you can't out-hormone a bad diet.

If you haven't yet had any hormonal changes, or you just have some of the first signs of the perimenopause, by following the plan you will make the transition smoother and even prevent some symptoms from happening at all. If you are mid-perimenopause, you will reduce and treat some symptoms. If you are towards the end of the perimenopause or into the menopause years, you will alleviate symptoms while bolstering your health for the future too. Remember that from now on, every little change you make, whether it's an extra vegetable a day, a relaxing bath in the evening or five minutes moving or meditation, is worth doing.

CHAPTER 3

The Food Framework

What to eat for hormonal balance

I say this to clients all the time: what you put in your mouth is one of the most important decisions you make every day. Food is powerful because you are literally building your body with each mouthful – your muscles, your neurotransmitters, your hormones. When you put rubbish in, you get rubbish out. But when you put in nourishing, nutrient-fuelled, natural, delicious and well-balanced food... you feel energetic, bright and well-balanced too. This chapter shows you how to eat to really fuel and look after your body now.

Perimenopause is a pivotal phase in a woman's life, as hormonal shifts profoundly change physical and emotional well-being. I've seen the impact that food can have on symptoms during perimenopause and I've seen thousands of women transform the way they feel, their energy levels and their weight by changing what they eat. One of my clients stopped her daily glass of wine and started filling half her plate with cruciferous veg at each meal. Her painful periods and sore breasts resolved in a month. Another client, who'd been a big snacker, gave up eating between meals, cut out all processed and sugary foods and went down to one coffee a day. Within two months, she found her periods became more regular and less painful.

You'd probably like a quick fix and to feel better tomorrow (or you might be thinking, *Actually, now please!*). You' may have felt tired, wired, irritable and out of sorts for weeks or months. Some women come to clinic having been stuck on a hormonal rollercoaster for years. And so the solution isn't going to be instant. Sadly, it's not as easy as popping an HRT pill or slapping on a patch. Even if you do decide to take HRT, you'll need to support your body with good food.

The Food Framework isn't an eating plan or diet. Rather, it's your blueprint for a way of eating that will support your hormones and your long-term health too. You may already be doing a lot of what I'm suggesting and just want to make a few tweaks, in which case, crack on! Or you may be here for a total overhaul. If that's the case, start with the 5 Foundations, then slowly work your way towards the longer list of rules that follow. It will seem like a lot at first. But you got to where you are over years, and so it's fine to take a while to develop new and lasting habits. In the Female Food Club, my online membership programme, we find that it takes around six months for women to adopt the changes so they stick.

You don't have to implement everything today – but whatever you can manage means you are looking after your body and mind, which you absolutely deserve.

The 5 Foundations

These five rules will, from now on, underpin your hormone-healthy way of eating. They are fundamental principles of fuelling your body that will help balance your hormones. If you're making changes, this is where to start.

1. START EVERY MEAL WITH TWO BITES OF PROTEIN

Eating protein first will help you feel satisfied earlier and helps to keep your blood sugar more even. It will also remind you that you need to eat a good portion of protein with every meal (see page 50). As you get into your forties and fifties, this becomes even more important; you need protein to build hormones, to prevent cravings, to fight fatigue and to build muscle, too.

2. LEAVE FOUR TO FIVE HOURS BETWEEN MEALS

That is between breakfast and lunch, and between lunch and dinner. If you need a snack, drink a glass of water and eat a small portion of protein (a boiled egg, a handful of nuts, quarter of a chicken breast, a slice of smoked salmon). Aim to finish eating by 7pm, leaving a 12-to-14-hour eating break until breakfast.

Leaving gaps between eating helps with blood sugar control, reduces insulin spikes and means you'll store less energy as fat. And being hungry will make your food taste more delicious! Having a break from eating overnight will support your digestion, gut health and liver function.

3. DRINK TWO LITRES OF WATER A DAY

Hydration helps keep your digestive system moving so you eliminate your waste products, which is important for hormonal balance. Aim for two litres per day – more if it's hot or you've exercised.

4. CHEW (UP TO) 30 TIMES

Chewing each mouthful until your food turns to mush slows down your eating speed, giving time for the fullness messages from your stomach to tell your brain you can stop eating. It will also reduce bloating, wind and constipation, and help you to get more nutrients out of your food. Take time to make your food look pretty on the plate and try to savour each mouthful. Finally, stay off your screen while eating.

5. EAT FOUR *DIFFERENT* VEGETABLES A DAY

Each day, eat four (or more) different vegetables. The next day, eat four different ones. Varying the plant foods you eat will supply you with different antioxidants and support the diversity of your gut microbiome. This includes the estrobolome, which is in charge of the bacteria that deal with processing oestrogen.

What to eat

PROTEIN

As we age, we lose muscle. And this loss speeds up in perimenopause due to the shift in hormones. Amino acids in protein are the building blocks of muscle, which is why eating enough protein at every meal is so important. Amino acids also build neurotransmitters, including serotonin and dopamine, and contribute to hormone synthesis too, so eating protein at every meal helps to regulate hormone levels. Protein is also very good for satiety, which is why I advise that your first two bites of any meal are protein. Aim for around 20–30g of protein per meal (you'll get this amount from eating around 110g raw fish, poultry, meat or tofu) and ideally 30g at breakfast.

All fish: Try to include at least two to three portions of omega-3-rich fish per week, such as mackerel, sardines, salmon, herring. Wild salmon is more nutritious than farmed. Buy tinned fish in spring water, brine or olive oil, not sunflower oil. N.B. Avoid tuna, as it's high in toxic mercury.

Portion size: minimum 110g, measured raw. Or one tin

All seafood: This has the bonus of being rich in zinc, as well as containing omega-3.
Portion size: minimum 110g, measured raw
Poultry: Chicken, turkey, duck.
Portion size: minimum 110g measured raw, e.g. one medium chicken breast, one leg portion
Red meat: Choose leaner cuts, such as pork fillet, lamb fillet and steak, beef fillet and sirloin, lean roast beef, lean mince, venison.
Portion size: minimum 110g, measured raw
Eggs: A medium egg provides around 6g of protein and all the essential amino acids. Choose free-range eggs for better quality fats.
Portion size: Two to three eggs (three is better)
Plant-based sources: Like animal and fish protein, tofu and tempeh are complete proteins, which means that they contain all the essential amino acids. Other plant-based proteins include beans and pulses.
Portion size: minimum 110g of tofu and tempeh. Half a tin of beans or pulses
Protein powder: A good quality whey, pea protein or bone broth powder. Avoid any with artificial sweeteners and flavourings. The brands I recommend are in Pippa Loves on my website.
Portion size: scoop containing 20g–30g protein

CARBOHYDRATES

During perimenopause, your blood sugar response to carbohydrates changes – and not in a positive way. As oestrogen levels fall, you become less responsive to the hormone insulin, which is supposed to mop up and store spare blood sugar (glucose) as energy. While you may have felt fine in your twenties eating toast for breakfast or chocolate between meals, you can find now that if you eat sugary food and/or white carbs, they cause blood sugar spikes and crashes that leave you hungry and/or exhausted.

Keeping glucose levels steady can help prevent hanger and keep mood swings to a minimum too. The best carbohydrates are low glycaemic (low GI), which are also called complex carbohydrates – that is, they release their energy into the blood steam slowly. They are high in fibre and/or whole grain, as the fibre is what slows sugar absorption. The added bonus is that they're higher in nutrients too.

Starchy vegetables: Sweet potato, butternut squash, parsnips, pumpkin, potatoes.

Whole grains: Buckwheat noodles, quinoa, oats, wild or basmati rice.

Fruit: Apples, cherries and all berries, kiwi fruit, plums, peaches, greengages and apricots, watermelon and honeydew melon, lemon, lime and grapefruit. Eat a maximum of two or three portions of fruit a day with meals.

FATS

This may be hard to believe but a lot of fats are nutritional heroes, not villains! They make cell membranes, are essential for synthesising hormones, are anti-inflammatory and are needed for you to absorb the fat-soluble vitamins A, D, E, and K. Making sure you're eating enough of the right fats really helps with satiety and balancing blood sugar, too.

Good fats and how to use them
For cooking:

- Extra virgin olive oil: anti-inflammatory, antioxidant and rich in monounsaturated fats, which are good for cholesterol levels.

- Coconut oil: contains medium-chain triglycerides (MCTs), which are rapidly converted into energy.

- Ghee: rich in butyric acid, which supports gut health.

N.B. Although it's a dairy product, ghee is free from both casein (milk protein) and lactose (milk sugar).

For salads, dressings and drizzling:
- Extra virgin olive oil
- Avocado oil: high in monounsaturated fats that are good for cardiovascular health.

For eating:
- Nuts and seeds: including flaxseeds, pumpkin seeds, sunflower seeds, almonds, chia seeds, walnuts, hemp seeds, Brazil nuts. Packed with essential fatty acids but also fibre and protein.
- Avocado: not only a fibre-packed vegetable but full of good fats too.
- Oily fish (mackerel, sardines, anchovies) and seaweed: rich in anti-inflammatory omega-3 fatty acids.

VEGETABLES

The nutrient powerhouses of our diets, vegetables are impressive multitaskers. They're packed with vitamins and minerals – some of which are antioxidants, meaning they reduce inflammation, which is important because this is high during perimenopause. They're also brilliant for the gut because each is packed with different polyphenols – chemicals produced by plants to keep themselves free of bacteria and fungi – as well as fibre, both of which feed beneficial bacteria. Polyphenols also enhance the liver's ability to process and eliminate toxins. Every plant food contains polyphenols but those that are very rich in them include berries, cacao, turmeric and citrus fruits.

All vegetables are great for you but these types have key midlife benefits:

Cruciferous vegetables: Contain compounds that support liver detoxification of used-up hormones.

Eat two types a day, at least. Choose from: broccoli, cabbage, cauliflower, kale, Brussels sprouts, red cabbage, bok choy, watercress, sauerkraut, Romanesco, mustard greens, turnips, rocket and radishes. Best of all are broccoli sprouts (you can buy them at some supermarkets or sprout them yourself). N.B. Chew your veg slowly for maximum benefits.

Vegetables that are rich in sulphur: Sulphur compounds contain glutathione, the powerhouse antioxidant that keeps the liver ticking over. The cruciferous vegetables listed above are a good source, but other sulphur-rich veg include garlic, onion, spring onions, shallots, beetroot, asparagus.

SUPER-POWER YOUR CRUCIFEROUS VEG

This process increases the beneficial sulforaphane content in broccoli and other cruciferous vegetables. Sulforaphane helps liver function, including its role in balancing oestrogen levels.

Chop the washed veg into pieces. Chopping breaks the cell walls, starting a chemical reaction between an enzyme called myrosinase and a compound called glucoraphanin, which produces sulforaphane. Leaving the chopped veg to sit at room temperature for 30 to 40 minutes before eating or cooking will increase levels of sulforaphane.

N.B. To help boost the availability of the sulforaphane content, add a source of myrosinase, such as mustard seed powder or radish.

Green leafy vegetables: High in calcium, which is needed for bone density. Eat all the cruciferous greens (see opposite) plus chard, chicory, endive, spinach, spring greens.

Bitter vegetables: These support bile production in the liver, which is needed to clear out toxins and used-up hormones. Eat rocket, watercress, dandelion, radishes, mustard greens, artichokes, turnip greens and chicory. Cooking with the spices fenugreek and turmeric is good too.

OTHER IMPORTANT FOODS

Polyphenol foods: Plants contain antioxidant substances called polyphenols which support multiple processes in the gut, liver and all over the body. Beetroot and lemon zest are particularly rich in liver-loving antioxidants. Eat a handful of berries and/or pomegranate seeds daily, as their purple and blue colouring is a powerful antioxidant. Cacao is not only rich in polyphenols that are good for the gut but also a calming chemical called anandamide (stick to 80 per cent+ cacao dark chocolate).

Gut supporting foods: Fermented foods contain probiotic bacteria, e.g. sauerkraut and kimchi, miso, coconut, sheep or goat yoghurt, coconut kefir. Foods containing prebiotic fibre, which feeds the good bacteria in your gut, include asparagus, leeks, onions, garlic, chicory, Jerusalem artichokes, chickpeas and all kinds of lentils and beans, flaxseeds and chia seeds.

Iron-rich foods: These are needed to produce energy and for the liver. Eat lean meat, liver, eggs, oily fish, game and the darker meat from poultry. If you're vegetarian or vegan, you can get iron from beans, pulses and dark green leafy vegetables.

Phytoestrogen foods: Phytoestrogens are compounds that occur naturally in a wide range of plant foods. They mimic your body's own oestrogens in a positive way, helping to regulate levels of oestrogen in the body. This makes them a daily go-to for the perimenopausal years. If you have symptoms of high oestrogen (see chapter seven), often the case earlier in perimenopause, they work to help reduce these. And when oestrogen is lower as you get closer to the menopause and beyond, they may help alleviate low oestrogen symptoms. Studies also suggest they could also help reduce appetite, improve skin and support bone health.

Good sources of phytoestrogens include GMO-free, organic, fermented soy, chickpeas, lentils and beans, alfalfa, beansprouts, grapes, peanuts, berries, tea, coffee. My number one phytoestrogen for this age and stage is flaxseeds (see 'How to do daily seed cycling box' on page 58).

Herbs and spices: Herbs and spices are little power packs of bioactive compounds that have health effects. Use them liberally in your cooking and sprinkle fresh herbs on food. Add these spices: turmeric, ginger, cinnamon, saffron. And these herbs: dill, parsley, rosemary, mint, oregano, sage.

You can make your own tea too, as this is a great way to get herbs in every day. Add one to two teaspoons of dried herbs (double that if fresh) to a small pot, add boiling water and leave to steep. You can use one herb or spice or a mixture. These are my favourite ingredients:

Anti-inflammatory tea: turmeric and ginger
Stress-reducing tea: chamomile, holy basil, passionflower, lemon balm, skullcap, oatstraw
Hormone balancing tea: sage, fenugreek and maca.

MAGIC HERBS AND SPICES

Coriander: Contains linalool, a compound known for its antioxidant and anti-inflammatory properties, which aid detoxification.

Cumin: Contains thymoquinone, an antioxidant that may have anti-cancer properties.

Fenugreek: Contains 4-hydroxyisoleucine, which aids in blood sugar regulation.

Garlic: Contains allicin, a sulphur-rich compound with known antibacterial properties.

Ginger: Rich in gingerol, which has potent anti-inflammatory and antioxidant effects.

Parsley: High in flavonoids including apigenin, which has anti-cancer properties.

Passionflower (for tea): Anti-anxiety and good for sleep.

Rosemary: Antioxidant, anti-inflammatory and antimicrobial activities. Can support the liver in its work of detoxifying used hormones.

Tulsi (for tea): An adaptogen (usually a herb or mushroom used in traditional medicine that helps the body adapt to stress). This one gives calm energy.

Turmeric: Known for its active compound curcumin, a potent anti-inflammatory.

Chamomile (for tea): Anti-anxiety and a mild sedative.

Dill: Contains phytoestrogens, so can help balance hormones (see page 68).

Lemon balm (for tea): Mildly sedative, calming, good pre-bed.

Mint: Helps digestion. Calming but also good for concentration. Soothing and cooling for hot flushes.

Oregano: Anti-bacterial so can potentially prevent pathogens. Calming and mood-lifting.

Sage: Contains phytoestrogens. Good for hot flushes and mood. An antioxidant and anti-inflammatory.

Skullcap (for tea): Calming and good for sleep and stress resilience.

Spearmint (for tea): Can help regulate high levels of testosterone. Also aids digestion.

Valerian (for tea): For better sleep and a calmer mind.

Wild oat (for tea): Calming and good for sleep and stress resilience.

HOW TO DO DAILY SEED CYCLING

This is a traditional naturopathic remedy to balance hormones which involves eating specific seeds during particular weeks of your cycle. And there's now evidence that seed cycling works. In a study of women who had been diagnosed with PCOS, the group that did seed cycling as well as portion control had better hormone balance at the end of three months. It's worth doing any time your hormones are out of balance and especially in perimenopause.

Seed cycling is based on the fact that different seeds contain different nutrients. Eating flaxseeds and pumpkin seeds in the first half of your menstrual cycle (roughly days

1 to 14 or the day you ovulate) helps regulate oestrogen. And eating sesame and pumpkin seeds in the second half (roughly days 15 to 28) helps regulate progesterone. If your cycle is irregular, start on day one of your period and follow the four-week plan. If your cycle has stopped, start day one of seed cycling on the first day of the new moon; it may be that seed cycling helps reboot your cycle. If you have low oestrogen symptoms, add an extra two tablespoons of ground flaxseeds every day (see page 159).

Days 1 to 14 (or the day you ovulate): *Eat 1 tablespoon each of freshly ground flax and pumpkin seeds per day, ideally in the morning with a glass of water.*

Days 15 to your next period: *Eat 1 tablespoon each of ground sunflower and sesame seeds per day.*

Foods to leave out or cut back on

You may find that a lot of the foods and drinks you could get away with when you were younger will no longer suit you when you consume them. Your body may give you that message loud and clear, by making perimenopausal symptoms worse or last longer, whether it's fatigue or moodiness, a hangover or a headache.

The following foods are the ones I tell everyone to be wary of. Please don't take this as a lecture – I'm not saying give up everything that gives you pleasure, or that you should never have a big night out or eat a pudding or a sandwich again. I'm a big fan of the 80:20 rule, of finding balance somewhere between pleasure and feeling good in your body. However, if you do have perimenopausal symptoms, you may want to avoid these foods completely for a few months, at least until your hormones are in better balance. Some women find that just cutting out the less helpful foods makes such a noticeable difference to how they feel that they never want to go back to eating them.

Gluten and (some) dairy: I advise everyone to try cutting out cow's dairy and gluten for 30 days. These are the two food types that people are most likely to have a sensitivity to. Reintroduce them separately after four weeks. If you get symptoms (such as nausea, bloating, achy joints, fatigue), you'll know you're sensitive (although it doesn't always mean you're sensitive forever). Sheep and goat milk and cheese is fine, as fewer people have problems with these. You can also have any plant milk without additives, coconut yoghurt and coconut kefir.

Processed foods: By this I mean fast food, junk food, packet foods, most takeaways, pretty much all the foods with a long list of ingredients and additives, any food that won't go bad in a week. Processed foods are low both in fibre and nutrients. They are bad for the health of the microbiome and affect blood sugar balance as well as how we process fats and detox hormones. They are also inflammatory – and as perimenopause is already an inflammatory state, you don't need to add more inflammation on top!

Processed meats: It's fine to eat some red meat, but avoid processed meats such as ham, salami, supermarket sausages, etc. They are full of nitrates that are known carcinogens and can be inflammatory.

White carbs and sugary foods: These cause rapid spikes in blood glucose, then an insulin spike, then blood sugar crashes. When your insulin response changes in perimenopause (see chapter two), the blood sugar and insulin spikes after eating processed carbs get even bigger. Eating too many of these foods for too long can lead to insulin resistance (see chapter 12) and increased fat storage. Plus, the blood sugar rollercoaster directly impacts serotonin and other mood-regulating neurotransmitters too.

Coffee: One to two coffees in the morning is fine – if you are someone who feels fine after one or two coffees. Some people are too sensitive to caffeine even to have one coffee. If you drink a lot of coffee, you'll feel better if you cut down: caffeine affects cortisol levels, which has a knock-on effect on progesterone levels. Some people find that when they do this, or give it up, their sleep and other symptoms improve. Drinking more than 400mg of caffeine day (a Pret cappuccino is 180mg, a Nespresso pod is 60mg to 90mg) can lead to jitters, increased heart rate and insomnia.

Alcohol: A lot of women say they have to stop drinking during the perimenopausal years and when it comes to alcohol, less is more. Our livers don't work as well in midlife; we just can't handle alcohol the way we used to. Used-up hormones are metabolised in the liver and drinking alcohol can interfere with this and make hormonal symptoms worse. The NHS limit for alcohol is 14 units a week, but this isn't necessarily the healthy limit. Ideally your glass of something will be occasional rather than regular.

Suggested supplements for perimenopause

I always say, 'Food comes first' because it's the fundamental building block of your body systems. However, I have seen that the following supplements can make a really profound difference to symptoms, too. If you're on HRT, they can be taken alongside it. In the brackets, you'll see suggestions from the range I've formulated, PCH.

- **B-complex vitamins** are fundamental for energy production and the proper functioning of the nervous system (PCH B-complex).

- **Magnesium** is known as the relaxation mineral; it is needed to help calm the nervous system and support sleep (PCH Magnesium Complex with Taurine).

- **Omega-3 fatty acids** help reduce inflammation and make hormones. N.B. Choose fish oil supplements or plant-based flaxseed oil (PCH Krill Oil).

- **Ashwagandha** is an adaptogenic herb. Adaptogens are herbs used in traditional medicine – Chinese and Ayurvedic – to support the body's ability to handle stress (PCH Ashwagandha).

- **Probiotics** may help to maintain a healthy gut flora, which in turn supports nutrient absorption and immune function (PCH Repopulate Probiotic).

- **Vitamin D** is needed for hormone receptors to work and helps to maintain bone health (PCH Vegan D3 complex with vitamins A and K2).

- A perimenopause blend to support your body systems through this stressful time. The one I formulated includes shatavari, a traditional Ayurvedic herb for the female reproductive system, as well as the Chinese herb dong quai, sage, maca, and the mushroom Tribulus terrestris (PCH Peri-Balance).

- An energy blend to support you as you make dietary and lifestyle changes. Mine includes three adaptogen herbs, includes rhodiola rosea, ginseng, liquorice root as well as co-enzyme Q10 (PCH Ener-Boost). Liquorice can increase cortisol levels, so it's good for people who've been under stress for a long time. N.B. do not take liquorice if you have high blood pressure.

FOOD FRAMEWORK: THE BASICS

1. Eat two bites of protein first and a good amount of protein at every meal. This will help you feel full and give you the building blocks of muscle and hormones.
2. Leave four to five hours between meals (if you can) to support digestion and gut health.
3. Drink two litres of water a day because it's good for all your bodily processes, including hormone processing.
4. Chew your food well to support your digestion and nutrient absorption. And enjoy your food!
5. Eat four different vegetables a day because diversity is great for your gut microbiome, which is key in getting rid of used up hormones. The veg to eat daily are those from the cruciferous family (the cabbage and broccoli family).
6. Make sure carbs are high fibre and/or wholegrain, so they help keep your blood sugar even, which helps with hunger and energy.
7. Eat gut-friendly foods, including fermented foods and prebiotic foods such as beans and lentils.
8. Eat phytoestrogen foods daily to support your oestrogen balance. The best source is flaxseeds but you can also eat fermented soy.

CHAPTER 4

Healthy Hormone Habits

Perimenopause symptoms are your wake-up call. Your body is telling you that, even if you managed without sleep, exercise and a healthy diet in your twenties and thirties, you simply can't now. If you don't look after your body with exercise, or if you are always 'doing' and never resting, during perimenopause this will come back to bite you.

When hormones change, your vulnerability to stress goes up. As you learnt in chapter two, the stress hormone cortisol stirs up a whole range of perimenopausal symptoms. This makes proper rest non-negotiable. If you find it hard to relax, consider this chapter as me giving you permission to stop. Here you'll find some pointers on how to achieve real rest, with meditation and breathwork, as well as getting quality sleep. I joke that you can tell the women who need to meditate the most because they're the ones who roll their eyes when I suggest it (also, if that's you, I used to be you!). However, if you can make a habit of consciously going into a relaxed state, your symptoms will improve.

Don't aim to do everything in this chapter all at once (it will only add to your stress!). Focus on your weakest link. You could start with your sleep, by turning off screens at 8.30pm and creating your own wind-down ritual. If you barely exercise, you could plan in five minutes, three times a day. Experiment with what works for you to find out what you'll keep doing. Just make a small change now, then another one in a week or so. You'll be surprised how quickly these changes add up.

Your toolkit for relaxation

People often ask me what they should do to relax and my answer is to find something that you will do consistently. Try out different styles of meditation to find the ones you like. I always found it really hard to sit and focus on my breath. I tried to get a meditation habit going for years and it was only when I invested in a meditation teacher that I finally managed it. I'm still lucky if I get a few minutes during a session when my mind is quiet, but those few minutes are gold for my mental state all day.

Meditation may not be for you at all. It really doesn't matter what you do from the list below – as long as you stick to it and do it regularly (just downloading the app won't give you any benefits!). You can keep it short, at least at first – a recent study showed that just five minutes of daily meditation or breathwork improves sleep and reduces anxiety. People also reported feeling calmer and more relaxed. Make this your new life rule: five minutes' peace (at least).

MEDITATION

The meditation that has been studied the most (and seems to be the most effective) in midlife women is mindfulness meditation. It's been shown to work for anxiety, depression, sleep and even to reduce hot flushes. It's clear that the more you practise, the better the results.

Mindfulness-based cognitive therapy (MBCT) is a structured course that's been shown to help with menopausal symptoms. You can find more information at oxfordmindfulness.org, but the most basic version of mindfulness meditation is simply to start in a sitting position, still and relaxed, breathing through your nose. Then focus on your breath moving in and out of your nose and observe the sensations that arise.

In loving kindness meditation, you repeat phrases of compassion towards yourself and others, for example, 'May they be safe, may they be loved, may they live with ease'. Some people prefer transcendental meditation (TM) because you learn at classes and you're given your own personal mantra to repeat. Or you might find a guided class easier, where you're talked through the meditation. A good place to start is to try one of the apps Calm, Headspace or Tamara Levitt's Daily Calm.

Some people like moving meditation, such as slow (hatha) yoga, qigong and tai chi. In a 12-week trial of people who'd been put into menopause due to breast cancer treatment, the group that did yoga and meditation had fewer psychological symptoms, less fatigue and an improved quality of life, but also fewer urogenital symptoms.

If, like me, you find meditation hard, you could also try the mindfulness exercise I invented – a version of Eye Spy. While I'm walking the dogs, as my eyes look at something, I say its name out loud. It keeps my mind on what's in front of me and what I'm experiencing in the now, rather than allowing my thoughts to wander.

BREATHWORK

This is a powerful way to calm your nervous system and reduce cortisol levels. It works because it sends a strong message to your body that you are safe, taking your body into rest and digest mode. A lot of women like to do five minutes first thing, even before getting out of bed. Some do it before meals. You can do it lying, sitting or while you're walking. You can do two minutes as a break from work, or when you feel stressed. You can even do it at red traffic lights (and especially when you feel road rage rising!).

How to do breathwork:
- **Cyclic sighing:** In a recent study, this came out as the most effective way to reduce anxiety and improve mood, over other types of breathwork and meditation. Inhale slowly through your nose until your lungs feel full, then inhale again until they feel very full. The second inhale will be short. Let your breath out slowly through your mouth.

- **Longer out breath:** Inhale until your lungs are full, then make your out breath longer. The version I do most often is to breathe out through my nose for eight counts, then in for six counts. But you could do five out and in for three; six out and in for four – whatever works for you. If you find this hard, start with four out then four in.

- **Box breathing:** Each breath and hold is the same length – as if you're breathing the four sides of a box. Breathing through the nose, inhale for four counts. Then hold your breath for four counts, then exhale for four counts, then hold for four counts.

MORE RELAXATION CHOICES

If meditation and breathwork don't appeal, these are some more options:
- Calming music. The app Endel has music to get you into various mind states such as 'focus' and 'calm'.

- Self-hypnosis. This has been shown to help with sleep but also hot flushes. Try the app Reveri.

- Bath, sauna or steam bath. Heat is not only relaxing but also makes you sweat, one of your key detox mechanisms.

- Yoga nidra. Also known as yogic sleep. Lying down, you listen to spoken stories that shut down your thinking mind and put you into a relaxed state somewhere between being awake and asleep, giving your mind and body deep rest.

- Calming stories. The app Calm has meditation stories, which is a good alternative if you find meditation hard.

- Sound baths. A soundtrack or live performance that's designed to take you into a deep state of relaxation.

- Going barefoot, a.k.a. grounding. Not only is this good for the many little muscles in our feet and ankles, but there is a small amount of research to show that being barefoot outside or on natural surfaces helps lower cortisol levels.

- Time in nature. Research shows that spending 120 minutes a week in nature leads to better wellbeing and health overall.

- Listening to music. Calming or uplifting music can improve mood and lower cortisol levels.

MORNING AND EVENING RITUALS

I'm a huge believer in doing the same thing every morning and evening, not least because a consistent waking and bedtime help your body get into restorative sleep. This is what I do but feel free to alter this so it works for you. Prioritise to see what you can fit in and when.

My morning ritual: *I swing my legs out of bed, sit up and drink a big glass of water containing some electrolytes, as you* *sweat out a lot of minerals at night, and the powder contains sodium, magnesium and potassium, which helps your body absorb the water and rehydrates your cells.*

I go downstairs and have a second glass of water – I'm already on my way to two litres a day! I feed the dogs and let them out, then have a cuddle with one of them, Honey, to put me in a good mood.

Then it's time to meditate for ten minutes. If the sun is up, I'll do it outside, as daylight helps raise cortisol, which is not only a stress hormone but in the morning is your get-up-and-go hormone. I'll often go barefoot and if the sun is out, I'll uncover my limbs to help make vitamin D.

Three days a week, I go straight to the gym for an intense 30-minute workout. I focus on strength training, sometimes add in some HIIT, then take a cold shower (though I skip this if I'm stressed because then it acts like extra stress rather than revival).

Sixty minutes after I've got up, I drink my coffee. Waiting a bit longer helps the coffee work more effectively and prevents an afternoon energy crash. If I haven't meditated first thing, I'll slot in a few minutes a few times throughout the day, often while I'm walking the dogs.

Evening ritual: *Just starting this ritual calms me down. As I'm a high energy person, I need to take a long run-up to bedtime in order to get quality sleep. At 8.30pm, I put my phone to bed for the night; I'm not allowed to pick it up again (I confess that some calls aren't silenced, and that's those from my children if they're not at home; it's hard to switch off from* *mothering!). I run a bath with two cups of Epsom salts and soak for around 20 minutes. This raises my body temperature and when it later drops, this helps put my body into sleep mode.*

At 9pm, I make what my husband James calls 'the witches' brew': a big pot of relaxing herbal tea for the two of us, with a teaspoon each of camomile, lemon balm, valerian and passionflower. I find that loose herbs have stronger effects (though teabags are great too). Then we watch TV – never anything too exciting and I wear blue-light blocking glasses – for around an hour. I'm usually in bed by 10pm, then I give my feet a 10-minute massage using half sweet almond oil and half sesame oil, which is not only good for circulation but relaxing and rebalancing. I read until around 10.30pm, when I turn my light off.

ARE YOU OVERDOING IT?

Some activities we assume are healthy can be too stressful when you're already having to cope with hormonal shifts. For example, exercising too hard is linked with higher cortisol and too much inflammation. I'm also seeing a lot of clients who put their body under stress by fasting for too long, or over too many days, or who are doing cold plunges or cold-water swimming despite feeling worse afterwards.

Without measuring cortisol levels, there are clues that you're overdoing exercise, cold exposure or fasting, which come from how you feel. If you need a nap or feel exhausted after an exercise session, or wake up sore and tired, you're

> *likely going too hard and/or for too long. If a cold plunge gives you a short-term high but then wipes you out, it may not suit you right now. If you don't feel good while fasting, or you get an energy crash or stop sleeping well, it may be that your eating window is too narrow or you aren't eating enough.*

Your exercise plan

Exercise really is like a magic pill that can counter the metabolic changes of midlife – it contributes to regulating insulin levels, supports liver function and helps process hormones.

The main thing is to be consistent: do something, anything, regularly. NHS guidance says to work out for two and a half hours a week – that's half an hour a day, five days a week. If you can't do 30 minutes, do 10 or 20. If you can't find longer periods of time, break it up into small five- or ten-minute chunks throughout the day. Try to stand up and move for at least five minutes every hour.

I find exercising first thing works for me, otherwise I don't fit it in. Experiment to find out when or what works for you, following the guidelines below. You will ideally include three kinds of exercise in your plan: strength-training, aerobic and mobility. Mix them up throughout the week.

STRENGTH-TRAINING/RESISTANCE EXERCISE

Strength training, two to three times a week, is non-negotiable for midlife women. A lot of women are nervous of building muscle but it's such a positive thing to do, not just to look good but because it counters the natural loss of muscle that comes with age, improves the lean muscle-to-fat ratio, plus muscle is metabolically active, so building it will help with blood sugar control.

If you're a beginner, start with bodyweight exercises – using your own weight against gravity rather than any equipment – and build up to using weights. It's good to get advice from an expert to make sure you're doing the exercises correctly, and especially if you have any health conditions or injuries. As you get stronger and move on to weights, remembering that the amount you're lifting doesn't matter – even if you're lifting 3kg and a friend is lifting 10kg – as long as it's at the right level for you.

For maximum gains, aim to get to the point where you're doing, for example, five to eight reps and the last two are hard – but not so hard you're left struggling to get on with your day afterwards. That said, if you are a newbie, you will feel some soreness the next day. Listen to your body.

What to do: Weight machines in the gym, any weights such as dumbbells/kettlebells, resistance bands, TRX straps – though do make sure you know what you are doing to avoid injury. Bodyweight exercises including Pilates, yoga and ballet count too, but weights will take the benefits to the next level.

CARDIO OR AEROBIC EXERCISE

As you go through perimenopause, your risk of cardiovascular conditions goes up, so exercise that works your heart is essential. A lot of women I see in clinic, especially runners, spend their exercise time doing mainly cardio. If that's you, there's a faster and more effective way to get the cardiovascular benefits of exercise by switching to HIIT, aka high intensity interval training. These are short bursts of exercise that take you to your cardio limit, followed by short but less intense recovery periods.

If you're starting out with exercise, you can get the benefits of HIIT by simply varying your pace as you walk, or by walking up and down hills rather than going at the same speed on the flat.

Serious runners often tell me they don't want to cut down on their usual big runs, but this isn't the time of life to run marathons or do endurance races. I usually advise hard runners to sub in some sessions of HIIT and at least one slow yoga day per week too. N.B. As you up the intensity of your exercise, research suggests consistency and rest are key.

What to do: Walking is the most brilliant exercise, especially if you do it outside, so you get the benefits of daylight and nature too. Aim to walk 6,000 to 10,000 steps per day, as many days as you can per week, which will take roughly 40 minutes to 90 minutes per day. You can break it up over the day. Turn walking and other workouts into HIIT, including running, swimming, cycling, dancing and roller skating, by alternating between fast and slow, or up and downhill.

FLEXIBILITY, BALANCE AND MOBILITY

The third part of your fitness regime is to keep bending and balancing, because hormone changes affect your stability and core strength as well as your mobility. Flexibility work may seem low priority if for example you're trying to lose weight, but your future self will thank you, especially as it reduces the risk of a serious fall, which increases with age. Pilates, yoga, qigong and tai chi also include an element of breath control, so help calm you as well as building muscle. There's some powerful research showing that yoga not only makes you bendy and helps with joint pain but can also improve perimenopausal mood changes and reduce hot flushes. It may be the meditative aspect that helps here: some women tell me that savasana, where you lie still at the end of the class, is the only time they get to relax.

What to do: Pilates, yoga, qigong, tai chi.

How I put my workout together

My basic gym routine is either just weights, or a combination of weights with some HIIT or power (such as box jumping) at the end. I'll do this in the gym or at home. Once a week I also go into the woods near my house and do some hill sprints (SIT – sprint interval training). This mix-and-match approach has been shown to be a really positive way to build and maintain muscle and bone.

If you're not certain how to plan your workout, a circuits class will include all three key elements. Or a fast yoga class will bring mobility, aerobic and strength benefits.

Though, if all this is sounding confusing, it's important to remember that all movement counts. Stand on one leg when you're brushing your teeth (don't forget to alternate legs!), stand up from your desk every hour and run up and down the stairs. You can have a lot of fun at workout classes or doing weekend walks with friends. And there are so many free resources for great workouts too. A couple of my favourites, which you can find on Instagram and via their websites, are from Sarah Gorman and Holly Active.

Sleep

Getting up for the loo yet again? Waking up sweating and hot? Finding yourself wide awake at 3am? A 2017 study by the American Menopause Society showed that 32 to 42 per cent of perimenopausal women have insomnia symptoms, compared to 16 per cent across all women. The main symptoms are: difficulty falling asleep, waking during the night, waking early in the morning and low quality sleep, meaning you don't feel refreshed when you wake up.

Disturbed sleep is often one of the first signs of perimenopause. Often, it's a lack of progesterone, the first hormone to change during perimenopause, that's to blame for sleeping less deeply (for more, see chapter one). Lower oestrogen levels can also contribute, as this hormone supports the production of the good mood brain chemical serotonin, which you need in order to make the sleepy hormone melatonin. If you weren't a great sleeper before perimenopause, your sleep can become worse. The real kicker to this is that deep sleep is exactly what you need to help keep hormones optimal for your age.

You likely already know the basic rules of sleep hygiene. I'm going to cover them below, adapted for midlife, plus some specific sleep hormone advice.

- Allow yourself enough time in bed to get the sleep you need – but not too much. You've probably heard you should aim for seven to eight hours' sleep. This is an average; you may feel good on less or more. Also, don't lie around in bed. If you feel good on six hours sleep, only spend seven hours physically in bed each night. If you sleep for seven hours, eight hours in bed will be enough.

- Train your clock. Your body has its own day/night clocks, which are kept in synch by a central clock. When this is working, your sleepiness – which builds up over the course of the day – will coincide with your physical and mental tiredness, and your readiness to sleep. Some people have to work a bit harder to make this happen.

- The morning is when your cortisol should be high to wake you up: it should peak around an hour to 90 minutes after waking. It should then go down during the day, which allows your sleepy hormone, melatonin, to rise in the evening. There are things you can do to optimise your clock. Think of it like sleep training a small baby – once you find what works, keep doing it!

- Good sleep starts first thing in the morning. Light entering your eyes sets your internal clock to daytime and helps you make serotonin, which you need to make melatonin. Ideally, get at least 10 to 30 minutes outside in daylight as early in the day as possible. Even better, as movement is also a waking signal, do some of your workout outside. If it's winter, you could use a light box (see 'Pippa Loves' on my website). This produces light that mimics daylight, so it's the closest thing to being outside.

- In the evening, go for low lighting. Going outside into the pink-tinged dusk is a powerful signal to your body that it's time to wind down for sleep. Try blue light-blocking glasses if you're looking at screens, although I always turn off my computer and phone at 8.30pm. When you sleep, you need pitch black. Put up blackout blinds or curtains, or wear an eye mask.

- There are some foods that are key to sleep. You need the amino acid tryptophan to make serotonin. Good sources are turkey, chicken, eggs, chickpeas and oats. You need to eat tryptophan with carbs in order to absorb it well. You also need enough vitamin D as well as B vitamins.

- If you wake at night, try not to worry or panic if you can't get back to sleep. Try the cyclic sigh breathing on page 68. If that doesn't work, get up and go to lie on the sofa in a dim light and read a book. Do not turn on any bright lights – ideally, not even in the bathroom. When you feel sleepy, go back to bed.

- Changing hormones can make your body thermostat over sensitive and over reactive, so temperature control becomes more important.

  - Keep your bedroom at 18 to 22 degrees Celsius – although some people find they prefer it to be even cooler, at 17 or even 16 degrees. You could keep a window open and/or turn off your bedroom heating.

  - Before sleep, your body temperature needs to dip by around half a degree Celsius. Bring this on by having a warm bath then getting cool before you get dressed for bed.

  - Stick to cool cotton pyjamas or a nightie and consider changing to a cooler summer-weight duvet.

- The sleep disturbing condition restless legs often starts during perimenopause. If this is you, make sure you're getting enough of the minerals sodium, magnesium and potassium (the supplement Bodybio E-Lyte Balanced Electrolyte Concentrate can help – see 'Pippa Loves' on my website).

ARE YOU BREATHING PROPERLY?

Age and especially weight gain raises your likelihood of snoring and sleep apnoea. Sleep apnoea is when you stop breathing briefly during sleep. This sends an alarm to your body that there's something wrong, and it wakes you up with the fight or flight response, taking you out of deep sleep. After a night of this, you'll wake up unrefreshed. The resulting rise in cortisol can have a negative effect on both testosterone and oestrogen levels.

- If you snore, ask someone if they can monitor your breathing; if you do stop breathing while you're asleep, see your GP. You may need a CPAP machine that blows oxygen into your airways while you sleep.

- According to Professor Andrew Huberman, creator of the Huberman Lab podcast, improving your capacity to breathe through your nose can help. You do this by practising breathing only through your nose while you exercise (not including swimming and very heavy exercise). It's surprisingly hard, but it does become easier over time.

PRACTICAL TIPS FOR GOOD SLEEP

- Keep your bedroom for sleeping only (oh, and sex). You might be used to lying in bed to work, eat breakfast or catch up on emails, or you might use your bedroom for exercise. But you need your brain to associate bed with rest, not socialising or work.

- If you share a bed, make it as big a bed as you have space for. Ideally, you'd be in a super king but you may not have enough room. You may also want to invest in separate, single duvets, as they have in Scandinavia, so you can wrap yourself up as much or as little as you want.

- Most people suit a 'medium firm' mattress. If it's too soft, your hips and shoulders will sink down too much. But if it's too hard, your shoulders will stick up, putting pressure on your neck.

- If your partner disturbs your sleep with snoring, ear plugs may not be enough. If you have another room, can one of you move rooms? Make the spare room bed or the sofa into

- a lovely place to sleep, with sheets, pillows and a duvet as cosy as the ones in your bedroom.

- You want your sleepiness to build over the course of the day. It's best to keep naps short and before mid-afternoon. Movement and being mentally taxed also increase tiredness.

- Caffeine has a half-life of five to six hours, so try cutting it out after lunch, or even earlier.

- In the evening, keep your brain calm by sticking to bland TV – and no scrolling!

- If you need more help, the insomnia intervention with the most evidence is called CBTi. The CBTi-based apps Sleepstation and Sleepio may be available via your GP (also, see page 128 for supplements that can help with sleep).

Clean up your environment

Many environmental toxins do their damage by mimicking your hormones. These kinds of endocrine-disrupting chemicals are widespread, for example bisphenol A (BPA) is a softener used in a lot of plastics. It is a xenoestrogen – it mimics oestrogen and fits into your oestrogen receptors, disrupting your hormonal balance. This can give you either high or low oestrogen symptoms.

On top of this, all toxins and used-up hormones need to be processed in the liver, so it makes sense to minimise your exposure to endocrine disruptors and other toxins where you can, including from the environment, in food and beauty products, from cigarettes and alcohol, as well as common drugs such as paracetamol that can be hard on the liver.

Endocrine disruptors include BPA and phthalates in plastic bottles, phthalates and parabens in skincare, some pesticides and herbicides in food.

- As much as you can, minimise your contact with plastic and non-stick pans, and especially the contact of your food with them. Replace non-stick and aluminium pans where possible with stainless steel, cast iron, ceramic or glass.

- Don't heat food or drinks in plastic. Where possible, don't store food in plastic or aluminium foil. Use glass, enamel, ceramic or stainless steel.

- Wash your fruit and vegetables to reduce residues of pesticides and herbicides. Rinse in a weak solution of vinegar or in Veggi Wash.

- Filter your drinking and cooking water where possible. Avoid water that's been bottled in plastic. I like the reverse osmosis method to filter water. See 'Pippa Loves' on my website for recommendations.

- Filter your air, especially if you suffer with environmental allergies. See 'Pippa Loves' for recommendations on air filter machines.

- Avoid taking till receipts. The thermal paper they're printed on is coated in BPA.

- Buy cleaning products, make-up and toiletries that are as natural as possible. In particular, buy formaldehyde-free nail polish.

- Take regular saunas or hot baths with added Epsom salts. Sweating hasn't been shown to help remove specific toxins from the body but it is another way that the body detoxifies.

- Dry skin brushing or any kind of massage before or after your bath will help stimulate the lymph system too, which is also key to detoxing, as well as removing dead skin cells that may be blocking pores.

- Finally, work on reducing your stress (see page 68). The stress hormone adrenaline is also broken down in the liver (see chapter five for more).

What else can help?

Therapy: At this time of transition, you may need help working out what the next part of your life should look like. Talking therapy can help with a larger perspective. Evidence shows CBT (cognitive behavioural therapy) works not just for emotional issues such as anxiety, stress and depression, but also for hot flushes, sleep and fatigue. It can help you manage your symptoms by reframing them and changing the way you think about them. Hobbies and learning help both mood and cognitive function. Everyone needs something for themselves – something other than the many other roles that occupy their lives. I am still looking for my thing!

Friends, groups, community and fun: This can be the missing piece, especially for women who say they only have time for work and family. Surround yourself with people who mean the most to you. You need peace in your life, so removing toxic relationships and friendships is a must, too. Support groups can help with peri/menopause symptoms as well as offering social support. The better your tribe, the better your vibe!

HEALTHY HORMONE HABITS | 83

> *EVERYDAY WAYS TO CALM YOUR MIND*
>
> *What to do if your thoughts are spinning out of control:*
>
> - *While walking, watch your feet planting on the ground, one after the other. It makes you present in every step.*
>
> - *While brushing your teeth, focus on each stroke and each tooth you clean.*
>
> - *Breathe in for four and out for eight. Set a timer to do this for two minutes, every hour.*
>
> - *Turn off the notifications on that pop up on your phone and/or make a noise. And adjust your settings so that only vital people can get through to you.*
>
> - *Massage your feet for ten minutes using a natural oil, doing what feels good, with a mixture of kneading and softer strokes.*

HORMONE HABITS: THE BASICS

1. Create your relaxation toolkit. It doesn't matter what you do – meditation, breathwork, nature or mindfulness – as long as you do something to calm your mind, every day.
2. Move your body. Aim for 150 minutes a week, combining balance/stretching, strength/weights and cardio.
3. Walk 6,000 to 10,000 steps a day. Our bodies were created to walk!
4. Make sleep a priority. Create a purposeful evening wind-down ritual with minimal screens, subdued light and relaxing activities.
5. Clean up your environment. As much as you can, go low and no chemical in household and beauty products.

Hayley's story

My first symptom of perimenopause was heart palpitations. They'd come on in the middle of the night. It felt as if someone was sitting on my chest as my heart beat harder and faster. I'd turn onto my side but the noise would be so loud, I could still hear it in my head. I'd get palpitations for two weeks, then not for two weeks, then they'd come back.

I used to think: *Am I having a heart attack? Is there something seriously wrong with me? Am I too stressed?* I have a busy, hectic job – which I love – running a marketing agency. When I went to see my doctor, I told him I was tired too. I tend to go at 100 miles an hour during the working week, but some weekends I couldn't get out of bed. To complicate things, I also have an autoimmune condition called scleroderma that causes skin inflammation. The GP said I was in burnout and put me on an antidepressant.

Next, I began to get hot sweats around the time of my period, but I blamed those on stress, too. Then my skin became really itchy. At work, I went from never forgetting anything to thinking: *Where on earth did I leave my car key?* I made sure the brain fog didn't affect my work by writing every single thing down. But still I'd wonder: *What's wrong with me?* I felt as if I was losing myself.

Over a few years, the symptoms either got worse or happened more often. I suspected I was in perimenopause, so went to see Claire, a nutritionist at Pippa's clinic. I did a DUTCH Cycle Mapping test that confirmed I was perimenopausal. But the levels of key hormones – oestrogen, progesterone and testosterone – were lower than Claire expected to see for my age. And my cortisol was massively high. I also did a DNA test that showed I was programmed not to produce a lot of serotonin or dopamine.

The key to improving my hormone levels and calming my symptoms, Claire said, was to get my stress and cortisol down, and to tweak my diet. I've always exercised regularly and eaten well due to my autoimmune condition and the food allergies to gluten, wheat and corn I've had since I was a teenager. Claire suggested I increase the anti-inflammatory power of my diet by varying my vegetables, eating the rainbow and getting as much colour on my plate as possible. She told me to add herbs and spices to every meal too. And to eat cruciferous vegetables every day – cauliflower and broccoli, cabbage and sprouts – to help with hormone balance.

Claire gave me a bespoke supplement regime, including PCH Vitamin D3, curcumin, PCH Chill (with saffron for mood and L-Theanine for relaxation). She advised me to focus on my sleep too. On a good night, I used to have four to five hours; on a bad night it would be two. I was having to get up at 2am and 5am to wee. So Claire suggested I stop drinking fluids at 8pm. And that I should cut down on drinking alcohol too, not only because I was using it to wind down too often but because it was sabotaging my sleep.

Now, most days, I make sure I cook good food, although I do eat out sometimes. Breakfast is fruit and yoghurt, or eggs, or a protein shake with PCH Super Greens. Lunch is protein plus vegetables. For dinner, I cook a stew, or veggies and fish. If I have carbs, it'll be sweet potato.

I've started to track my cycle so I know when it's the week before my period. Then, if I feel down or I'm going crazy, or am tempted to reach for wine to get a dopamine hit, I can catch myself before I do it.

I make sure I relax every day. I've learnt to make time for myself, and to stop saying yes to everyone and everything. I love cooking, particularly making bread. I've adapted a sourdough recipe so I can make gluten-free focaccia and rolls. And I have learnt to make gluten-free pasta too. I love walking my two dogs and looking after my other animals – three horses and three chickens. They calm me down. I do hot and cold therapy at least three times a week too, between an ice bath and sauna, finishing off in the hot tub.

If I don't have enough sleep, I've noticed that all my good intentions go out of the window. So I have a regular evening routine: I have a bath with magnesium salts, then I lie on my spiky shakti mat for 20 minutes, which works via acupressure. I found a device called Sensate that helps me meditate – it vibrates on your vagus nerve and puts you into relaxation mode, plus it plays calming natural sounds.

I'm thinking about starting HRT at some point, but I will see how my symptoms go. I'm not getting palpitations any more but the hot flushes come back occasionally. I'm much calmer and I have a lot more energy now. Claire has made me more aware of what's going on in my body and given me the tools to look after myself. I can't do everything she says all of the time, but I can do most of it most of the time.

Part 3

Solving Your Symptoms

This section is where you'll work out your personal hormonal formula to help reduce your perimenopausal symptoms. Everyone will feel benefits from following the Food Framework and the Hormone Habits we've just been looking at in chapters three and four. However, the PCM helps you personalise the plan to your hormonal needs, because we're all different and we will all have a variety of different symptoms in perimenopause. Your symptoms will depend on a combination of your genetics and constitution, your lifestyle and nutrition, and whether you're taking HRT (and the dosage too).

Sometimes, women assume their symptoms are simply part of being a woman: nuisances to be ignored or 'powered through'. But don't do this – it can tank your quality of life and put a strain on your relationships. It affects your long-term health too, including brain function (especially memory and concentration), the strength of your bones, the risk of high blood pressure and cardiovascular disease.

What are your symptoms?

Each chapter within this part of the book opens by detailing a set of symptoms that correspond to a particular hormonal imbalance that's common at this time of life. When I explain these sets of symptoms to women, they are often relieved to know there's something real going on and that there are specific things they can do to improve these symptoms.

If you have three or more of the symptoms in each section, it's very likely you have that imbalance – at least at some times of the month. You can read and follow the advice for ALL the sets of symptoms that sound like yours.

Remember, your hormones are always in flux during perimenopause, and your symptoms will change over the coming months and years too. Each time you have a new symptom, you can come back to the lists that follow and see if there are any additional ways you can help yourself.

Symptom checklist

Let's start by identifying your symptoms so you can head to the chapters that cover that particular hormone imbalance first. Afterwards, you might like to read the other chapters too, to help you recognise any groups of symptoms that you might experience in the future, rather than automatically putting them down to tiredness and stress, as so many of us do.

ADRENAL DYSFUNCTION

- ☐ Fatigue. Do you feel tired, even after a night's sleep?
- ☐ Needing caffeine. Is it unthinkable to get through the morning without coffee?

- ☐ Brain fog. Do you find it impossible to focus or concentrate?
- ☐ Weight gain. Have you gained weight around the middle that's hard to shift?
- ☐ Dizziness. When you get up, do you feel light-headed, especially when getting up from lying down?
- ☐ Overwhelmed and down. Are you more teary, reactive and less resilient when stressful things happen?
- ☐ Soreness. Do you have sore muscles and achy joints? Are you slow to recover after exercise?
- ☐ Energy crashes. Do you find your energy bottoms out in the afternoon?
- ☐ Craving salty and/or sweet foods. Are you unstoppable around crisps and nuts or cakes and chocolate?
- ☐ Low immunity. Are you getting sick more often? Are any injuries slow to heal?

If this sounds like you, see chapter 5

PROGESTERONE DROP

- ☐ Irregular menstrual cycle. Can you no longer plan around your period because you're not sure when it will come?
- ☐ Heavy menstrual bleeding. Are your periods heavy? This means having to change your protection every one to two hours, or your menstrual cup more often than is recommended, having to use two kinds of protection or a period that lasts more than seven days.
- ☐ Mood swings. Do you have attacks of anxiety or sadness that feel more than ordinary ups and downs? Do you feel less able to cope with stressful situations, so they hit you harder?
- ☐ Worried, anxious, low and/or depressed. Are you persistently

SOLVING YOUR SYMPTOMS | 91

anxious about things without being able to pinpoint a reason? Have you lost your love for life, so you can't see the point?

- ☐ Sleep problems. Are you having difficulty falling asleep or staying asleep? Or waking up tired? Is your sleep being disturbed by having to go to the loo more than once?
- ☐ Night sweats. Are you waking up in the night feeling hot and sweating, perhaps so that your sheets are soaked?
- ☐ Weight gain. Have you gained weight despite not changing your eating or even after trying to eat less?
- ☐ Bloating. Do you often feel bloated and puffy, as if you're holding onto water? (When your period comes, this feeling may go away.)

If this sounds like you, see chapter 6

OESTROGEN DOMINANCE

- ☐ Rage and/or irritability. Are you easily frustrated or annoyed? Do you find yourself accelerating from irritable to angry in a heartbeat?
- ☐ Weight gain. Have you gained weight despite not changing your eating or trying to eat less?
- ☐ Premenstrual syndrome (PMS). Have your PMS symptoms, such as mood swings, abdominal cramping, fatigue and irritability, become worse or are they lasting longer? Or have you got PMS for the first time?
- ☐ Fatigue. Do you constantly feel drained and low in energy?
- ☐ Headaches/migraines. Have you got new headaches, or are your headaches are more frequent or more intense?
- ☐ Endometriosis, fibroids, cysts. Have you been diagnosed with any of these?

- ☐ Breast tenderness and swelling. Do your breasts feel particularly sensitive? This may be towards the run-up to your period, from around day 18 to 20 up to 28, or from around day 3 of your period.

If this sounds like you, see chapter 7

OESTROGEN DEFICIENCY

- ☐ Hot flushes. Do you get suddenly overcome by heat, especially over your face, neck and chest? You may also feel heart palpitations and anxiety too.
- ☐ Vaginal dryness. Have you noticed vaginal dryness or soreness? Or that sex is more uncomfortable or painful? Are you getting UTIs more regularly?
- ☐ Weight. Have you noticed you're putting on weight around your mid-section? And/or that you're losing the definition of your waist?
- ☐ Insomnia. Are you sleeping for less time than you used to? Do you wake up feeling less refreshed?
- ☐ Fatigue. Do you feel you don't have the energy levels you used to have? Do you feel subpar, although you can't pinpoint why?
- ☐ Cognitive issues. Is your memory not as good as it used to be? Is it hard to pay attention and to understand some information?
- ☐ Joint pain. Do you have more aches and pains than you used to?
- ☐ Skin changes. Is your skin drier than it used to be, so you have to use a thicker moisturiser? Does it feel thinner and less springy, more saggy? Do you feel you've lost your glow?

SOLVING YOUR SYMPTOMS

- ☐ Bone issues. Have you been diagnosed with osteopenia or osteoporosis? Or have you broken a bone when you wouldn't have expected to?

If this sounds like you, see chapter 8

ANDROGEN DOMINANCE

- ☐ Acne and oily skin. Are you getting spots on your face or body? Are breakouts happening more often or are they more severe?
- ☐ Facial and body hair. Have you noticed new growth of facial or body hair, particularly on your chin, upper lip or abdomen?
- ☐ Hair thinning. Is your hair lacking its usual volume? Is your scalp more visible along the parting or hairline or on the temples and/or on the crown?
- ☐ Weight gain. Are you putting on weight despite sticking to the same eating and exercise habits?
- ☐ A short fuse. Are your emotions on an unpredictable roller-coaster, so you can easily find yourself irritated and angry?

If this sounds like you, see chapter 9

ANDROGEN DEFICIENCY

- ☐ Low libido. Has your level of desire dropped? Has the idea of sex become less appealing? Are you less aroused than you used to be?
- ☐ Low energy and fatigue. Do you often feel tired or drained even after a night's sleep? Does this fatigue stop you getting on with life?
- ☐ Loss of muscle mass. Have you noticed a loss in muscle tone or definition, but you haven't changed your eating or exercise?

- ☐ Difficulty concentrating. Are you finding it hard to focus or concentrate on tasks? Are you more easily distracted than usual?
- ☐ Vaginal dryness. Have you noticed vaginal dryness or soreness? Or that sex is more uncomfortable or painful? Are you getting UTIs more regularly?
- ☐ Feeling flat and unmotivated. Do you have low mood that won't shift? Or have you lost interest in activities you once enjoyed? Do you find it increasingly difficult to motivate yourself to do work, fun things or chores?

If this sounds like you, see chapter 10

LOW THYROID FUNCTION

- ☐ Feeling tired or sluggish. Do you find you need a lot of sleep to function? Or do you always need an afternoon nap?
- ☐ Feeling cold. Do your hands and feet often feel cold? And/or do you feel cold at times when other people don't?
- ☐ Weight gain. Do you find that you put on weight easily? Or are you gaining weight despite not changing what you eat?
- ☐ Constipation. Do you go to the loo less than once a day? Does your digestion feel sluggish or do you feel bloated?
- ☐ Loss of outer third of eyebrow. Look at your brows: is the outside third very thin or thinner than it was?
- ☐ Thinning and shedding hair: Have you noticed you're losing a lot of hair? Does your hair clog up your hairbrush or the plughole? Is your hair looking thinner all over?
- ☐ Indigestion after rich food. Do you feel queasy or get a tummy ache after eating fatty foods? Or have you noticed that your poop is pale and floats?

SOLVING YOUR SYMPTOMS | 95

- ☐ High LDL cholesterol. Has a blood test shown that your levels of HDL (bad) cholesterol are high?

If this sounds like you, see chapter 11

BLOOD SUGAR DYSREGULATION

- ☐ Hanger. Do you feel both hungry and angry when you haven't eaten for a while?
- ☐ Fatigue after eating. Does it feel as if you go into a 'food coma' after meals, so that you could fall asleep?
- ☐ Waking at night. Do you often wake up during the night, in particular before 3am?
- ☐ Brain fog. Do you find it especially hard to focus either before eating or afterwards?
- ☐ Weight gain. Are you carrying weight around the middle? In particular, is your waist over 35 inches (89cm)?
- ☐ Sweet or carby cravings. Do you feel hungry even after eating? Do you crave sweets or carbs but when you eat them, you don't feel better?

If this sounds like you, see chapter 12

CHAPTER 5

Adrenal Dysfunction

- Fatigue. Do you feel tired, even after a night's sleep?
- Needing caffeine. Is it unthinkable to get through the morning without coffee?
- Brain fog. Do you find it impossible to focus or concentrate?
- Weight gain. Have you gained weight around the middle that's hard to shift?
- Dizziness. When you get up, do you feel light-headed, especially when getting up from lying down?
- Overwhelmed and down. Are you more teary, reactive and less resilient when stressful things happen?
- Soreness. Do you have sore muscles and achy joints? Are you slow to recover after exercise?
- Energy crashes. Do you find your energy bottoms out in the afternoon?
- Craving salty and/or sweet foods. Are you unstoppable around crisps and nuts or cakes and chocolate?

- Low immunity. Are you getting sick more often? Are any injuries slow to heal?

Stress is a factor for almost every client I see – and it probably is for you too. That's why this chapter, which explains how stress affects your hormones, comes before all the other hormone imbalance chapters. Stress either creates or worsens a whole range of perimenopausal symptoms.

Most of the women I see in clinic tell me they've felt under constant stress for years. They may have got away with living this fast-paced, high-pressure life during their twenties and early thirties. But once perimenopause hits, they suddenly find they can no longer do this. In fact, stress is one of the major reasons – along with diet, lifestyle and genetics – that perimenopause symptoms can hit women like a ton of bricks, rather than being a gradual transition.

What's the stress-hormone connection?

When you come up against a stress, your body acts as if you are in danger. The communication system between the brain and adrenals, called the hypothalamic-pituitary-adrenal (HPA) axis, that we met in chapter one, tells your adrenal glands to make stress hormones, including adrenaline and cortisol. These help give you a burst of energy. In evolutionary terms, this response was designed as a short-term fix, just to escape the immediate danger, like being confronted by a predator.

Once the danger has passed, a feedback loop should send a message around the HPA axis to switch off the production of adrenaline and cortisol. Then, you can return to your recovery or 'rest or digest' relaxed state.

However, modern stress – work challenges, ageing parents,

ADRENAL DYSFUNCTION | 99

children's exams – tend to be more long term, which means that the adrenals will keep on producing cortisol. This is a problem because cortisol is inflammatory. Eventually, the HPA axis will register that there has been too much damaging cortisol hanging around for too long and so, for self-protection, it will scale production right down.

But this causes an even worse problem: low cortisol. As well as being a stress hormone, cortisol is your get-up-and-go hormone. It's supposed to be high in the morning – it gives you that kick to get out of bed – then it should reduce towards the evening, so you're relaxed for sleep. If you don't have enough cortisol, you're tired all the time (if you have cortisol that's too high, you're more likely to feel tired and wired).

The name that used to be given to this was 'adrenal fatigue'. But in fact, this name is misleading. It's not that the adrenals are exhausted, it's that the communication system between the brain and the adrenals, the HPA axis, has become dysregulated. Treating this HPA dysregulation can help to restore healthy cortisol levels.

SEX HORMONES UNDER STRESS

During perimenopause, the negative effects of the drop in sex hormones are amplified by HPA dysfunction. In your fertile years, you make most of your sex hormones in your ovaries and some in your adrenals. If you had some adrenal dysfunction in your fertile years, it wouldn't have made much of a difference to your levels of sex hormones. However, over the course of the perimenopause, as your ovaries wind down as a hormone factory, your adrenals should take over, to make the small amount of oestrogen and progesterone that you need. But when HPA comms are disrupted by stress, this causes three major glitches in your sex hormone manufacturing system.

As you read in chapter one, your hormones are made in a cascade, one from another. The raw material for most hormones is cholesterol. It's used to make the grandmother hormone, pregnenolone, which becomes the mother hormone, DHEA, then testosterone and, finally, oestrogen. Mother hormone DHEA is actually made in the adrenals. When you're stressed, your adrenals will prioritise making stress hormones – cortisol – instead of making DHEA, so you won't have the raw materials available to make testosterone and oestrogen. This makes sense: in times of stress, the body prioritises survival over fertility. Also, the raw materials needed for cortisol are diverted from making the sex hormone progesterone, so you make less progesterone too.

Finally, the production of testosterone and oestrogen in the ovaries has its own communication channel to and from the brain – the hypothalamus-pituitary-ovarian or HPO axis, as you can see in this diagram.

WHERE HORMONES ARE MADE

The diagram shows how your adrenals make both stress hormones and sex hormones . . . The manufacture of stress hormones will always take priority over sex hormones.

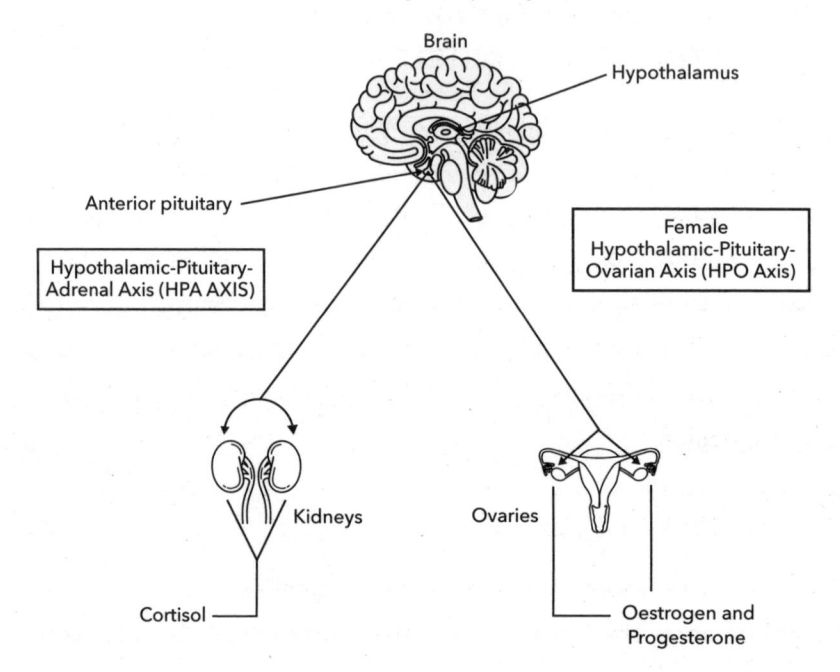

- Brain
- Hypothalamus
- Anterior pituitary
- Hypothalamic-Pituitary-Adrenal Axis (HPA AXIS)
- Female Hypothalamic-Pituitary-Ovarian Axis (HPO Axis)
- Kidneys
- Ovaries
- Cortisol
- Oestrogen and Progesterone

When brain-to-adrenal communication breaks down due to stress, a.k.a. HPA dysregulation, this affects the HPO axis too. Your body doesn't get the signal to make testosterone and oestrogen as it should.

Three key reasons for adrenal dysfunction

1. CHRONIC STRESS

How would you rate your stress levels? And how stressed have you been for the past 10 or 20 years? Stress comes in many forms. There is the big stuff, such as losing someone you love, losing your job, serious illness, having a child who's struggling, going through a relationship break-up. But there's also the everyday stuff: commuting, life admin, traffic jams, losing keys. When the HPA axis becomes dysregulated in the face of persistent stress, this can lead to symptoms that affect many of the body's key functions: metabolism, immunity and sleep.

2. A DIET THAT CREATES STRESS

What you eat can either support or undermine your adrenal function. Diets high in sugar and refined carbohydrates can lead to fluctuations in blood sugar levels, which can tax the adrenal glands. Too much coffee can put more stress on the adrenals, as caffeine triggers the release of adrenaline and cortisol, perpetuating a cycle of stimulation and crash. The effect is magnified if you don't get enough of the nutrients your adrenals need – including vitamin C, B vitamins, zinc and magnesium.

3. BAD SLEEP PATTERNS

Cortisol levels should decline to their lowest level during the early stages of sleep, then peak in the early morning to help wake you up.

This circadian rhythm can easily be put off track by a variety of factors, from shift work to not getting daylight, bright lights at night or not going to bed at a regular time. This can then put out your cortisol rhythm, so it stresses your adrenals even more.

You can't stop the hormonal changes of perimenopause; your production of sex hormones is inevitably reducing. But now we will talk about how you can look after your adrenal health and so mitigate the negative effects of stress on your sex hormones. This will not only help your hormone levels to be the best they can be at this point in your life but will help relieve your symptoms, too.

Adrenal dysfunction: what to eat

STABILIZE BLOOD SUGAR LEVELS

Fluctuations in blood sugar can stress the adrenals, so it's crucial to maintain steady levels throughout the day.

- Fill your plate with a mix of foods that are low on the glycaemic index (GI), which refers to the extent to which blood glucose rises after eating a food. Include protein, fat (nuts and seeds), non-starchy vegetables and greens, legumes and high-fibre, slow-release carbs (see chapter three). By following the Food Framework, you're already excluding high-GI foods most of the time, including sugary foods, white carbs and processed foods.

- Aim for 30g of protein at breakfast, and include complex carbohydrates in your evening meal, such as starchy vegetables or whole grains.

MAXIMISE NUTRIENTS

Eat a colourful diet that's rich in a variety of fruits and vegetables for the widest range of vitamins, minerals and antioxidants. This will give you the building blocks for adrenal hormones. Good sources of nutrients are dark leafy greens, berries, nuts and seeds.

- Eat foods high in vitamins C and B: the adrenal glands have one of the highest concentrations of vitamin C in the body and the stress response uses up B vitamins too.
- For vitamin C: citrus fruits, strawberries, bell peppers, cruciferous vegetables.
- For vitamin B: meat, liver, chicken, eggs, fish, seafood, mushrooms, lentils, chickpeas, avocado, leafy greens.
- Stay hydrated: being dehydrated can increase cortisol levels. Aim for two litres of water a day. You can also hydrate by eating high-water foods, such as cucumber, celery and melons.
- Stress and particularly high cortisol can be inflammatory to the brain. Turmeric, with its active compound curcumin, has anti-inflammatory properties (plus, see page 128 for adaptogenic herbs like ashwagandha that may help the body manage stress).

HEALTHY FATS

Healthy fats, such as those found in cold-water fish like salmon and mackerel, flaxseeds, chia seeds and extra virgin olive oil provide the fatty acids necessary for building adrenal hormones.

LIMIT STIMULANTS

Although caffeine, sugar and alcohol may feel as if they're giving you an energy boost, what goes up does come down. They can cause blood sugar crashes that strain the adrenals.

Adrenal dysfunction: lifestyle guidelines

TELL YOUR BODY THAT IT'S SAFE

If you're stressed, you're living in a state of high alert, also called fight or flight. Focus on telling your body that it's safe. Put together an anti-stress toolkit that works for you (see chapter four). This might include a bath, a sound bath, yoga nidra or self-hypnosis. I tend to know which clients really need to do this kind of work as they protest the most when I recommend it! But there are a lot of choices and you can start with just a minute a day.

EAT SLOWLY AND CALMLY

It's tempting to rush your food when you're stressed. But not only will eating slowly in a calm, non-distracted place signal to your body that you're safe, it will improve digestion and the absorption of nutrients. Sit at a table for meals, ban screens, chew thoroughly, and keep listening to your body's hunger and fullness cues.

SLEEP DEEPLY

Good sleep is exactly what you need but the irony is that when you're stressed, good sleep is hard to get. All the sleep advice in chapter four is key for you. In particular, help to regularise your daily cortisol rhythm by going to bed and getting up at the same time, even on weekends. Also go outside for ten minutes in daylight first thing to set your body clock for the day, and ideally at dusk too as this tells it that it's time to wind down. After this, keep lights low and screens to a minimum.

MODERATE EXERCISE

Regular exercise can help buffer the effects of stress and regulate cortisol levels. But with your hormonal profile, you have to be careful not to go too long and/or work out too hard, as overtraining will stress your body further. Low to moderate intensity exercise is the sweet spot for you, such as brisk walking, cycling, swimming or any other form of exercise that you enjoy. If you exercise in the morning, you should be able to go about your normal day (without a nap!) and if you exercise later in the day, you shouldn't feel tired the next day.

DON'T PUSH YOURSELF

When you've lost your resilience to stress, you're not sleeping and you can't think straight, it's counterproductive to put any extra stress on your mind or body. This is true for exercise (as above) but also for food and for life, too. It means thinking about where you can cut back, asking yourself: What can I do less of? Where can I ask for help? Who can I say no to? It's not a time for cold plunges, keto or long periods of fasting – rather, it's a time for rest and nourishing yourself with food.

FAMILY AND FUN

Social isolation is a stressor but spending time with good friends and/or close family is the opposite. Nurture your relationships and make new ones by joining groups where you have a shared interest – whether it's hiking, pottery or roller skating – as that will bring you extra joy.

Key symptoms and how to treat them

1. FATIGUE

This is a core symptom of HPA axis disruption, linked to abnormal daily rhythms of cortisol, the stress hormone. When cortisol is either too high or too low, it can leave you feeling lacking in energy and exhausted.

Food: Eat according to the principles of the Food Framework.

Lifestyle: Think about ways to improve your rest, relaxation and sleep (see above and chapter four for more).

Suggested supplements: Rhodiola rosea – an adaptogenic herb that's traditionally used for boosting energy. (It can be found in PCH Ener-Boost, along with liquorice and ginseng. N.B. Don't take rhodiola in the evening and don't take liquorice if you have high blood pressure.)

Also, stress uses up a lot of B vitamins, so take B-complex (PCH B-Complex).

2. RELYING ON CAFFEINE

Coffee spikes cortisol, so if you cannot do without coffee in the morning, it may be because your cortisol levels are low. If you tried to give it up and you couldn't, this might be applicable to you. The problem is, drinking too much caffeine can put even more stress on a dysregulated HPA axis. Try the following...

Food: Gradually cut back on caffeine until you're having none – or just one cup. If you are going to drink coffee, time it right to get the maximum effect from it. Have it with breakfast, around an hour after waking. Or replace it with herbal teas or decaffeinated coffee, or with green or matcha tea. Green tea contains some caffeine but also high levels of calming L-theanine, which balances out the effect of caffeine.

Lifestyle: Exposure to daylight first thing in the morning to tell your body that it's daytime. Morning exercise can be energising too.

Suggested supplements: Rhodiola rosea, as above, and liquorice, which can support adrenal function. (N.B. Don't take rhodiola in the evening and don't take liquorice if you have high blood pressure. Both can be found in PCH Ener-Boost).

3. BRAIN FOG

Your brain is full of oestrogen receptors and so brain fog during perimenopause is often due to fluctuating levels of oestrogen. Plus, chronic high levels of cortisol affect memory and learning.

Food: Eat a brain-healthy diet that's rich in omega-3 fatty acids (in fatty fish, walnuts and flaxseeds) and in antioxidants (colourful fruits and vegetables). The brain also likes a steady supply of energy; eat to keep blood sugar even (see page 220).

Lifestyle: Focus on sleep and stress reduction (see chapter four).

Suggested supplements: Vitamin B12 and folate (B9) both help maintain brain health (in PCH B-Complex).

4. WEIGHT GAIN

Fluctuating cortisol levels and reduced oestrogen can both influence metabolism and encourage the storage of fat around your middle. Plus, adrenal dysfunction can lead to imbalances in blood sugar levels and insulin sensitivity, which may further contribute to weight gain.

Food: Eat to keep blood sugar even (see page 220). At the beginning of each meal, eat two bites of protein to help you feel fuller, sooner.

Lifestyle: Develop your stress toolkit plus do regular gentle exercise (see page 104).

Suggested supplements: Chromium helps keep blood sugar regulated and cayenne pepper raises your temperature, speeding up the metabolism. (Both can be found in PCH Meta-Boost.)

5. DIZZINESS

When cortisol is low, it can lead to a low blood pressure condition known as orthostatic hypotension. When you sit up or stand up from lying down, you feel light-headed. Women with low cortisol often have low blood sugar too, which can also make you feel dizzy and weak.

Food: Make sure you're drinking enough water. And don't skip meals, especially breakfast. They should include a balance of protein, healthy fats and complex carbohydrates, which can not only stabilise blood sugar but also blood pressure levels. You may also find eating a small protein snack mid-morning and mid-afternoon helpful.

Lifestyle: Taking transitions slowly, such as sitting on the edge of the bed before standing, can prevent sudden drops in blood pressure. Strengthening exercises, especially those that target the lower body and core, can improve circulation and blood pressure regulation.

Suggested supplement: Liquorice may help maintain stable blood pressure levels. (N.B. Do not take liquorice if you have hypertension. Found in PCH Ener-Boost.)

6. OVERWHELMED AND DOWN

Low cortisol can reduce your resilience to stress, which can leave you feeling overwhelmed, emotionally drained, low and/or anxious.

Food: Eat plenty of vegetables, fruits and whole grains to make sure you're getting your B vitamins, which are vital for energy and cognitive function. Protein-rich foods contain amino acids that are important for restoring cortisol levels too.

Lifestyle: As above, take regular exercise and put together your own stress toolkit.

Suggested supplements: Siberian ginseng, Korean ginseng and Rhodiola rosea are adaptogen herbs that help support the body's response to stress and adrenal health (found in PCH Ener-Boost).

7. SORENESS

Cortisol is anti-inflammatory, so when it's low, you can have more inflammation, pain and soreness.

Food: Anti-inflammatory foods can help, such as fish rich in omega-3 fatty acids, turmeric and berries. Also, make sure you're getting enough electrolytes (sodium, potassium, magnesium) by adding a pinch of Himalayan pink salt to meals.

Lifestyle: Take gentle to moderate exercise and focus on rest and sleep. Ease soreness with warmth: a sauna, steam or a bath with Epsom salts.

Suggested supplement: Curcumin, the active ingredient in turmeric, known for its anti-inflammatory properties (found in PCH Curcumin).

8. ENERGY CRASHES

Cortisol is supposed to peak in the morning and gradually decline throughout the day. It's natural to have an afternoon energy dip, but when cortisol is out of balance, this dip can feel more like a sharp decline. This can be made worse by fluctuating blood sugar levels, which are also partly regulated by cortisol.

Food: Focus on following a low GI diet. If you find you're hungry between meals, try to work out if you are eating enough protein. Aim for 20g to 30g at each meal, ideally 30g at breakfast. If you are still hungry, try having a protein-rich snack, such as a handful of nuts.

Lifestyle: It may seem counterintuitive but move more rather than less. Exercise helps with blood sugar control and increases circulation of energy and oxygen. Plus take short, frequent breaks throughout the day to stand, stretch or walk.

Suggested supplements: B-complex vitamins support energy production at the cellular level (PCH B-Complex).

9. CRAVING SALTY AND/OR SWEET FOODS

The adrenal glands produce a hormone called aldosterone, which regulates salt balance. When this is disrupted, it can manifest as a craving for salty foods. Also, imbalanced cortisol affects blood sugar and insulin function, leading to a desire for quick energy sources like sugary treats.

Food: To reduce salt cravings, eat foods rich in minerals, particularly magnesium and potassium, such as sweet potatoes and leafy greens. For sweet cravings, eat low-GI and high-fibre foods to regulate blood sugar levels. To satisfy a sweet tooth, eat fruit (some berries, an apple, a pear) or a pudding of coconut yoghurt with berries and cacao nibs.

Lifestyle: Staying well-hydrated is key; sometimes the body misinterprets signals of dehydration as hunger. If you are a stress or emotional eater, be mindful of your triggers and keep working on reducing stress. Mindfulness techniques can help you become more aware of true hunger cues versus emotional eating (see chapter four for more).

Suggested supplements: Chromium can aid in blood sugar stabilisation, potentially decreasing cravings. (Found in PCH Meta-Boost.)

10. LOW IMMUNITY

Cortisol plays a critical role in regulating the immune response. When cortisol levels are dysregulated, either too high or too low, it can make you more likely to get ill and cause you to heal more slowly.

Food: Foods high in vitamins C and E, zinc and selenium can bolster the immune response. Eat citrus fruits, berries, nuts, seeds and green leafy vegetables. Eating enough protein is also critical for healing from injuries.

ADRENAL DYSFUNCTION | 111

Lifestyle: Both good sleep and moderate exercise are key (see pages 72-78).

Suggested supplements: Vitamin D is important for immune health and is often low during perimenopause (PCH Vegan D3 Complex). Probiotics can support a healthy gut microbiome, which is crucial for a robust immune system (PCH Repopulate Probiotic).

> ### EASY WIN: A MINUTE'S BREATHING
>
> *Every hour, do a minute of breathing in for four, out for eight. The longer out breath puts the body into relaxation mode, plus taking a minute out gives you space and time to process your feelings and experiences.*

Jane's story

It was hard to know which symptoms were due to the perimenopause and which were due to the accident. Five years ago, aged 51, I was trampled by cattle. As well as physical injuries, the accident left me with severe PTSD, claustrophobia, anxiety and panic attacks. Not long afterwards, I started having hot flushes too. They'd always seem to manifest at the most inappropriate time, such as in the middle of a board meeting. I'd feel hot and panicky, overwhelmed by fear that people were looking at me, thinking, *What on earth is wrong with her?*

The double whammy of trauma plus hormones left me feeling as if my world had fallen apart. I am very task-focused, so I thought, *What can I do to fix this?* HRT seemed to be the answer, so I booked an appointment at a private clinic, had a consultation and came home with a prescription for oestrogen, progesterone and testosterone.

For a couple of years, my symptoms went away. Then, I got Covid. I only discovered that I had it because I wear an Oura Ring, which told me that my body temperature, heart rate and sleep were all over the place.

Not long after I recovered, I noticed that the anxiety was back, I was feeling quite depressed and my moods had become very volatile, although the hot flushes hadn't returned. I was putting on weight too. I've always been a fairly constant size eight but my clothes were starting to get tight. I couldn't understand why: I watch what I eat and I rarely drink, except for the odd glass of fizz. I walk the dogs twice a day, I have a personal trainer three times a week and I can deadlift 120kg! There was no reason why this weight was going on but when I got on some scales, I discovered

I'd put on just over a stone. I felt bloated all the time. I have a pair of jeans that I use as my guide and I couldn't do them up. It was depressing not being able to get into my clothes.

My moods were all over the place too. I'd go into an incandescent rage over things that, in hindsight, weren't a big deal, like my partner forgetting to put out the recycling. I tried to bottle it up, but I'd feel the fury and resentment building up. I could also burst into tears for no apparent reason.

There was a lot going on at the time – not least lockdown. My role at work, in a company where I'd worked for 25 years, was made redundant. I went to stay with my parents in rural Spain for two months, as they were having a lot of health issues and complex legal and admin problems. It was all very tricky to sort out, especially in lockdown.

I got another job quickly, another high-pressure role. Then, the week I started, Dad died from Covid. That left Mum living in the middle of nowhere with seven dogs, semi-blind and immobile. At first, I couldn't travel because of lockdown, so I had to organise Dad's funeral remotely. Then, when restrictions were lifted, I was going back and forth, trying to sort out all the problems and care for Mum. I felt so guilty because she wasn't coping. The admin was like a full-time second job.

The stressors were piling on from all angles. My beloved dog, Alfie, died a few months after Dad, which was unexpected. Then my partner's mum passed away after a battle with dementia and cancer.

As much as I looked as if I was coping, inside I was all over the place. I had next-level mental fog. Really, it was amazing that I was still functioning. The more stressed I felt, the worse my menopause symptoms got. I started bleeding and when I went back to the menopause clinic for check-ups and blood tests, I told the doctor how bad I was feeling. She put up my dose of oestrogen but also progesterone to counteract the bleeding. She advised me to have an ultrasound scan to check that there weren't any issues with the lining of my womb thickening – thankfully, this was fine.

Then, unexpectedly, Mum died. I was left with massive legal issues over their house, plus a battle with the care company about what had happened to her.

When I went back to the menopause clinic almost a year later, I told the doctor that I was weepy and anxious all the time, and still bleeding a little. She put up my oestrogen dose yet again, to six pumps of Oestrogel, and suggested that having a Mirena coil inserted instead of taking progesterone might help the bleeding. She also suggested that I could consider taking antidepressants. Neither of these I wanted to do.

My mood didn't get any better. I felt alternately ragey or weepy. I didn't have any interest in anything, or any joy or energy. I had to drag myself to the gym. Even if you'd told me that I'd won millions on the Pools, I wouldn't have reacted with any happiness. And I normally go to the loo frequently but I wasn't. I felt bloated and bunged up.

The weight gain was very frustrating. In two months, as well as all my usual exercise, I walked 400km but the scales didn't budge. People say that you have to accept weight gain in middle age but I felt miserable and wasn't prepared to.

Two weeks after the HRT clinic, I booked in to see Kate at Pippa's clinic, in the hope of finding an answer. Kate told me that stress affects hormones a lot and it was possible that having Covid had affected them too. She suggested I do a DUTCH test. The result came back that my testosterone was a bit low, my progesterone was fine, but my oestrogen result was wildly different to the blood results that they'd seen in the menopause clinic. It showed my oestrogen as off-the-scale high, in the red zone. This might be because while the blood test is a single moment in time, the DUTCH looks at it over the whole course of the day, or it might be due to my hormones on the day I took the test.

The DUTCH test also showed my DHEA was low and my cortisol was non-existent. Cortisol should peak half an hour after getting up but mine was flat, which Kate said was my body's protective response to me being under so much stress. It was no wonder that I had so little energy because as well as being a stress hormone, cortisol is your get-up-and-go hormone. Kate told me that because my hormones were not in balance, my metabolism wasn't working as it should. I cried because I finally understood that I was not going mad; there was something real and biological happening to me.

Kate said my body was giving me a clear message to slow down and look after myself and that I should stop fighting it. I've always eaten good food but Kate tweaked it. I continued to start my day with a big smoothie, putting in protein powder and good fats such as avocado (Kate advised switching from peanut butter). Lunch is often now eggs or smoked mackerel salad with quinoa, heavy on the veg but light on the carbs, as they make me sleepy in the afternoon. Dinner is usually fish and vegetables or a big salad.

Kate suggested I take the supplements DIM and calcium D-glucarate to help my liver process used-up oestrogen. She also recommended I carry on using my meditation apps and Sensate, a vibrating meditation device which I'd bought to help with the anxiety.

Just a couple of weeks later, I felt much better. I decided to experiment and drop my oestrogen dosage by two pumps – none of the symptoms came back. I thought that was interesting. So I decided to stop taking oestrogen altogether, but some of my hot flushes and anxiety came back. I went back up to two pumps, but then felt bloated and bunged up again. Then I went down to one and I felt fine. Eventually, I decided to stop taking all the HRT. If things get bad again, I know I could always restart.

The bloating and stomach cramps have completely gone. My moods have stabilised and even though I am still having to cope with stress and the challenges of Mum's death, I feel far more in control. While I haven't dropped all of the extra weight, I have lost nine pounds and my jeans fit again! Kate said that it will take a little more time because of my age and because I need to balance my hormones first. But now that I can see everything that I'm doing is having an effect, I don't mind.

CHAPTER 6

Progesterone Drop

- Irregular menstrual cycle. Can you no longer plan around your period because you're not sure when it will come?

- Heavy menstrual bleeding. Are your periods heavy? This means having to change your protection every one to two hours or your menstrual cup more often than is recommended, having to use two kinds of protection or a period that lasts more than seven days.

- Mood swings. Do you have attacks of anxiety or sadness that feel more than ordinary ups and downs? Do you feel less able to cope with stressful situations, so they hit you harder?

- Worried, anxious, low and/or depressed. Are you persistently anxious about things without being able to pinpoint a reason? Have you lost your love for life, so you can't see the point?

- Sleep problems. Are you having difficulty falling asleep or staying asleep? Or waking up tired? Or is your sleep being disturbed by having to go to the loo more than once?
- Night sweats. Are you waking up in the night, feeling hot and sweating, perhaps so that your sheets are soaked?
- Weight gain. Have you gained weight despite not changing your eating or even after trying to eat less?
- Bloating. Do you often feel bloated and puffy, as if you're holding onto water? (When your period comes, this feeling may go away.)

Progesterone doesn't get top billing of the female hormones, despite having more than 300 roles in your body. Star status usually goes to its better-known sister hormone, oestrogen. However, in this book, progesterone is coming before oestrogen because it's the first to drop in the years leading up to menopause. This usually happens when women are in their forties, but it can happen your mid-to-late thirties too.

The other reason I've prioritised this hormonal change is because I've seen the massive effect the drop can have on women's lives. You need some progesterone in order to counterbalance oestrogen and keep your cycle regular, as well as for mood. Women with low progesterone can be consumed by low confidence and are often sleeping badly. They describe being anxious, even having heart palpitations, feeling as if their heart is jumping out of their chest.

It may make you feel better to know that you're not imagining things. As well as being a hormone, progesterone is a brain chemical. It increases the brain's sensitivity to the calming neurotransmitter gamma-aminobutyric acid (GABA), which is anti-anxiety, pro-sleep and pro-relaxation. This is why a drop in progesterone can shorten your sleep and tank your mood. One clue that a low mood or any of the symptoms listed above are due to low progesterone is that they are more likely to be worse in the second half of your cycle, although they can come and go.

What happens when progesterone goes down?

Progesterone acts like your menstrual cycle's air traffic controller, driving the timing of your cycle, regulating your period and balancing out the effects of oestrogen. When it's working well, the up and down rhythm of these two hormones thickens the womb lining for a fertilised egg and then, if there's no pregnancy, sheds the womb lining as your period. It's a very neat system: after the egg is released at ovulation, the empty follicle (casing) transforms into the corpus luteum, which then starts to produce progesterone.

During perimenopause, your adrenals should take over from your ovaries and start to make low levels of progesterone and moderate levels of oestrogen. However, in clinic, tests show that a lot of women have progesterone levels that are even lower than the expected range for their age, along with the symptoms above. Stress is often a big factor in this because of 'the progesterone steal'. The stress hormone cortisol is made from the same raw materials as progesterone. If it's under stress, the body 'steals' those raw materials from progesterone in order to make cortisol.

When progesterone goes down, it can start a ripple effect that affects the body's other hormones. For example, low progesterone can have a knock-on effect on thyroid function (see chapter 11 for more). And if progesterone is no longer doing its job of counterbalancing oestrogen, it can lead to oestrogen dominance (OD), the subject of the next chapter.

Four key reasons for the progesterone drop

1. YOUR EGG STORE IS RUNNING LOWER

The menopause marks the end of your ovaries' store of eggs. In the years leading up to menopause, you'll increasingly have cycles when you don't ovulate, called anovulatory cycles. And if you don't ovulate, the corpus luteum never forms and you produce less progesterone.

2. YOU'RE ALWAYS OR OFTEN STRESSED

As explained, stress is a key reason for progesterone dip. Although we talk about stress as a normal factor in modern life, we don't often think about how constant stress can make a serious dent on the proper workings of our hormonal system, making lowering progesterone levels even lower. On top of that, stress can make it less likely that you'll ovulate, thus lowering progesterone levels even more.

3. NUTRIENT DEFICIENCIES

Some nutrients – for example, zinc and B6 – are crucial in making progesterone. A deficiency in one or more of these can, indirectly, lower progesterone levels.

4. LOW THYROID FUNCTION

Fertility clinics usually test a woman's thyroid hormone levels because these can have a big impact on the menstrual cycle. This is because having low thyroid function can lead to low progesterone. Conversely, you also need enough progesterone in order to have well-functioning thyroid.

You can never get back the progesterone levels of your reproductive years – but if you're getting the symptoms listed above, it's likely that there are other factors lowering the levels rather than simply perimenopause alone. And this you can do something about. By using food, lifestyle changes and the right supplements, you can slow down the decline – and feel better.

CAN I TAKE PROGESTERONE ON ITS OWN AS HRT?

By Dr Klaudia Raczko

In the UK, NICE guidelines advise that women should be given oestrogen and progesterone together (if they have a womb) or oestrogen on its own after womb removal (hysterectomy). In my practice, I have found that some women do benefit from taking progesterone only. This is especially true early in perimenopause, as progesterone is usually the first hormone to start to decrease, sometimes as early as in your thirties. If your ovaries are still producing a good amount of oestrogen or your oestrogen level is fluctuating (it can be high on some days), which often happens in perimenopause, taking extra oestrogen on top of this can sometimes make you feel worse, rather than better. As no one size fits all, it may be worth talking to your GP if your current HRT isn't working as you expected.

Is there a difference between progestin and progesterone in HRT and Mirena?

Yes. Body identical progesterone (Utrogestan) is the natural form of the hormone, identical to what our ovaries produce. It helps protect bones and is calming in the brain as well as balancing out oestrogen. Progestins are synthetic forms of progesterone. They are in some contraceptive pills, some older HRT formulations and in the Mirena coil.

> *In HRT, doctors give progesterone or progestin alongside oestrogen to women who have a womb. This stops the womb lining building up, which is a risk factor for endometrial cancer. Doctors also give the Mirena coil in perimenopause because it works as contraception too.*
>
> *The problem is, progestins do not have the same body and brain benefits as natural progesterone. Progesterone does around 300 jobs in the body, as well as protecting the lining of the womb. And so if you have anxiety, or sleep issues, or water retention during perimenopause, having Mirena or another progestin alongside oestrogen HRT will not help with those symptoms.*
>
> *Additionally, because progestins don't behave like natural progesterone, they won't balance your hormones, so you can end up with too much oestrogen (oestrogen dominance, see chapter seven). If you experience breast tenderness, tearfulness, emotional reactivity, headaches and/or bloating, it may mean that your oestrogen and progesterone are out of balance. On top of this, the progestin levonorgestrel (in Mirena) is androgenic – that is, it acts like a male hormone. Some women can get acne and hair loss when they start it.*

Progesterone drop: what to eat

Slow release, low GI carbs such as sweet potato or quinoa (see chapter three for more examples). You won't do well eating keto or low carb because you need carbs to make progesterone. If you're not sleeping well, eating carbs in the evening will help with sleep quality.

- **Plenty of protein:** Protein provides the amino acids needed for making hormones. Eat: lean meats, fish, and plant-based sources like lentils and chickpeas (see chapter three).

- **Healthy fats:** Hormones including progesterone are made from cholesterol and eating healthy fats can support the body's cholesterol production. Eat: avocado, salmon and walnuts (see chapter three for more healthy fats).

- **Vitamin B6-rich foods:** Vitamin B6 helps you to absorb and metabolise hormones. Eat: turkey, potatoes, eggs and spinach.

- **Magnesium-rich foods:** Another essential for progesterone production. Eat: leafy greens, almonds, black beans and dark chocolate.

- **Zinc-rich foods:** Zinc plays a role in hormone creation and balance. Eat: pumpkin seeds, beef, cashews.

- **Berries:** Low GI but rich in antioxidants that help with cellular repair and anti-inflammatory processes.

- **Fermented foods:** Foods including sauerkraut and kefir can help improve gut health, which is key to hormonal balance.

- **Hormone-balancing herbs:** Herbs that contain rosmarinic acid, such as rosemary, sage, mint and basil, help to balance hormones. Add them into your meals or take as supplements.

> **EASY WIN: FIVE MINUTES OF CYCLICAL SIGH BREATHING**
>
> *Research has shown doing this kind of breathing for just five minutes a day cuts stress and causes a surge in joy, energy and peace. It does this by breaking our cycle of physical tension and anxiety.*
>
> **How to do it:** *Set a timer for five minutes. Breathe in through your nose. When your lungs feel full, take a second sip of air to expand your lungs as much as you can. Exhale through your mouth, very slowly and completely. Repeat.*

Progesterone drop: lifestyle guidelines

YOUR RELAX TOOLKIT

There may be some stresses from your life that you can't change (though perhaps there are some you can?). But you do need to carve out time for proper rest and relaxation. That might be through one of the following, or see chapter four for more ideas:

Meditation. If you haven't yet managed to start a meditation practice, now is a brilliant time to get into it. Research shows that meditation reduces cortisol levels and it works best for people with high levels of stress.

Breathwork. People often find breathwork even more powerful than meditation. A recent study compared breathing techniques and found that cyclic sigh breathing was most effective at cutting stress – in particular, sigh breathing, although others were good too. See box above. The key thing to know here is that brief structured respiration practices enhance mood and reduce physiological arousal.

EXERCISE CALMLY AND CONSISTENTLY

Aim to do moderate exercise regularly, at a level that may be a little more gentle than you're used to or expect. Research shows high-intensity exercise ups your cortisol level, while low-intensity exercise can lower it.

A handful of studies have shown that yoga helps reduce stress and cortisol. The meditative part helps but so does the stretching, which can activate the relaxation response. Swimming is good too, particularly if you are someone who finds being in the water calming. Other good forms of exercise are Pilates, low-impact cardio such as walking, dancing to music that you find uplifting and gardening.

As you know, strength training is vital in midlife for bone mass and insulin sensitivity, but in addition to this, it's also been shown to aid in stress reduction when done consistently. This has the added benefit of making your progesterone feel more potent, even with lower levels.

SLEEP: THE SECRET WEAPON

Poor sleep leads to a cascade of hormonal issues, including progesterone deficiency. Follow the advice in chapter four and don't forget to focus on sleep quality rather than on the number of hours. One way to do this is not to drink alcohol (see chapter three) – even moderate drinkers tend to have less restful sleep.

You could also try a white noise app: research suggests this helps people who have noisy bedrooms (from outside noise) get to sleep faster and/or wake less at night.

Treating symptoms

1. IRREGULAR MENSTRUAL CYCLE

In a textbook cycle, while oestrogen tells the endometrial lining of the uterus to thicken for the (potential) fertilised egg, progesterone tells the lining exactly how much. And if no fertilisation happens, it tells the lining when to shed as your period. However, when progesterone is low, the endometrial lining doesn't get the right signals and this process becomes erratic and unpredictable. You may get your period more often or you may skip a period or a few periods.

Food: Eat foods high in vitamin B6, needed to make progesterone, particularly turkey, potatoes, eggs and spinach. Also try seed cycling, which supports your cycle with the right nutrients at the right time (see page 58).

Suggested supplement: Vitex agnus castus, which is known for its ability to regulate menstrual cycles and relieve PMS symptoms.

2. HEAVY MENSTRUAL BLEEDING

Another role of progesterone is to keep oestrogen in balance. When progesterone is low, high oestrogen encourages the womb lining to grow too thick, leading to heavier periods with more clotting. If you notice you often have a less heavy month followed by a heavy one, it may be because faulty progesterone signalling has meant you haven't shed the lining completely one month; this build-up then makes the next period much heavier.

Food: Make sure you are eating enough iron-rich foods to compensate for blood loss. Low iron and anaemia levels are very common in women with heavy periods. Ask your GP for a test if you think you may be anaemic (symptoms include tiredness, shortness of breath). Iron from animal sources, haem iron, is better absorbed.

Vegetarians should combine green leafy vegetables with vitamin C foods – for example, baby spinach leaves in a citrus dressing.

Suggested supplement: Yarrow is a herb traditionally used to staunch bleeding and for heavy periods. It's also anti-inflammatory.

3. MOOD SWINGS

Not only does low progesterone decrease the brain's sensitivity to calming GABA, but it has other brain effects too. It affects the neurotransmitter dopamine, so a lack of it can lead to feelings of joylessness or even depression. It also affects serotonin, a neurotransmitter that's crucial for mood stability. Finally, progesterone is anti-inflammatory, and brain inflammation is linked with both depression and anxiety.

Food: Oily fish, such as mackerel, sardines and salmon, is rich in omega-3 fats needed to build cell membranes and for helping better receptor binding and neurotransmission. In short, omega-3 is vital for a well-functioning brain.

Lifestyle: Exercise increases the sensitivity of the GABA receptor in the brain, making it more effective at lower concentrations of GABA.

Suggested supplements: L-theanine is a calming amino acid found in tea that helps you into a state of relaxed alertness (in PCH Chill). A recent study showed that taking saffron twice a day improved both anxiety and depression scores by a third in perimenopausal women (also in PCH Chill).

4. WORRIED, ANXIOUS, LOW AND/OR DEPRESSED

If this is how you feel, you'll be pleased to know that tweaking your eating and lifestyle in the ways covered in chapters four and five will help. Specifically, do these things too:

Food: Eat some protein that contains an amino acid called tryptophan, needed to make serotonin. Good sources are turkey and chicken, nuts and seeds, oats, dark chocolate.

Lifestyle: Mind-body techniques such as meditation have been shown to reduce inflammatory chemicals that exacerbate depression. They also help balance the effects of low progesterone by regulating cortisol.

Suggested supplements: Ashwagandha is a traditional Ayurvedic herb that can regulate cortisol levels (in PCH Ashwagandha). 5-HTP is an amino acid that's converted to the mood neurotransmitter serotonin (in PCH Mood & Sleep). (N.B. 5-HTP can interact with antidepressant medications.)

5. SLEEP PROBLEMS

Due to its effect on GABA, progesterone acts as a sedative, helping you fall asleep and keeping you sleeping for longer. Progesterone also has a role in the body's daily circadian rhythms that regulate sleep-wake patterns. A lack of progesterone can not only throw off your daily sleep-wake cycle but can lead to more fragmented and less restorative sleep.

Food: You need magnesium to make serotonin and the sleepy hormone melatonin, both of which are critical for sleep regulation. Eat: green leafy vegetables, beans and pulses, nuts, cacao.

Lifestyle: You've probably heard you shouldn't use your phone before bed, but I'd suggest a cut-off of 8.30pm. You could also invest in some blue-light blocking glasses, as blue light from screens slows production of melatonin. Finally, create your own evening ritual to signal to your body that it's time to wind down (see page 70 for mine).

Suggested supplements: Magnesium quiets neural activity and is a natural muscle relaxant (in PCH Magnesium Complex). 5-HTP is converted to serotonin, which is then converted to melatonin, needed for sleep (in PCH Mood & Sleep, which also contains calming passionflower and chamomile).

6. NIGHT SWEATS

Progesterone and oestrogen together regulate the body's heat thermostat. When progesterone is low, you can become over-sensitive to even minor changes in body temperature, leading to overheating and night sweats.

Food: Some women find that seed cycling (see page 70) helps ease symptoms.

Lifestyle: Always make sure you're properly hydrated as this helps to regulate body temperature.

Suggested supplement: Vitex agnus castus is a herb that's known to support levels of progesterone. It can take two to three months to notice the difference. Please note, it may not work for all women.

7. WEIGHT GAIN

It's common to gain a pound or even two per month in the peri-menopausal period, despite not changing what you eat or how you exercise. A key factor in this is progesterone's effects on insulin, the fat storage hormone. When progesterone is low it can lead to insulin resistance, meaning your cells no longer respond well to the hormone insulin. The result is higher blood sugar levels which can lead to weight gain. In addition to this, body fat contains receptors for progesterone, and low progesterone gives the biochemical go-ahead to store more fat. Also, if you're stressed, high cortisol levels lead to cravings for high fat, high sugar foods.

Food: Make sure you are eating plenty of fibre-rich foods. These help to regulate the insulin response by slowing down the absorption of sugars. Aim for 30g of fibre a day. Good sources are ground flaxseed, chia seeds, pulses, vegetables, nuts and fruit. N.B. If you have a low fibre breakfast (e.g. eggs on sourdough) and a low fibre lunch (e.g. a sandwich) it will be almost impossible to get your 30g.

Lifestyle: Strength training increases insulin sensitivity in muscles and raises the potency of the progesterone you do have.

Suggested supplement: Chromium enhances insulin sensitivity, helping you use up glucose in cells rather than storing it as fat. This should reduce cravings for sugary foods (in PCH Meta-Boost).

8. BLOATING

Progesterone is a natural diuretic, allowing the body to lose excess water. When progesterone is low, you can feel puffy and waterlogged. This happens particularly in the lead-up to your period. Having low progesterone can also interfere with the rhythmic contractions of the gut muscles that move food along the gut.

Food: Diuretic foods and drinks will help to eliminate excess water. Eat cucumber, celery and lemon. Drink dandelion leaf tea.

Lifestyle: Try cutting down on the amount of salt you eat – so resist adding salt to meals but also reduce salty foods – to see if it minimises bloating.

Suggested supplements: Potassium balances out sodium (salt) and so helps to get rid of excess water.

Yasmin's story

Six years ago, when I was aged 48, I noticed my periods had changed. My cycle, which had pretty much always been 28 days, had got shorter and heavier. I sometimes had painful joints too.

I went to the GP, who advised me to have the Mirena coil fitted. But it did not suit me at all. I bled every day for six months until I had it taken out.

Then, nobody was really talking much about perimenopause. So I didn't do anything for a few years, until I was 52. By this time, I had terrible joint pains every morning and my ankles were really stiff. I was putting on weight. My periods were getting heavier and I was having a lot of blood clots and flooding. I had brain fog too. I had heart palpitations at night, once or twice a month. They feel as if you have a butterfly where your heart is. The scariest moment is when they stopped, as I'd think my heart had stopped too. My doctor sent me for an ECG, which showed my heart was fine.

Then I had two big panic attacks. After that, I'd had enough. I'd seen a lot about HRT in the media and thought it could be the answer. I rang my GP but she said I couldn't have HRT, that I'd only be allowed it for two years as it's not safe for women aged over 54 (I've since found out that this isn't the case). So I booked in to see a private doctor. She was happy to prescribe me HRT – oestrogen spray (Lenzetto) and progesterone tablets (Utrogestan).

The joint pain went away but the anxiety didn't. When I went back to the doctor three months later, she offered me testosterone on top of the other two hormones. I wasn't sure about taking it, so I decided not to. By this time, I had to go to bed for a day every month with period pain so bad that I had shooting pains down my legs. My periods were so heavy that I'd flood for a few days.

I went to see a different NHS GP. She sent me to have a scan, to check if I had fibroids. It turned out there were a few little cysts. I also had a hysteroscopy, which is when they put a camera inside your womb. Then I was sent to the gynaecologist. She offered me three options for the bleeding: the Mirena coil, endometrial ablation (where the lining of the womb is removed) or, as a last resort, a hysterectomy. I didn't want any of these.

I went to Pippa's clinic, where I had the DUTCH Cycle Mapping test. It measures all three kinds of oestrogen and all three were extremely high, into the red zone of the graph. It appeared that my oestrogen levels had already been high, then oestrogen HRT had added even more on top. I decided I would come off the oestrogen slowly and try to manage my symptoms with diet and lifestyle.

By the time I had reduced the oestrogen spray down to nothing, I felt better. It took a few months, but the bleeding finally stopped. During this time, I also changed a lot about my eating and lifestyle. Now, I only drink alcohol one night a week as when I used to drink more, I paid for it with worse symptoms. I prioritise my sleep and I do daily stress management: fresh air and light on my 30-minute morning dog walk, plus breathwork. I try to do 10 to 15 minutes of yoga a day, stretching to music, and I do ten minutes of weights a day.

I have ginger tea first thing, then I love my coffee mid-morning, and I make sure I drink lots of water all day. I eat protein with every meal. For breakfast, I eat eggs or I make a smoothie with pea protein powder, a piece of frozen cauliflower, Greek yoghurt, two tablespoons of ground flaxseed, some frozen mango and a little bit of vanilla kefir.

For lunch, I eat a big salad with lots of greens and chicken or feta, pomegranate seeds, olive oil, apple cider vinegar and pumpkin seeds. At night, we usually have a family meal, which is a curry or a stir-fry or some kind of meat with vegetables, plus some sweet potato, rice or potato. If I really need a snack, I might have an apple, oatcakes with hummus, or maybe a couple of squares of dark chocolate.

My joint pain hasn't come back. When I feel myself getting anxious, I take PCH Chill, which contains L-theanine and saffron. I take a supplement called phosphatidyl choline for brain fog.

I discovered that HRT wasn't for me. I have realised that in order to feel well, I have to manage my stress and eat good food. The practitioner explained that as my hormones change, what works for me now may not work for me tomorrow, but that's fine. It helps to acknowledge that if I get anxiety now, it's not me, it's my hormones. And that I need to be kind to myself, and that this time will pass.

CHAPTER 7

Oestrogen Dominance

- Rage and/or irritability. Are you easily frustrated or irritated? Do you find yourself accelerating from irritable to angry in a heartbeat?
- Weight gain. Have you gained weight despite not changing your eating or trying to eat less?
- Premenstrual syndrome (PMS). Have your PMS symptoms, such as mood swings, abdominal cramping, fatigue and irritability, got worse or are they lasting longer? Or have you got PMS for the first time?
- Fatigue. Do you constantly feel drained and low in energy?
- Headaches/migraines. Have you got new headaches, or are your headaches are more frequent or more intense?
- Endometriosis, fibroids, cysts. Have you been diagnosed with any of these?
- Breast tenderness and swelling. Do your breasts feel particularly sensitive? This may be in the run-up to your

period, from around day 18 up to 28, or from around day 3 of your period.

It often surprises women when I tell them that oestrogen tends to be high rather than low in perimenopause, particularly in the earlier years. And that oestrogen often doesn't start declining until closer to menopause.

Remember the ups and downs of your mood during puberty? A lot of the blame for that emotional rollercoaster – in particular, the highs – can be put down to fluctuations in oestrogen. Perimenopause has been described as a second puberty because it has a similar pattern of oestrogen fluctuations. This might explain why, in perimenopause, you may have found yourself going from laughing to crying to rage, all in the space of a few minutes.

Oestrogen is the hormone responsible for sexual development but there are oestrogen receptors all over the brain as well as the body, due to its many functions. In the reproductive years, each month it builds your womb lining and co-directs your cycle with progesterone. It helps your skin stay firm, keeps your metabolic rate high, your temperature regulated, your brain sharp and your mood good. However, too much oestrogen – and in the hormonal havoc of perimenopause, it's common to have too much – can send all of these body systems out of whack, which can lead to any (or even all) of the symptoms above.

In addition, I also see women in clinic who have itchy skin, hives, hay fever that's got worse and/or who report that they've started reacting to wine or champagne. These histamine symptoms can be caused by a high level of oestrogen. Antihistamines often don't work, however, because they don't deal with the root cause of the problem.

What causes oestrogen dominance?

The phrase 'oestrogen dominance' (OD) sounds as if your oestrogen level is simply too high, but OD is always more nuanced than that. There are five common patterns that can lead to OD.

- You have always had too much oestrogen. You may look at the symptoms of oestrogen dominance above and think, *I've felt like this for the whole of my whole fertile life!* You may also have been diagnosed with fibroids or endometriosis. In clinic, I see women of all ages who have oestrogen dominance as an underlying issue, and one reason is polycystic ovarian syndrome (PCOS). Being overweight is another: fat is an active organ that increases levels of oestrogen.

- Your body has started to make too much oestrogen at some times of the month. A common pattern is that oestrogen will start to surge earlier in the cycle than it would do normally, around day three. It's as if your brain is shouting at your ovaries, 'Last chance for a baby, go for it!' This leads to an earlier ovulation too, at around day 10 instead of day 14. This is a very common reason for shorter cycles during the perimenopause.

- Your oestrogen is too high in relation to progesterone. In the right proportions, oestrogen and progesterone balance each other in hormonal harmony. But in the ten or so years leading to menopause, your progesterone level drops. So you may have the symptoms of low progesterone (see chapter eight) as well as those in this chapter.

- You're taking HRT. Women are often given HRT while their oestrogen levels are still going up and down – this can lead at times to high oestrogen.

- Your liver isn't processing oestrogen properly. As explained in chapter two, after being used, oestrogen needs to be processed in the liver then in the gut, then finally carried out of the body via the stool. If any of this doesn't happen, because these stages of processing aren't working properly, the used oestrogen ends up recirculating in the body, causing oestrogen dominance. This can happen even if your levels of oestrogen aren't high and your levels of progesterone aren't low. This is a pattern I see very often in women during perimenopause but it is also common in younger women.

Looking back, I had OD in my late teens and twenties. I suffered from PMS, rage, irritability and being very emotional. Sometimes I was so spacey that I found it hard to carry out normal daily tasks, as if my brain was wading through treacle. Then my period would arrive and my symptoms would disappear – until two weeks later, just after ovulating, when they were back for another two weeks.

It was only in my early thirties that I discovered these symptoms were due to not clearing out my used oestrogen properly. You'll hear a lot more about detoxing oestrogen in the rest of this chapter, but by making some eating and lifestyle changes, I became (thankfully) symptom free.

Then, in my mid-forties, my symptoms returned. By this time, I was a nutritionist. I did a DUTCH test and saw that I had high oestrogen levels. I had to research even more ways to help my body to process the overload of oestrogen, advice which I share here.

There's one more big contributor to oestrogen dominance: environmental chemicals. Every day, our bodies now encounter chemicals that act like oestrogen in the body, called xenoestrogens or 'dirty oestrogens', that also need to be detoxed. (We mentioned these in chapter two.) In this chapter, you'll learn how to do this, while also reducing your exposure.

Three key reasons for oestrogen dominance

1. INFLAMMATION

When the body is in a state of inflammation, it can upset the balance between oestrogen and progesterone by affecting hormone receptor sites and changing hormone production. Common reasons for inflammation include stress, a less than healthy diet and lack of exercise. Inflammation also impairs gut health, another crucial player in hormone balance, as certain gut bacteria are responsible for metabolising oestrogen.

2. ENVIRONMENTAL FACTORS

Endocrine-disrupting chemicals (EDCs) present in our environment can mimic oestrogen and attach to oestrogen receptors, exacerbating oestrogen dominance. These chemicals are often found in plastics – for example, BPA in water bottles and food packaging – as well as toiletries.

3. POOR DETOXIFICATION (OFTEN REFERRED TO AS OESTROGEN METABOLISM)

Some people have a genetic tendency to be less efficient at detoxifying oestrogen in the liver and even the gut. This can also be affected by stress, lifestyle and your liver being overloaded with toxins. Each step of dealing with used-up oestrogen requires specific nutrients, and so eating the right foods will really support the whole process.

Oestrogen dominance is really satisfying to treat because with the right choices in diet, exercise and stress management, plus some key supplements, women can feel transformed. Most women start to notice some improvements within a few weeks of making these changes. However, changes in symptoms that relate to menstrual cycles or more chronic conditions like endometriosis or fibroids may take several months to a year or more to make themselves felt.

Oestrogen dominance: what to eat

As we now know, your liver has to work hard to metabolise used oestrogen and your gut needs to be in good order to eliminate it. These foods will help support that process:

FOODS TO SUPPORT LIVER DETOXIFICATION

- Eggs: they are rich in choline, essential for methylation, one of the liver detox processes.
- B vitamins: good sources include leafy greens, oily fish such as salmon and mackerel, organ meats (including liver), nuts and seeds.
- Spices: garlic, ginger, turmeric in particular come with multiple benefits for liver health
- Cruciferous vegetables: broccoli, cabbage, cauliflower and kale, among others, contain glucosinolates, needed to make key compounds (indole-3-carbinol I3C and sulforaphane) for liver detoxification processes. Eat two portions a day. See the full list on page 54.
- Antioxidant foods: including green tea, grapes, pomegranate and berries. These are rich in antioxidants that help reduce oxidative stress in the liver.

FOODS THAT HELP BILE FLOW

Bile carries used oestrogen out of the liver into the gall bladder. When you eat fat, it's then released into the digestive system. Eat bitter greens such as chicory, watercress, dandelion greens and rocket, as well as artichokes, lemons and beetroot to support this process.

GUT-FRIENDLY FOODS

The right balance of bacteria will regulate an enzyme called beta-glucuronidase, helping reduce the chance of old oestrogen being recirculated. Eat plenty of prebiotic foods (e.g. garlic, leeks, onions) and probiotic foods (e.g. kimchi, sauerkraut, kefir, kombucha) to help support a healthy balance of the gut microbiome.

OTHER FIBRE-RICH FOODS

There are two kinds of fibre, soluble and insoluble. Soluble fibre is found in foods such as chia seeds, avocado and fruit, and insoluble fibre rich foods include quinoa and legumes. You need plenty of both to bind to oestrogens and carry them out of the gut promptly. Foods high in lignans, a type of insoluble fibre found in abundance in flaxseeds and sesame seeds, are expert at this job (see box on seed cycling, page 58). And fibre in carrots – especially in the skin, so don't peel them – is good at this too.

Oestrogen dominance: lifestyle guidelines

REST FOR MIND AND BODY

Work on rest, anti-stress and sleep as a priority. Ask yourself: *What will help me feel content in mind as well as body?* Build your anti-stress toolkit with activities that work for you (see chapter four).

This might also include talking therapy with an expert as well as practices you can do yourself.

CONSISTENT PHYSICAL ACTIVITY

For advice on exercise, see chapter four. Ideally, you'll be doing 150 minutes a week of movement. As well as strength training and aerobic exercise, include flexibility and stretching (Pilates, yoga) and balance exercises too (tai chi, qigong).

TAKE THE STRAIN OFF YOUR LIVER

Some environmental toxins called xenoestrogens can flood your oestrogen receptors and give you symptoms of OD. They need to be processed by your liver in the same way as your own used-up oestrogen. So although it's impossible to avoid all environmental toxins, it's a good idea to minimise your exposure and therefore the work your liver needs to do.

> ### EASY WIN: EAT BROCCOLI SPROUTS DAILY
>
> *Some supermarkets and health food stores sell boxes of broccoli sprouts, though if you have the space and a little time to look after them, you can grow your own. It's well worth the effort because the green shoots from these just-germinated seeds contain up to 25 times as much liver-supporting sulforaphane as cruciferous vegetables – though it's still a good idea to eat the veg every day too. Sprinkle on salads or eggs for a nutrient boost.*

Treating symptoms

1. RAGE AND/OR IRRITABILITY

Your brain is full of oestrogen receptors. Too much oestrogen leads to fluctuating levels of mood neurotransmitters, including serotonin, dopamine and norepinephrine. It can also sensitise the HPA axis, magnifying the effect of stress. Plus, it can lead to cognitive overload – that feeling of being overwhelmed and unable to make decisions.

Food: All of the food listed in the section above can help, but especially leafy greens, oily fish, avocado and legumes.

Lifestyle: Work on building that stress toolkit (see chapter four). You could also try cognitive behavioural therapy (CBT), which can help you better understand your emotional triggers and responses.

Suggested supplements: Magnesium is key in neurotransmitter function (in PCH Magnesium Complex), and L-theanine, found naturally in green tea, helps promote relaxation without sedation (also in PCH Chill).

2. WEIGHT GAIN

Too much oestrogen affects fat storage directly, but also affects how you process sugar and carbohydrates, encouraging your body to store this energy as fat. It impacts ghrelin, the hunger hormone, and leptin, the hormone that signals you are full. It can make the thyroid, which controls your metabolism, behave as if it's underactive. It can also undermine your stamina, so you move less. And as fat stores produce oestrogen, putting on weight leads to a vicious cycle of putting on more weight.

Food: Fibre-rich foods help with satiety and balancing blood sugar levels, while lean proteins (see page 62) are important both for muscle repair and to keep you fuller for longer.

Lifestyle: Regular exercise is key, and particularly strength training, which raises metabolic rate and reduces fat storage.

Suggested supplements: Green tea extract is known for its thermogenic (energy-burning) properties and is therefore useful for boosting the metabolism. Berberine – a plant-derived compound – helps to improve insulin sensitivity and regulates fat storage. N.B. Only use it for eight weeks maximum if not under practitioner guidance.

3. PREMENSTRUAL SYNDROME (PMS)

PMS is a reaction to the rise in progesterone after ovulation, which in turn leads to mood swings and irritability in the second half (luteal) phase of the cycle. During perimenopause, it's thought you become more sensitised to hormonal changes, which is why PMS may feel worse or you develop it for the first time.

There are other things going on too. During the luteal phase, there's a rise in the production of inflammatory chemicals called cytokines. These add fuel to any existing inflammation, causing abdominal cramps and breast tenderness. Fluctuating hormones can also mess with your sensitivity to the hormone insulin, leading to cravings for sugar and carbohydrates.

Food: Slow-release carbs will stabilise blood sugar, which can help keep your mood more even. Avoid sugary foods and white carbs (even if you want them!). Having enough magnesium can help alleviate cramps and irritability. Good sources include leafy greens, nuts and seeds.

Lifestyle: It might not be exactly what you fancy doing but regular exercise and movement will improve mood and energy by stimulating endorphin production. Add in mindfulness meditation to your routine to help regulate mood and reduce stress. Over time, it can disrupt the cycle of habitual responses to stress and pain.

Suggested supplements: B vitamins are essential for mood regulation and proper metabolism of neurotransmitters, including serotonin (in PCH B-Complex). Calcium-D-glucarate assists the liver in clearing oestrogen.

4. FATIGUE

OD saps your energy in multiple ways, and especially in the luteal phase of your cycle. With OD, your cells struggle to meet the energy demands of your body, leading to fatigue, muscle weakness and taking longer to recover from exercise. OD can also deplete your mental energy because too much oestrogen can overstimulate your nervous system. It also affects the function of your thyroid, which controls the speed of your metabolism (see chapter 11 for more).

Food: Walnuts are rich in anti-inflammatory omega-3 fatty acids plus antioxidants that may help liver function. Pumpkin seeds provide a rich source of magnesium, zinc and healthy fats – all nutrients that play a role in energy production and hormonal balance.

Lifestyle: Keep exercise balanced. Overexertion can lead to adrenal fatigue and worsen symptoms.

Suggested supplement: Rhodiola rosea is an adaptogenic herb that's good for energy, stamina and mental clarity. It works by supporting the adrenal glands and improving the body's response to stress. (In PCH Ener-Boost, along with liquorice and ginseng.)

5. HEADACHES/MIGRAINES

High oestrogen stimulates immune cells to produce more pro-inflammatory chemicals, which can increase pain. Having high oestrogen (and in fact also the drop from high to low oestrogen premenstrually) can trigger headaches and/or migraines by causing a microscopic traffic jam in blood vessels in the brain. Plus, it sensitises pain receptors in the brain, so cranks up the volume of your headache.

If you're still having a cycle, a headache that's due to OD might happen around day 3 of your cycle in the run-up to ovulation or just after ovulation in your luteal phase, days 19 to 22.

Food: Ginger contains anti-inflammatory properties that can help reduce headaches. Magnesium is also anti-inflammatory and supports neurotransmitters involved in migraine. Good sources include almonds, leafy greens and pumpkin seeds.

Lifestyle: The traditional Chinese medicine techniques acupressure and acupuncture aim to balance the body's energy flow and can be effective in headache relief.

Suggested supplements: Again, magnesium can reduce the frequency and severity of migraines. It goes very well with taurine, a calming amino acid that can also help to prevent migraines (PCH Magnesium Complex). Vitamins B2 and B12 may also help reduce the severity of migraines (PCH B-Complex, PCH B12).

6. ENDOMETRIOSIS, FIBROIDS, CYSTS

Oestrogen is a pro-growth hormone. One of its jobs is to grow the endometrial lining and so when there's too much oestrogen compared to progesterone, this lining can become thicker, which can cause heavy periods. Oestrogen that's not balanced by progesterone can act like a fertiliser that you don't need, causing unwanted growth in other areas too. This is true of endometriosis, where endometrial cells grow outside the uterus and oestrogen dominance can also lead to the growth of fibroids and ovarian cysts.

Food: Berries and turmeric are handy for their anti-inflammatory and antioxidant properties.

Lifestyle: You probably already know that a hot water bottle or heat pad is good for cramps, because heat relaxes the uterine muscles. I'm also partial to a hot bath with Epsom salts, which are rich in calming magnesium. Stress exacerbates inflammatory conditions so spend time finding the stress management strategies that work for you – and that you enjoy. If you like them, you'll do them! (see chapter five).

Suggested supplements: Curcumin, the active ingredient in turmeric, is known for its anti-inflammatory properties (PCH Curcumin). Plus, omega-3 fatty acids can help alleviate inflammation (PCH Krill).

7. BREAST TENDERNESS AND SWELLING

Breast pain and tenderness is a real clue that oestrogen levels are too high. You may feel it all the time (this is common if you take HRT) or for just some of your cycle. It's usually due to a combination of factors. Oestrogen stimulates breast tissue and too much of it encourages fluid retention. Plus, it can prompt the release of inflammatory substances like histamine. An imbalance between oestrogen and progesterone can also exacerbate pre-existing breast conditions, such as lumpy breasts or a tendency to have cysts.

Food: Cucumber and green tea, both of which are natural diuretics and so good for countering fluid retention.

Lifestyle: Reduce salt intake as sodium can exacerbate fluid retention.

Suggested supplements: Evening primrose oil is known to relieve breast pain, while vitamin E has antioxidant properties that can alleviate symptoms of breast tenderness.

Julie's story

When I was 46, I went to see a private doctor who specialises in HRT. She gave me a list of perimenopause symptoms and I ticked more than three quarters of them, even though I still had regular periods.

The symptoms that I found the worst to live with were brain fog and problems with my memory, especially when I was at work. This scenario was typical: I was talking to someone I'd met at a work event, then a colleague I'd worked with for years came up to us. I went to introduce her ... and totally blanked on her name. When those kinds of things happened it was horrible and made me feel so stupid.

On top of the brain symptoms, there were others: night sweats, difficulty sleeping, bloating and craving sugar, weight gain, feeling tense, anxious, nervous, low and/or irritable, difficulty concentrating, plus I kept getting headaches and tingling in my fingers and I had vaginal dryness. I usually work out five times a week, a mixture of strength and cardio, but it was hard as I felt so tired and lacking in energy. I just did not feel myself – at all. I felt apathetic with no motivation and I had a sense of lethargy that I just couldn't shake.

A few of my friends had been to the GP for similar symptoms and had been prescribed antidepressants. I definitely did not want to take those – I wanted HRT. So I took myself off to see the menopause doctor.

The doctor gave me a whole series of blood tests, testing over 50 markers from thyroid to cholesterol and my hormones too. She prescribed me Oestrogel (body-identical oestrogen gel), Utrogestan (body-identical progesterone pills) and Vagifem (topical oestrogen for the vaginal area). The Vagifem worked but otherwise I didn't feel any different.

When I had my next appointment two months later, I told the doctor that I didn't feel an awful lot better. She looked at my blood tests and said that my level of testosterone was low. She suggested I start on testosterone cream too (AndroFeme), which I did.

I have a very good friend, Caroline, who is paralysed from the waist down after a horse-riding accident. That summer, she had a flare-up of inflammation and arthritis in her hands. She needs her hands to get into her chair, so she spent two full weeks in bed.

I listened to a podcast about how eating a plant-based diet can reduce inflammation and I suggested to her that she try it. She said, 'No way, I've got enough restrictions in my life!' I said, 'Let's both go plant-based for a month. And if neither of us feel better, we can write it off as a bad job.'

She agreed and we started. And within a few weeks, we both did feel better. I was quite strict for the first six months, eating no meat or fish or milk or cheese (although I did eat eggs and butter). I began to feel better, a lot better than from any of the HRT medication I took. And eating like this alongside Caroline made it so much easier, as we shared recipes and supported each other.

Around that time, when I was looking for more information about nutrition online, I found Pippa on Instagram. I liked the way she explained nutrition, so I booked in to see one of Pippa's practitioners in the clinic. She asked me about my symptoms in detail. When I described the extent of my digestive issues – bloating especially after eating bread, burping and gas, heartburn, diarrhoea, thrush, craving starchy and sweet foods and hangovers getting worse even with small amounts of alcohol, she said she thought there was something going on besides perimenopause.

The practitioner suggested I do a stool test, to find out what was going on in my gut. When the results came back, they were fascinating. I had an intestinal protozoa, a type of parasite. And I had Dientamoeba fragilis, a bad bacteria that you can get from dirty water. My microbiome was on the very low end of diversity, the opposite of what it should be, plus I had an overgrowth of candida yeast. The practitioner said that a lot of the symptoms I'd ticked at the menopause clinic – in particular, the brain fog – were probably down to the candida. While I was feeling so down and tired, my go-to comfort food had been bread, which had probably fed the candida.

The strict anti-candida diet lasted eight weeks, excluding bread, yeast and sugar. The practitioner gave me an oral microbiome toothpaste plus a whole protocol of supplements to get rid of the parasites and to increase my gut diversity.

My next consultation was about my hormones. I had a DUTCH test and the results of that were even more interesting. I was still taking the same HRT, and my testosterone levels were within range for my age. But my oestrogen levels were off the chart, as high as someone who was pregnant. And my progesterone levels were on the floor, like someone fully in menopause.

I also had a series of DNA tests, one of which looked at how I metabolise hormones. It explained some of my hormone results. It showed that that I was metabolising testosterone too quickly and I wasn't detoxifying used-up oestrogen, so a lot of my symptoms were due to having too much oestrogen.

The practitioner wasn't overly happy that I was completely plant based. In particular, she said I was missing out on the amino acid tryptophan, which is important for making the good mood brain chemical serotonin and the sleepy hormone melatonin, so she advised me to eat chicken. I gradually started eating some chicken, then fish, and now I do eat some meat too, although I'm plant based around 80 per cent of the time.

To support my liver, I did a complete overhaul of all my beauty products, using the Yuka app to identify and minimise harmful chemicals in my new products. And to help my liver detoxify used-up oestrogen, I eat a lot of cruciferous, bitter and sulphur-rich veg. I seed cycle to help balance my hormones and I drink goats milk kefir for my gut. I'm taking some supplements too, including magnesium, phosphatidyl choline, vitamin D, fish oil, PCH Just Ashwagandha, PCH Chill and PCH Mood & Sleep. I've also started making sure I have a proper overnight fast.

After a few months, I felt so much better, with so much more energy, that I decided I didn't want to take HRT any more – at least, for the time being. When I came off HRT, I didn't get any symptoms back, which is what I told the doctor at my HRT follow-up.

I've found that I can go to the gym more now, as I've got more energy. I train with weights most days but I've also introduced Pilates to help my flexibility. And I've created my own protocol of breathwork that I do for five to ten minutes every night.

The plan is to retake the stool test soon, to find out how my gut microbiome looks. And I'll also retake the DUTCH test, now I'm no longer taking HRT. The best thing that's come out of all of this is that I'm no longer in that lethargic place I was in before. I now feel 100 per cent different – and better.

CHAPTER 8

Oestrogen Deficiency

- Hot flushes. Do you get suddenly overcome by heat, especially over your face, neck and chest? You may also feel heart palpitations and anxiety too.
- Vaginal dryness. Have you noticed vaginal dryness or soreness? Or that sex is more uncomfortable or painful? Are you getting UTIs more regularly?
- Weight. Have you noticed you're putting on weight around your mid-section? And/or that you're losing the definition of your waist?
- Insomnia. Are you sleeping for less time than you used to? Do you wake up feeling less refreshed?
- Fatigue. Do you feel you don't have the energy levels you used to have? Do you feel subpar, although you can't pinpoint why?
- Cognitive issues. Is your memory not as good as it used to be? Is it hard to pay attention and to understand some information?

- Joint pain. Do you have more aches and pains than you used to?

- Skin changes. Is your skin drier than it used to be, so you have to use a thicker moisturiser? Does it feel thinner and less springy, more saggy? Do you feel you've lost your glow?

- Bone issues. Have you been diagnosed with osteopenia or osteoporosis? Or have you broken a bone when you wouldn't have expected to?

Hot flushes are the classic symptom that people associate with perimenopause. But in fact, they are often a symptom of later perimenopause, as you approach the end of your periods, and menopause itself, a year without periods. That's because hot flushes tend to be a symptom of low oestrogen.

In early perimenopause, oestrogen levels often fluctuate, but they tend to be high more than low. Then, as periods become less and less frequent, and as you approach your final period, oestrogen is more likely to be low.

It's often assumed that, after menopause, women have zero oestrogen. In fact, your body still produces oestrogen, although at a lower level than in your fertile years, and a different kind. As your ovaries wind down, most of the job of producing oestrogen is taken over by your back-up system, the adrenals. To make this new oestrogen, the body ramps up the activity of an enzyme called aromatase, which turns testosterone (more of which is now being made in the adrenals) into oestrogen. Aromatase is found in fatty tissue. So the more fat stores you have, the more aromatase you have and the bigger potential you have to make more oestrogen. This new kind of oestrogen is called estrone (E1). It isn't as potent as your fertile estradiol (E2) oestrogen but, if everything is working, it's strong enough and plentiful enough that the transition from fertile to your third age is symptom-free – or, at least, bearable.

However, for many women, this isn't the case. In clinic, I often see women in later perimenopause and around the menopause itself who are being hit by wave after wave of hot flushes as well as other low oestrogen symptoms. Less often, I see women who have lower than normal oestrogen in the early stages of perimenopause, while they still have periods. I also see women who've either had a surgical menopause (they've had their ovaries removed) or are taking medication to stop their cycle – for example, after breast cancer. Their drop in oestrogen is sudden and happens overnight, and symptoms can be severe.

Finally, it's very common for me to see women who zigzag between symptoms of high oestrogen (see chapter seven) and the low oestrogen symptoms and as they get closer to menopause, they tend to be more low oestrogen.

The women who have low oestrogen naturally are often living with chronic stress. Their adrenals are working hard to produce stress hormones rather than making oestrogen. These women also may have a less than good diet, low body weight and/or can be over-exercising.

Three key reasons for oestrogen deficiency

1. YOUR OVARIES ARE GOING OFFLINE

As you ovulate less frequently, the ups and downs of oestrogen during the perimenopause slowly turn into more downs. Once your periods have stopped for a year – menopause itself – you will have an oestrogen level that's much lower than in your fertile years (unless you're taking HRT).

2. XENOESTROGENS

We encounter endocrine-disrupting fake oestrogens all the time, such as bisphenol A that's used as a softener in plastics (see page 80 for more). Your body sees these as real oestrogen. Xenoestrogens are so powerful that they can flood your oestrogen receptors and give you symptoms of high oestrogen. But they can also fool your body into thinking that you have enough oestrogen and so you produce less, giving you symptoms of low oestrogen.

Xenoestrogens are detoxed in the liver, so it's important to support that nutritionally. And eating phytoestrogens (see opposite) can also help rid your body of xenoestrogens. When phytoestrogens also bind to oestrogen receptors, they leave less space for xenoestrogens to attach.

3. STRESS

Continued stress can lead to an increased production of cortisol, which can disrupt the balance of sex hormones, including oestrogen. During late perimenopause, as the ovaries go offline, the adrenals ideally produce enough oestrogen to keep symptoms at bay. But if the adrenals are already busy making cortisol, they won't have the capacity. This makes sense: why would your body prioritise fertility when it's constantly getting a message that you're in a life-threatening situation?

This is the most important time to prioritise looking after yourself. You are coming to the end of a massive shift for your hormones, body and brain. This chapter explains the factors that will help keep your low oestrogen symptoms at bay for the foreseeable future, by making sure that your new factory for oestrogen – the adrenals – can do its job.

Oestrogen deficiency: what to eat

PHYTOESTROGENS

Phytoestrogens are plant compounds that, like xenoestrogens, mimic oestrogen in the body. However, unlike xenoestrogens, they are generally beneficial. The best studied phytoestrogens in menopause are isoflavones, found in soy products like edamame, tofu and tempeh, which may help alleviate symptoms of oestrogen deficiency. Buy non-GMO organic soy products. Flaxseeds are brilliant at helping reduce symptoms too; I suggest you take them daily (see page 159). They're an excellent source of phytoestrogens called lignans.

FAT

Eating fat is crucial for oestrogen production. Make sure you get enough omega-3 fatty acids, found in oily fish like salmon, because they're also anti-inflammatory. If you're veggie, eat chia seeds, pumpkin seeds and walnuts. Finally, the monounsaturated fats found in avocados and olive oil are integral for building healthy cell membranes, including those of hormones.

FIBRE

Not only will eating fibre help you to eliminate used-up oestrogen, but it will also support a steady release of energy, preventing spikes in blood sugar that can disrupt hormonal balance. Make sure you have plenty of vegetables, whole grains and fruits in your diet.

LIVER-SUPPORTING FOODS

The liver has the job of packaging up used oestrogen for excretion, and to help it do its job properly, make sure you're eating foods from each of the following three categories of nutrients daily.

Foods to focus on are: B vitamin-rich foods such as spinach, kale, beans and lentils, sulphur-rich foods such as egg yolks, garlic and onions, and cruciferous vegetables such as broccoli, Brussels sprouts, cabbage and kale.

Oestrogen deficiency: lifestyle guidelines

AVOID XENOESTROGENS

Follow the advice in chapter four to help reduce your exposure to oestrogen-mimicking chemicals. Eat organic (especially animal products) where you can. Go plastic free for food storage and when cooking and heating food. Buy natural cosmetics and cleaning products that are free from parabens, phthalates and other chemicals.

WORK ON YOUR STRESS

Your third age is a time to rethink what's important to you and to start taking care of yourself. This is when to actively work on managing stress, setting boundaries and avoiding overcommitting. What will help you feel content in mind as well as body? Would it help to have some sessions with a therapist? Can you say 'no' more often? Can you carve out non-negotiable time for yourself? Have you got friends and/or family who make you feel good and who you can rely on? There's lots you can do. For example, you can make your exercise routine more restorative by doing yoga. You can do meditation or deep breathing exercises while walking or making tea. By exploring these options and more, and seeing what works, you can develop your own anti-stress toolkit. Go back to chapter four if you need a reminder on how to do this.

CONSISTENT PHYSICAL ACTIVITY

For advice on exercise, see chapter four. Ideally, you'll be doing 2 hours and 30 minutes a week of movement. As well as strength training and aerobic exercise, it's good to include flexibility and stretching (Pilates, yoga) and balance exercises too (tai chi, qi gong).

QUALITY SLEEP

Sleep is important for hormone synthesis and balance; see page 75 for how to maximise your rest time.

> **EASY WIN: TWO TABLESPOONS OF GROUND FLAXSEED A DAY.**
>
> *Flaxseeds contain phytoestrogens which help balance oestrogen levels in the body. They're also packed with both the soluble and insoluble kinds of fibre which can help carry used-up hormones out of the body via your stool. Put ground flaxseeds in your protein smoothie (see recipe on page 238) or sprinkle onto coconut yoghurt.*

Treating symptoms

1. HOT FLUSHES

These feel like a rush of intense heat in the face, neck and chest, plus redness, sweating and sometimes a rapid heartbeat. Changes in oestrogen levels make the hypothalamus, the part of the brain responsible for regulating body temperature, overly sensitive to changes in body temperature. When the hypothalamus senses that you're too warm, hot flushes are its attempt to cool you down.

Food: Eating phytoestrogen-containing foods (see page 157) daily may help reduce the frequency and intensity of hot flushes by mildly boosting oestrogen levels or by mimicking oestrogen's effects.

Lifestyle: Current research isn't conclusive that exercise helps reduce hot flushes and if it does, about the kind of exercise that works best. However, we do know regular aerobic exercise helps improve your vascular health.

Suggested supplement: Soy isoflavones are the best studied phytoestrogen when it comes to reducing hot flushes (PCH Oestro-Balance contains soy isoflavones plus magnesium, zinc and chromium).

2. VAGINAL DRYNESS

Both oestrogen and testosterone help to maintain the thickness and elasticity of the skin of the vagina and vulva. A drop in hormones can lead to less lubrication, less elasticity and thinner vaginal walls, causing dryness, itchiness, soreness and pain during sex. It also makes vaginal and urinary tract infections more likely.

Your GP will offer you topical oestrogen (as a tiny pill or pessary you insert, or as a cream or gel) to replace the oestrogen locally. This is not the same as taking HRT. Plus, he/she may suggest you use a vaginal moisturiser. Look for one that's all natural and made from hyaluronic acid, such as Yes! There's also a DHEA (androgen) pessary (the DHEA turns into oestrogen and testosterone) but it's not available from all GPs. Your GP or menopause specialist can help you find the right treatment (see box on page 26).

Food: Eating essential fatty acids (such as omega 3 fats) found in foods including chia seeds and walnuts can improve skin hydration and help keep cell membranes healthy.

Lifestyle: Drink water. So simple but so vital. Hydration is crucial for maintaining the health of mucosal barriers including vaginal tissue.

Suggested supplements: Vitamin E – some women find it helpful to apply it directly to the vaginal area. PCH Oestro-Balance, which contains soy isoflavones that are good at balancing oestrogen levels.

3. WEIGHT GAIN

This is a high-risk time for weight gain. As oestrogen levels go down, weight tends to go up, especially around the mid-section. Hunger signals and appetite become stronger, you are more likely to eat for emotional reasons and your sleep gets disturbed, which can all contribute to weight gain. At the same time, muscle mass and metabolic rate both decline with age.

Food: Increase the amount of quality protein you eat, to 20g to 30g each meal. A protein-rich meal is good for blood sugar balance and satiety, and provides the building blocks for neurotransmitters and muscle.

Lifestyle: Ideally, do aerobic exercise (e.g. walking, swimming or cycling) plus strength training to support metabolism and muscle mass. Research suggests that blood sugar control is best when exercise is regular and includes resistance exercise, that you move around the time of eating (after is best but you can do it before if that suits you better), and that you break up your day with regular three-minute bouts of any exercise, also called exercise snacks. Plus, better sleep and targeted daily relaxation can help weight indirectly.

Suggested supplements: Cayenne and chromium can both help increase metabolic rate and decrease appetite (both are found in PCH Meta Boost).

4. INSOMNIA

Oestrogen is needed to make serotonin, which supports the production of the sleepy hormone melatonin. It helps regulate your sleep-wake cycle and lulls you into a deeper sleep. So when it drops, so does your sleep quality and often the hours you sleep, too.

Food: Include lots of magnesium-rich food, such as leafy greens, like spinach, kale and Swiss chard, plus nuts, seeds, legumes and whole grains, as magnesium helps to calm the nervous system and is needed to make melatonin. Some foods contain small amounts of melatonin too – namely cherries, nuts and oats.

Lifestyle: All the advice in chapter four on creating a consistent sleep schedule and good sleep hygiene is particularly relevant for you.

Suggested supplements: Valerian, a herb traditionally used to improve sleep quality. 5-HTP can help to increase serotonin levels, which can be converted to melatonin. Magnesium helps relax you and regulates the sleep-wake cycle (in PCH Mood & Sleep, which contains 5-HTP, magnesium and the relaxing herb, passionflower - see also PCH Magnesium Complex). N.B. Do not take 5-HTP alongside SSRI antidepressants.

5. FATIGUE

If you have fatigue, you are not alone: nearly half of women in perimenopause report symptoms of physical and mental exhaustion.

Lower oestrogen affects the adrenal hormones (see chapter five), thyroid (see chapter 11) and brain function, all of which can leave you feeling exhausted in both mind and body. And research shows that in late menopause in particular, as oestrogen falls lower, fatigue can add to stress, which makes you more tired.

Food: Follow the Food Framework in chapter three for sustained energy. Around a third of women have low iron levels, so make sure you're eating enough iron-rich foods, especially if your periods have become heavier. These include lentils, spinach and red meat.

Lifestyle: Work on sleep hygiene, moderate exercise, plus proper rest and relaxation (see chapter four).

Suggested supplements: B vitamins for energy production and the proper functioning of the nervous system, specifically B12 (PCH B-Complex, PCH Vitamin B12).

6. COGNITIVE ISSUES

A drop in oestrogen influences neurotransmitter systems, neural plasticity and blood flow to the brain, affecting memory, learning and your ability to concentrate – so-called brain fog. There isn't conclusive evidence about what can help, but as this is an inflammatory state, eat an anti-inflammatory diet, as explained on page 194. The good news is that brain fog that's due to hormones typically doesn't last beyond menopause.

Food: Eat more antioxidants; they help combat oxidative stress which contributes to brain ageing and cognitive decline. Berries, such as blueberries, strawberries and blackberries, contain flavonoids that have been shown to improve memory and cognitive functions. Other antioxidant-rich foods include leafy greens, nuts, seeds and dark chocolate. Foods high in omega-3 fatty acids, such as fatty fish, flaxseeds and walnuts, support brain health.

Lifestyle: Regular exercise has an anti-inflammatory effect on the brain and reduces cognitive decline.

Suggested supplements: DHA, a type of omega-3 fatty acid, is particularly important for maintaining the health of brain cells (PCH Krill Oil).

7. JOINT PAIN

Having enough oestrogen helps to reduce inflammation and sensitivity to pain, and it also helps maintain healthy collagen and cartilage in the joints. As oestrogen drops, women report experiencing more inflammation, stiffness and pain in their knees and hips, as well as in their hands and feet.

Food: Eat anti-inflammatory foods, such as those high in omega-3 (oily fish, flaxseeds and walnuts), and foods high in antioxidants (berries, leafy greens and tomatoes). Add in anti-inflammatory spices turmeric and ginger. Stay hydrated and limit inflammatory foods (processed foods, sugars, alcohol and caffeine).

Lifestyle: Stretching and flexibility exercises (Pilates, yoga) can help keep joints mobile. You may find lower impact exercise, such as walking or swimming, easier on your joints. Strength training will strengthen the muscles around the joints, improving stability and reducing pain. It's also a good idea to manage body weight, as more weight means more stress on the joints (see my previous book, *Eat Right, Lose Weight* if you require more information on this).

Suggested supplement: Curcumin is anti-inflammatory including for the joints (PCH Curcumin).

8. SKIN CHANGES

As oestrogen levels decrease, so does your production of collagen and elastin. Skin becomes thinner and less elastic, and circulation drops, causing wrinkles, dryness and a decrease in skin's overall plumpness and firmness.

Food: Eat enough protein (see page 50) at every meal. Vitamin C helps collagen synthesis, and antioxidants help to counteract the effects of reduced collagen and elastin. Eat citrus fruits, berries, nuts, seeds, tomatoes, sweet potatoes and carrots. Omega-3 fatty acids, found in fatty fish, flaxseeds and walnuts, also support skin health by reducing inflammation and helping to keep it hydrated. To improve circulation, eat flavonoid-rich foods, such as dark chocolate, green tea, and a mix of colourful fruits and vegetables.

Lifestyle: Protect your skin from sun damage with SPF (stick to natural SPF, e.g. zinc oxide) because sunlight also damages collagen and increases pigmentation. Stay hydrated.

Suggested supplements: A collagen supplement provides the amino acids necessary for collagen production in skin, supporting elasticity and hydration (PCH Marine Collagen).

9. BONE ISSUES

Oestrogen plays a critical role in bone health: it helps to regulate the balance of osteoblasts (cells that build bone) and osteoclasts (cells that break down bone), maintaining bone density and strength. When oestrogen levels decrease, this balance is disrupted, which can lead to decreased bone mineral density (osteopenia) and to weaker bones with a higher risk of fracture (osteoporosis).

Food: Eat enough calcium, vitamin D, magnesium and vitamin K2. Calcium-rich foods include green leafy vegetables, sesame seeds, tahini, almonds, tofu and the bones of tinned sardine and mackerel (in brine rather than oil). For vitamin D, 20 minutes of morning sun exposure on your legs and arms is ideal plus it's in oily fish, egg yolks and fortified foods. Magnesium-rich foods include nuts, seeds, whole grains and leafy greens. Vitamin K2-rich foods include egg yolk and butter, as well as fermented foods, such as miso, sauerkraut and natto (fermented soybeans).

Lifestyle: Impact on bones strengthens them: walking, jogging, dancing and skipping are all good for this. Resistance training also stimulates bone formation. N.B. If you've been diagnosed with osteopenia or osteoporosis, get professional or medical advice about the kind of exercise you can do. Smoking and alcohol are both bad for bone health. And try to stay at a healthy weight; being underweight can increase the risk of bone loss and fractures.

Suggested supplements: Before you supplement vitamin D, you may want to test to see if you're deficient. A recent UK survey showed that half of Asian people aged 40 to 69 are deficient, around a third of Black people and 12 per cent of white people. You're also more likely to be deficient in winter and spring (the stores you build in summer only last so long) and if you live in the north rather than the south of the UK. If you have dark skin, you're more likely to be deficient. Vitamin K2 helps in the regulation of calcium deposition in the bones. It's often recommended to take vitamin K2 alongside calcium and vitamin D to enhance their bone-protective effects (PCH D3 Vegan Complex contains vitamin D3, K2 and A).

Amanda's story

My perimenopause started relatively early. I was aged 41 and my daughter was just two. I started waking up in the night with horrendous night sweats and having mood swings during the day too.

I went to the GP who did blood tests on my hormones and said my levels were fine. And so I carried on living with those symptoms for three or four years. Then I began to get five to six hot flushes every day, so bad that the nape of my neck would get drenched. My moods were going up and down even more, so sometimes I'd be raging then crying. And my memory had started to get worse too.

I didn't want to go on HRT because I'd heard horror stories about it increasing the risk of breast cancer. I was determined to fix my symptoms naturally. So I went to see a nutritionist who specialised in women's health. She gave me the herb black cohosh and some dietary advice, such as don't eat spicy foods and don't drink alcohol. The herb didn't work for me. Cutting down on alcohol helped to a degree. It helped me to sleep better and I had fewer hot flushes – but it didn't solve things completely. The rest of her advice wasn't that useful.

So I just carried on living with the hot flushes, trying all kinds of different things that I read about or people suggested. At times, I was so desperate to feel better I would have done anything.

I thought stress might be a factor, so I swapped running for walking and yoga. I tried going dairy free at one point. I stopped eating any processed foods at all. I gave up alcohol almost entirely. Someone suggested I try fasting but it made me feel worse. For six months, I had acupuncture every week. I enjoyed it and initially I thought it helped, but then I became unsure it was making a real difference.

Then one Friday I went to see a client. During that meeting, I had two hot flushes, one straight after the other. As soon as I got back, I called the GP for an emergency appointment. I told her, 'It's awful, I'm not even living.'

By 6pm, I had picked up an HRT prescription. That weekend we were away for my parents-in-law's wedding anniversary, and I put a patch on. I'd been dreading the weekend as I knew I'd have hot flushes. But I didn't have even one. And in bed that night, I didn't have night sweats either. I was absolutely thrilled. I thought, *Now I can live a normal life!*

I had been one of the first in my friendship group to get perimenopausal symptoms. But by this time, my close friends all had symptoms too, and quite a few of them were taking HRT. They told me that HRT had not only got rid of their hot flushes but it had cured their brain fog too. They said they felt back to being themselves. The only thing HRT had done for me was stop the hot flushes.

I learnt to manage my memory problems by putting alarms on my phone and making notes on everything. But I still had mood swings, rage and tearfulness, joint pains, and no sex drive, and I still felt disconnected from the world. In a way, some of those symptoms were harder to live with than the hot flushes. There were other symptoms creeping in too: bloating and digestive issues, and weight gain.

Because I still felt bad, I went to see a private hormone doctor. She did a blood test that showed my testosterone was really low and suggested I add that to my HRT. I started taking it and it really helped with the joint pain, clarity of mind and libido. It changed me too: around that time, I went skiing and I found myself on the hard red runs, when I'd always stuck to blue or green before! But it had a downside: it made my stomach issues so bad that I dreaded eating.

I was being healthy, eating probably 50 different plants in a week, lower carbs and zero processed foods, but I was still not feeling as good as you'd imagine from eating that well.

I started researching what could be wrong with my gut, and that's when I came across Pippa's clinic and booked in to see one of the practitioners. She suggested I do a DUTCH test. It showed that I was oestrogen dominant and it looked as if I was converting testosterone to oestrogen too fast. It also showed that my cortisol was flatlining – I'd been stressed for so long that I had stopped making enough cortisol.

I decided to reduce my oestrogen to see if I felt better. So I cut back slowly and now I'm down to half a pump a day. At the same time, I focused on getting my gut healthy. I've always eaten well, but now I'm taking it to the next level. I'm eating a lot more plant based, lots of pulses, lentils, beans and less meat. When I do eat meat, I have good quality chicken or steak. If I'm making a salad, I'll add sprouted seeds. I've also switched to natural beauty products and cleaning products, to take the pressure off my liver so it can process the used-up oestrogen. When I'm eating well, I want to exercise too, to go for a walk in the fresh air, rather than feeling sluggish, so that's great.

Now, three months later, my dress size has gone from 12 to 14 down to my normal 10 to 12, and my stomach is a normal size too. I still had some gut symptoms, so I did a stool test. That showed I had an overgrowth of candida, a type of yeast. I'm on a supplement programme to help with this. I'm also taking supplements to help me process oestrogen better.

I did try coming off HRT completely, but sadly my symptoms returned, so I'm back on a low dose again. I am working on my stress levels with breathwork, meditation and a calmer lifestyle. I hope to try and come off HRT again soon. To me, it feels like a sticking plaster to put over the real issue.

CHAPTER 9

Androgen Dominance

- Acne and oily skin. Are you getting spots on your face or body? Are breakouts happening more often or they're more severe?
- Facial and body hair. Have you noticed new growth of facial or body hair, particularly on your chin, upper lip or abdomen?
- Hair thinning. Is your hair lacking its usual volume? Is your scalp more visible along the parting or hairline, or on the temples or the crown?
- Weight gain. Are you putting on weight despite sticking to the same eating and exercise habits?
- A short fuse. Are your emotions on an unpredictable rollercoaster, so you can easily find yourself irritated and angry?

> **THE MAIN PLAYERS**
>
> **DHEA:** *Dehydroepiandrosterone is an androgen hormone produced by in the adrenal glands. It's the precursor to testosterone.*
>
> **Testosterone:** *An important androgen sex hormone.*
>
> **SHBG:** *Sex hormone-binding globulin binds to sex hormones (including testosterone) to control the amount that's active.*
>
> **DHT:** *Dihydrotestosterone is an androgen made from testosterone.*
>
> **5AR:** *5-alpha reductase is the enzyme that turns testosterone into DHT.*

It's a close-run competition as to which hormonal imbalance women find the hardest to live with, but this might be the one. Having excess androgens can not only make you feel tired and angry, but women say it makes them feel self-conscious, unattractive – even desperate – when they can't find a solution. In clinic, the symptom women most often report as being especially distressing is acne. Breakouts tends to concentrate around the chin and be of the painful, cystic kind that can take a long time to heal.

Another symptom that's hard to deal with – and it only comes second because it's a little less common – is hair loss. Then there's hair growing in places you don't want it – chin, nipples, upper lip. Add to that weight gain, especially around the middle, and you've got a perfect storm of unwanted symptoms.

You may think of androgens as male hormones, but women need them just as much as men, just not too much. Androgens are in charge of bone density, libido, muscle growth and maintenance, mood and libido. You also need to them to make oestrogen. The androgen DHEA, which I call the mother hormone, is made in your ovaries and your adrenal glands. Then some of this is transformed into testosterone, and some of the testosterone changes into oestrogen too.

There are two kinds of women who come into clinic with this hormone imbalance. In one group, there are the women who've been androgen dominant since puberty. If this is you, you might, for example, have suffered from persistent acne and now it's flared up again. And you're firmly in this group if you've been diagnosed with polycystic ovarian syndrome (PCOS). (N.B. Some of the symptoms of PCOS can settle down after menopause but not all symptoms and not for everyone).

The second group develop androgen dominance for the first time in midlife. It happens when oestrogen drops towards the end of perimenopause. While the actual amount of testosterone isn't that high, it is in comparison to other sex hormones, namely oestrogen and progesterone. Then, women who've never before had androgenic symptoms suddenly find they are getting adult acne, hair loss, a moustache and hair growing on their chin.

These symptoms that women find so hard to live with are in fact due to a product of testosterone, called DHT. DHT is five to eight times more powerful than testosterone.

Four key reasons for androgen dominance

1. INSULIN RESISTANCE

Oestrogen helps us be more sensitive to insulin, so when it declines, you're at higher risk of insulin resistance. This is when the body's cells become unresponsive or less sensitive to insulin (see chapter 12 for more on this). Insulin resistance becomes more common as you get older too. It can hyper stimulate the ovaries and adrenal glands to produce more androgens. This can then create a negative feedback loop: high insulin drives up androgens; high androgens then drive up insulin resistance. One way to stop this cycle is to eat to keep blood sugar levels as even as possible.

2. LOW SEX HORMONE-BINDING GLOBULIN (SHBG)

SHBG is a protein made in the liver that helps to control the amount of testosterone and DHT that's active or 'free' for your tissues to use. When SHBG binds to these hormones, your tissues can't use them. However, when oestrogen goes down during the perimenopause, SHBG levels go down too, and so free testosterone and DHT go up. There are specific foods you can eat to support your body to make SHBG, which I've listed on page 175 in the 'What to eat' section.

3. POLYCYSTIC OVARY SYNDROME (PCOS)

PCOS is an endocrine disorder that's the most common cause of infertility, with 5 to 18 per cent of women thought to have it. One key feature of PCOS is that the ovaries make too many androgens. Another is that you don't ovulate properly and so your ovaries end up with multiple small cysts, leading to irregular periods. Lastly, PCOS comes along with insulin resistance, as explained above, which drives up free testosterone and DHT levels.

4. RELATIVE ANDROGEN DOMINANCE

Androgen dominance, like all hormonal imbalances, is part of the whole picture of hormonal imbalances at this time. During your reproductive years, oestrogen, progesterone and androgens are in a delicate balancing act (if you don't have PCOS or another hormonal issue). But during the perimenopause, when oestrogen is high and fluctuating, and progesterone drops, androgens can be left in charge, leaving you in a state of relative androgen dominance.

Treating the symptoms of androgen dominance starts with the bigger hormonal picture, the advice in chapters three and four. Then, the advice in this chapter targets this imbalance in two ways. The idea is to balance blood sugar and so increase levels of SHBG, leaving less free testosterone available to act in the body. And secondly, to reduce the amount of testosterone that changes into the more damaging DHT, by blocking the enzyme 5-alpha reductase (5AR).

> ### EASY WIN: TWO CUPS OF SPEARMINT TEA PER DAY
>
> *Spearmint tea has been shown to reduce free (active) testosterone levels. Steep one tablespoon of fresh or one teaspoon of dried leaves in boiling water for 5–10 minutes. Drink two per day. For an extra boost, add green tea. It contains substances called catechins which inhibit 5AR. It only needs to be steeped for 2–3 minutes so put it in the pot later. Add a slice of lemon to help absorption.*

Androgen dominance: what to eat

EAT TO KEEP BLOOD SUGAR STABLE

Over time, this will help to improve insulin sensitivity and so help stop the negative spiral of androgen production.

- Eat 20 to 30g protein for breakfast (ideally 30g). For example, eggs, salmon, mackerel, chickpeas, hummus, protein shake. N.B. two eggs is 12g protein, so you will need more eggs or another source. I'm a big fan of leftovers for breakfast!
- Include protein, fat and carbs in each meal – for example a salad with chicken, avocado and quinoa. Choose slow-

release, high-fibre carbs that don't make your blood sugar go up fast. Try quinoa, lentils and pulses, and sweet potato (especially when cooked then cooled).

- The spices cinnamon, fenugreek and ginger have a positive effect on blood sugar.

EAT TO SUPPORT SHBG

SHBG helps to keep levels of free (active) testosterone down.

- Make sure you include enough antioxidant-rich foods, as oxidative stress has been shown to reduce levels of SHBG. Good sources include all types of berries, dark chocolate, nuts and seeds, green tea.

- Vitamin E and coenzyme Q10 (CoQ10) foods will help with this too. One study showed that supplementing with CoQ10 and vitamin E led to a rise in SHBG levels and a drop in total testosterone. For vitamin E, eat sunflower seeds, peanuts, almonds, avocados, oily fish, olive oil and spinach.

- The best source of CoQ10 are organ meats (e.g. liver) but it's also in oily fish, meat. Veggie sources include soy, sesame seeds, spinach and broccoli.

- Phytoestrogen foods, such as soy foods, flaxseeds, sesame seeds and lentils, can raise SHBG.

LIVER-SUPPORTING FOODS

All hormones need to be processed in the liver, so liver health is very important. This is what to eat to support your liver function:

- Cruciferous vegetables such as broccoli, cauliflower, Brussels sprouts and cabbage, help the liver detoxify used-up hormones, including testosterone.

- Garlic and onions are sulphur-rich, supporting detoxification in the liver. They also contain quercetin, a flavonoid that plays a supportive role in the body's detoxification pathways, which in turn can help in the regulation of androgen levels.

- Turmeric is rich in curcuminoids; this helps support liver detoxification too.

Androgen dominance: lifestyle guidelines

LESS STRESS, BETTER SLEEP

- Stress raises androgen levels, so make sure you put together your personal anti-stress toolkit, plus, if you need to, find ways to improve your sleep (see chapter four).

FIND YOUR MOVES

- Cardiovascular exercise improves insulin sensitivity, which reduces androgen levels. In one study, cycling at an intensity of 60 to 70 per cent for 30 minutes, three days a week, was effective. High intensity interval training (HIIT) – short bursts of intense activity – has been shown to reduce levels of the androgen DHEA-S. N.B. Whatever you do, consistency is key.

- Women with androgen dominance had lower testosterone levels after doing regular strength training for 16 weeks.

- After three months of doing yoga, women with androgen dominance had lower levels of free testosterone and reported better mood as well as reductions in anxiety and depression.

Treating symptoms

1. ACNE AND OILY SKIN

Raised insulin and high androgens stimulate the sebaceous glands in the skin to produce more sebum, the oily substance that's the skin's natural moisturiser. However, excessive sebum can trap bacteria and dead skin cells in the pores, causing inflammation and acne.

Food: Make sure you are eating slow-release carbs, as keeping blood sugar levels balanced can reduce the production of sebum. Also, include plenty of anti-inflammatory foods – particularly berries, turmeric and leafy greens.

Lifestyle: High cortisol levels can increase sebum production, so proactively think about what you can do to make yourself feel less stressed, such as meditation, yoga and breathing exercises.

Suggested Supplements: Zinc is antibacterial and acts as an anti-inflammatory, while saw palmetto extract, made from the fruit of the palm, reduces DHT, the most potent of the androgens.

2. FACIAL AND BODY HAIR

High androgens, particularly DHT, bind to the follicles and prompt the conversion of the fine, peach fuzz hair on your face or body into thicker, darker hairs. You will have a genetic predisposition as to how sensitive your follicles are to DHT.

Food: Flaxseeds are rich in lignans, phytoestrogen compounds that work to inhibit 5AR.

3. HAIR THINNING

When DHT binds to the follicles on the head, its action is the opposite to that on the body. It shortens the hair growth cycle and miniaturises follicles so that, over time, they become finer and shorter. Not all areas of the scalp are equally sensitive to DHT, which is why hair loss occurs in specific patterns, including receding hairline or widening of the parting, a.k.a. female pattern hair loss. The sensitivity of your follicles to DHT is primarily determined by genetics.

Food: Being low in iron, which a lot of women are, affects hair growth. Eat iron-rich foods such as red meat, liver, legumes. Also, omega-3-rich fish, nuts and seeds provide healthy fats to support scalp health and so the hair follicles. Eggs are high in biotin and zinc, which contribute to hair strength.

Lifestyle: Regular scalp massage improves blood circulation, providing more oxygen and nutrients to the hair follicles. And – our old nemesis again – stress can make hair loss worse. So don't forget to work on your own stress toolkit. Drink green tea: it contains substances called catechins which inhibit 5AR. To maximise catechins, steep good-quality loose leaves in hot water (just below boiling) for 2-3 minutes only. Add a slice of lemon to help absorption.

Suggested supplements: Stinging nettle and saw palmetto both target 5AR, reducing DHT. One study showed that out of all the medicinal mushrooms, reishi are the most powerful anti-androgen.

4. WEIGHT GAIN

Hormonal changes make it more likely you'll put on weight, particularly around your middle. This raises your risk of inflammation, insulin resistance, high glucose levels, type 2 diabetes, heart disease and fatty liver disease, particularly if the fat is around your organs, which is called visceral fat. N.B. A key mechanism for weight gain if you have high androgens is insulin resistance – see chapter 12 for more information if you suspect that may be you.

Food: The soluble fibre (see page 141 for more on this) in plant foods such as legumes, sweet potato and apples encourages the microbiome to produce substances called short chain fatty acids, that can help reduce belly fat.

Lifestyle: Research shows HIIT increases the amount of energy and fat you burn after exercise more than steady state aerobic exercise.

Mindful eating: This has been shown to help make you more sensitive to leptin, the fullness hormone. The principles of this are in the 5 Foundations (page 48). Start by making what's on your plate look appealing. Sit down and really savour eating with no distractions from screens – enjoy the colours, smells and flavours. Eat slowly, chew well and stop when you're no longer hungry.

Suggested supplements: Chromium picolinate improves insulin sensitivity and blood sugar levels, helping with appetite (PCH Meta-Boost).

5. A SHORT FUSE

High levels of testosterone interfere with the balance of brain chemicals, specifically serotonin (the feel-good neurotransmitter), dopamine (essential for rewards and pleasure) and calming gamma-aminobutyric acid (GABA).

Food: B vitamins are needed to convert amino acids from proteins into neurotransmitters. One of the richest sources is liver. Others are meat, chicken, eggs, fish, seafood, mushrooms, lentils, chickpeas, avocado, leafy greens. (N.B. Vegetarians and vegans may need to supplement – see page 145). You also need the amino acid tryptophan to make serotonin, this is found in good quantities in turkey, chickpeas and spinach. Eat with some carbohydrates.

Lifestyle: The regular practice of mindfulness and meditation has been shown to support levels of key neurotransmitters. Learning some cognitive behavioural therapy (CBT) techniques might be a good idea too, as CBT teaches us techniques to help break the cycle of mood swings by replacing unhelpful thought patterns.

Suggested supplements: White peony and liquorice. High levels of testosterone can come from lower aromatase activity (lower conversion of androgens to oestrogen). White peony (a traditional Chinese remedy) and liquorice are both aromatase inducers – that is, they encourage conversion. N.B. Do not take liquorice you have high blood pressure.

CHAPTER 10

Androgen Deficiency

- Low libido. Has your level of desire dropped? Has the idea of sex become less appealing? Are you less aroused than you used to be?

- Low energy and fatigue. Do you often feel tired or drained even after a night's sleep? Does this fatigue stop you getting on with life?

- Loss of muscle mass. Have you noticed a loss in muscle tone or definition, but you haven't changed your eating or exercise?

- Difficulty concentrating: Are you finding it hard to focus or concentrate on tasks? Are you more easily distracted than usual?

- Vaginal dryness. Have you noticed vaginal dryness or soreness? Or that sex is more uncomfortable or painful? Are you getting UTIs more regularly?

- Feeling flat and unmotivated. Do you have low mood that won't shift? Or have you lost interest in activities you once enjoyed? Do you find it increasingly difficult to motivate yourself to do work, fun things or chores?

Androgens are so potent that I call them 'Goldilocks' hormones' because, just like Goldilocks with the porridge, you need just enough, relative to the other sex hormones. You can get symptoms if your levels are too high or too low. Androgen levels decline from early adulthood to middle age, so by the age of 40, your levels of testosterone will be roughly half your levels at age 20.

Androgens do produce typically 'male' characteristics, such as hairiness and increased muscularity, but they aren't strictly male hormones. The 'mother hormone', DHEA, is an androgen that's made in the adrenal glands. It's turned into testosterone and, finally, into oestrogen.

In clinic, we frequently see women with levels of DHEA that are lower than they should be for their age. This is often down to long-term stress, which impacts DHEA production. Stress in this case can be psychological (such as trauma, a relationship split, losing a loved one, having a high-pressure job) or it could be physiological (such as a bad diet, drinking too much alcohol or smoking). Stress can also be what you might think of as 'positive stress': for example, cold plunging, long-term fasting or over-exercising. Even those things can have a negative impact if the cumulative effect is too much.

Androgens are important in both men and women for muscle growth and maintaining bone mass, as well as keeping the metabolism revved up, plus emotional stability and overall life satisfaction. Low levels can slow your metabolism so you put on weight and lose muscle. In clinic, the symptom I hear most often from women with low testosterone is that they are low in energy.

I also hear about low libido. Sometimes women (and their partners) assume that taking testosterone replacement therapy will 'cure' this.

But sex drive isn't just a hormonal issue – it's psychological and relationship-related too. However, if your desire has dropped, it can be a message from your body that you have low levels of androgens.

Another clear clue is when a woman says that she's lost her mojo or that she has no get-up-and-go. Androgens also seem to be important for staying enthusiastic about life. If she's a regular exerciser, she'll report that she doesn't feel like exercising. And if she's exercising, she may say she's not seeing the results she used to and she'll likely also report that she's put on weight around her middle.

> ### THE MAIN PLAYERS
>
> **Testosterone:** *One of the male sex hormones.*
>
> **Mitochondria:** *The batteries of the cell and where hormones are made inside the ovaries and adrenal glands.*
>
> **Adrenal glands:** *In charge of making stress hormones and – increasingly over perimenopause – some sex hormones too.*
>
> **The HPA axis:** *The hypothalamic-pituitary-adrenal axis is how the brain (hypothalamus) communicates with the adrenal glands.*
>
> **DHEA:** *Dehydroepiandrosterone is a male hormone produced in the adrenal glands. It's the precursor to testosterone.*

Three key reasons for androgen deficiency

1. YOUR OVARIES ARE WINDING DOWN

During the perimenopause, the ovaries get less consistent at making androgens (as well as oestrogen) and they're making less of them too. The drop in testosterone during this time is not as big as the drop in oestrogen, but because androgens are so potent, it can have big effects.

While no diet can reverse the ageing process of the ovaries, good nutrition can support them to maintain their hormone production, easing some androgen deficiency symptoms. Androgens are manufactured inside a type of cell called mitochondria, inside the ovaries and adrenals. Mitochondria act like cell batteries, generating energy needed to power cells as well as make hormones. As we age, the power of mitochondria goes down, a bit like a battery running out of juice.

2. YOU'RE TURNING MORE ANDROGENS TO OESTROGEN

As we talked about in chapter one, the raw material for all your sex hormones is cholesterol. Your body turns it into pregnenolone (the grandmother hormone), then DHEA (an androgen and the mother hormone), then testosterone, and some of that to oestrogen. Testosterone is converted to oestrogen by an enzyme called aromatase, in a process called aromatisation. If you put on weight around your middle (which most people do in midlife), or you have an inflammatory diet, or you have high insulin levels, you produce more aromatase, and so convert more testosterone to oestrogen.

3. YOUR DHEA IS LOW

Your adrenals make stress hormones including cortisol, as well as sex hormones including the mother hormone, DHEA. Levels of DHEA are affected in different ways by short- and long-term stresses. In the short term, stress will usually prompt the adrenals to make more of both cortisol and DHEA. DHEA balances out high cortisol, giving you resilience to stress. This is what happens if you, for example, do a cold-water dip when you're not stressed or you're only in the early stages of more long-term stress.

However, as you learnt in chapter five, long-term stress dysregulates the HPA axis, leading to low cortisol levels and exhaustion. But long-term stress also leads to DHEA levels that are lower than they should be for your age – and so you don't have the capacity to make enough testosterone.

To improve symptoms caused by low androgens, you'll focus on improving the function of both the ovaries and the adrenal glands, with a particular focus on mitochondria, where hormones are made. During the reproductive years, a quarter of testosterone is made in the ovaries and a quarter is made in the adrenals (the rest is in body tissue).

Because some of the work of making testosterone happens around the body, general health is important too. You'll also look at your sources of stress and recovery, including sleep, because as ovaries go offline during perimenopause, this leaves your adrenals in charge of making testosterone (although it seems that post menopause, your ovaries do still produce a little testosterone; studies disagree as to how much). And so you may also want to follow the advice in the chapter on the adrenals (chapter five), as well as the advice below.

CAN I HAVE TESTOSTERONE HRT?

By Dr Klaudia Raczko

Testosterone is not part of the routine HRT recommendations in NICE and NHS guidelines. However, it can be prescribed by an NHS GP for low desire or libido, after considering other treatments.

I have heard a lot of evidence from clinicians who see that testosterone can be life-changing for some patients. And there are a lot of plausible explanations as to why testosterone works to increase psychological and physical energy and wellbeing, to help build bones and muscle and to keep the brain healthy and sharp. My patients often say that while taking testosterone, they feel more motivated, more on point and assertive, and that it's easier for them to make decisions, for example. However, at the same time, we don't have enough quality research on women to back this up. Also, a woman's testosterone level will not always significantly decrease with age, even after menopause, as our adrenals can produce a good amount of this hormone. Therefore, measuring blood level, as well as looking at symptoms, may help with deciding who may be a good candidate for testosterone replacement.

Does testosterone work to increase libido?

Although testosterone is one of the treatments for low libido, it isn't a wonder drug. Lack of libido doesn't equal a lack of testosterone. There are psychological factors at play too here: the relationship with your partner, feeling safe and being comfortable in your own skin.

There's a lot of shame around having a lack of desire, especially when women have a supportive and loving partner. There are also physical issues associated with low testosterone, including vaginal dryness or a more severe condition called vaginal atrophy. The first line of approach for this is oestrogen replacement (see page 26). We also know that suboptimal oestrogen level is linked to lower libido in women.

The main problem with prescribing testosterone is that most testosterone formulations (except Androfem) are used 'off label', which means they have a licence for one type of use but are being used for a different one. In this case, the formulations were originally designed for men, but can be prescribed off label for women. The result is that the dose per pump is too high for women. This makes it very hard to be precise about dosage because you may be told, for example, to use a one fourth of a single pump or a tiny pea-sized amount of gel from the tube. For one product, a full pump might be 20mg, but a common dose for women is 5mg. There are bioidentical versions designed for women that are available privately which give a more precise dose. This allows us to start with much lower doses, which work especially well for women who can't tolerate high doses or who are sensitive to male hormones (for example, having a history of PCOS). We are always looking for the lowest effective dose.

While taking testosterone, some women report not only libido benefits (interestingly, we have testosterone receptors in the vagina) but also improved energy levels, better focus and more mental clarity. Plus, long term, they may also see a change in body composition. When you train, taking testosterone increases your ability to build muscle mass, which in turn also helps with blood sugar control.

Before recommending testosterone for low libido, doctors first need to consider any vaginal symptoms in general, such as dryness and/or discomfort. Pain can create a cycle of not wanting to have sex or to engage with your partner. Taking systemic (whole body) HRT, in particular oestrogen, can help reduce vaginal symptoms. If this isn't improving symptoms, it may be worth considering the vaginal application of oestrogen

> (oestradiol, oestriol) which is available on the NHS. One of the benefits of prescribing privately is that we can create bespoke products that combine different hormones and add other ingredients that help with vaginal symptoms, such as moisturising hyaluronic acid.

Androgen deficiency: what to eat

SUPPORT YOUR MITOCHONDRIA

- Make sure you're having enough proteins and good fats, as high quality sources of both will help support mitochondrial function.

- Eat seafood and fish, particularly oily fish such as salmon and sardines, ideally at least one to two servings a week. N.B. Wild-caught salmon is better, as farmed can contain toxins that affect how well mitochondria work. Nuts and seeds are powerhouses of healthy fats but also deliver nutrients crucial for mitochondrial and ovarian health, such as phosphatidylcholine, magnesium and zinc. Almonds, walnuts, Brazil nuts, flaxseeds, sunflower seeds, pumpkin seeds and hemp seeds are all great to include in your diet to support the mitochondria. Eggs contain protein and phosphatidylcholine.

- Zinc-rich foods. Zinc is important to help regulate testosterone levels. It is found in oysters and other seafood, broccoli, beef, pork, chicken, pumpkin seeds, cashew nuts and mushrooms.

- Grass-fed beef and liver are good sources of iron, a mineral that's essential for maintaining mitochondrial function.

- Extra virgin olive oil contains coenzyme Q10 (CoQ10) and alpha lipoic acid (ALA), which shield mitochondria from oxidative damage and encourage the growth of new mitochondria too.
- Liver is packed with B vitamins and vitamin D, as well as iron, supporting various aspects of ovarian health, including mitochondrial function.

CONVERSION-REDUCING FOODS.

To reduce the production of aromatase, the enzyme that converts testosterone to oestrogen, it's a good idea to eat high-fibre foods, flaxseeds, soy, green tea and white button mushrooms.

Also see the dietary advice in chapter five, 'Adrenal Dysfunction', as stress is a key player in this hormone imbalance.

Androgen deficiency: lifestyle guidelines

WEIGHTS AND HIIT

As we now know, every woman needs to do weights, particularly during midlife when if we are not making muscle, we are losing it. Research also suggests that lifting weights and large compound movements such as squats and deadlifts are good for testosterone levels, at least in the short term.

If your usual workout is cardio – for example, running, cycling or swimming – can you switch to intervals? Research suggests that interval training is good for mitochondrial function.

Alternate faster sprints (for example, one or two minutes) with the same length cool down. When running, that might mean running up a hill, then walking down to get your breath back. In the pool, it could be a fast crawl, followed by a length of slow breaststroke. Remember your mobility work, which could be yoga or Pilates, or part of your cool down.

DON'T FAST

Aside from planning your meals so you do a 12–14 hour overnight fast, you are probably not a great candidate for longer fasting, as research suggests it lowers testosterone levels.

LOOK AT YOUR SLEEP

It's worth putting some time into improving your sleep. A study showed that when midlife women had less than six hours sleep or more than nine hours sleep, they had lower testosterone levels than those who slept seven to eight hours.

BUILD YOUR STRESS TOOLKIT

It's worth finding healthy ways to relieve stress that don't involve alcohol or smoking as both reduce testosterone – and, of course, are also generally unhealthy! See chapter four for more.

AVOID ANTI-ANDROGENS

A whole range of chemicals, anti-androgens, have been shown to disrupt androgens. A lot of anti-androgens are also xenoestrogens, and they can be found in particular phthalates and in BPA in plastics, for example, in food packaging, but also fungicides and pesticides. See page 80 for ways to go low chemical.

Treating symptoms

1. LOW LIBIDO

Low testosterone impacts levels of brain chemicals (neurotransmitters) such as dopamine and serotonin that are essential for sexual arousal. However, testosterone is by no means the only factor in desire, so raising testosterone levels isn't the only answer.

Food: Research shows that having more zinc in the diet helps raise testosterone – and sex drive – in midlife women with low sex drive. Meat, liver, shellfish, pumpkin seeds and other seeds, legumes and eggs are all good sources.

Lifestyle: Having sex can increase testosterone – which is rather ironic if your libido is low. If you have pain or discomfort during sex, see your GP (also see below). Therapy can help with relationship and body image issues. Pelvic floor exercises can also help; read *Strong Foundations* by pelvic health physiotherapist Clare Bourne.

Suggested supplements: There is good research available to suggest that the adaptogens Tribulus terrestris and maca improve libido.

2. LOW ENERGY AND FATIGUE

Not only can low mitochondrial function lead to low testosterone, but low testosterone can play a role in the function of mitochondria (cell batteries) too. A decline in testosterone can result in less efficient energy production.

Food: In general, eat a well-balanced diet (as described in chapter three) to keep energy at a stable level, with a focus on the foods listed above. Make sure you're getting enough vitamin B12 as this is important for supporting energy levels. It's found in salmon, red meat and liver. If you're veggie or vegan, you may need a supplement.

Lifestyle: As described in the lifestyle guidelines above, exercise can help mitochondrial function.

Suggested supplements: Chrysin, found in honey, propolis and some passionflowers, has been studied for its potential to inhibit aromatase. Also, Rhodiola rosea, an adaptogen, may reduce fatigue by improving cellular energy utilisation and reducing oxidative stress. (It's included in PCH Ener-Boost, along with liquorice and ginseng. N.B. Don't take liquorice if you have high blood pressure.)

3. LOSS OF MUSCLE MASS

Decreasing levels of androgens affect muscle maintenance and growth. This results in muscle wastage and reduced physical strength.

Food: Eating enough protein is key; it provides the building blocks for muscle (see page 50 for protein guidelines).

Lifestyle: Build muscle by strength training, gradually increasing the load on muscles. If you're a beginner, even simple bodyweight exercises can have a dramatic effect on muscle preservation, particularly after midlife (see chapter four for more).

Suggested supplements: Creatine monohydrate and amino acids have been researched for their benefits in muscle growth and maintenance.

4. DIFFICULTY CONCENTRATING

Research suggests low DHEA may be a key factor if you're finding it hard to focus, affecting neural pathways involved in memory and concentration. Hormonal imbalance can lead to mood swings, which is also bad for concentration.

Food: Antioxidant foods such as berries, dark chocolate, turmeric, lemons, limes and extra-virgin olive oil help support cognitive function. as do anti-inflammatory foods such as turmeric, ginger, rosemary, thyme, oregano and cinnamon.

Lifestyle: Reducing stress and improving sleep is key to helping to reduce the production of stress hormones and inflammation, allowing your body to produce optimal DHEA levels.

Suggested supplements: PCH Ashwagandha and Bacopa monnieri (also called brahmi), traditional Ayurvedic herbs, have been studied for potential benefits in cognitive function.

5. VAGINAL DRYNESS

There are both oestrogen and testosterone receptors around the vagina and vulva. Low testosterone can cause a lack of natural lubrication, which can lead to soreness. This can be made worse by low oestrogen levels, common at this time.

If you tell your GP you have vaginal symptoms, you may be offered topical oestrogen (as a tiny pill or pessary you insert, or as a cream or gel – see page 26 for more on this). There's also a DHEA (androgen) pessary that's prescribed privately called Intrarosa. The DHEA turns into oestrogen and testosterone.

Food: Essential fatty acids found in foods including chia seeds and walnuts improve skin hydration and help keep membranes healthy.

Lifestyle: Don't forget to drink water: hydration is crucial for maintaining the health of mucosal barriers, including vaginal tissue.

Suggested supplements: You may want to use a vaginal moisturiser. Look for one that's all natural and made from hyaluronic acid, such as Yes! Some women find that topical application of vitamin E oil is helpful in restoring tissue hydration.

6. FEELING FLAT AND UNMOTIVATED

Low testosterone impacts levels of feel-good neurotransmitters such as dopamine and serotonin. Less testosterone can lead to feelings of apathy, flatness, lack of motivation and a diminished sense of wellbeing.

Food: Foods that support neurotransmitter production include protein-rich foods such as turkey, chicken and fish, and green leafy vegetables.

Lifestyle: Cognitive behavioural therapy (CBT) can help reframe negative thought patterns. Mindfulness practices such as meditation and mind-body practices like yoga and tai chi can also improve mood and motivation.

Suggested supplements: Ashwagandha is often used to boost energy and improve mood (PCH Ashwagandha). Also, the amino acid L-tyrosine has been linked to the production of dopamine and may enhance motivation.

EASY WIN: ONE TEASPOON OF MACA DAILY

Maca is the powdered root of a vegetable that's native to Peru. It's a herb that's traditionally used to help support hormone symptoms associated with low androgens. Maca is in the cruciferous family, so is related to broccoli and kale. You can put it in your smoothie or sprinkle it on your breakfast – it has a malty flavour.

CHAPTER 11

Low Thyroid Function

- Feeling tired or sluggish. Do you find you need a lot of sleep to function? Or do you always need an afternoon nap?

- Feeling cold. Are your hands and feet often cold? And/or do you feel cold at times when other people don't?

- Weight gain. Do you find that you put on weight easily? Or are you gaining weight despite not changing what you eat?

- Constipation. Do you go to the loo less than once a day? Does your digestion feel sluggish or do you feel bloated?

- Loss of outer third of eyebrow. Look at your brows: is the outside third very thin or thinner than it was?

- Thinning and shedding hair. Have you noticed you're losing a lot of hair? Does your hair clog up your hairbrush or the plughole? Is your hair looking thinner all over?

- Indigestion after rich food. Do you feel queasy or get a tummy ache after eating fatty foods? Or have you noticed that your poop is pale and floats?

- High LDL cholesterol. Has a blood test shown that your levels of HDL (bad) cholesterol are high?

It is so common to see clients with an underactive thyroid in clinic. This isn't surprising – firstly, thyroid dysfunction is ten times more common in women than men. Secondly, it very often develops – or gets worse – in the perimenopausal years. You're most likely to be diagnosed between the ages of 30 and 50.

You may be reading this chapter because you have been diagnosed with an underactive thyroid. Or you may suspect you have one. Women who come to my clinic have sometimes had a blood test at their GP and been told that their thyroid function is in the 'normal' range,' but when we do our more extensive testing, we often find that they do, in fact, have an underactive thyroid.

The thyroid is a butterfly-shaped gland in your throat, just below your larynx. It's like the thermostat of your metabolism, in charge of how quickly or slowly your cells use energy. It has a role in lots of other body processes, including regulation of body temperature, appetite and digestion, cognition, reproduction and the healthy growth of hair and nails. This is why the symptoms are so wide-ranging (though not everyone will get every symptom, of course). The most common symptom caused by thyroid issues is fatigue. Women with low thyroid function often tell me they cannot get through the day without a nap in the afternoon.

The thyroid system, the stress system and the reproductive system are all linked. The same part of the brain – the hypothalamus – is ultimately in charge of the level of sex hormones your ovaries produce, how much stress hormones your adrenals put into the bloodstream and how much thyroid hormones your thyroid makes and releases too. So, you have an HPO axis (the brain-to-ovaries communication system), an HPA axis (the brain-to-adrenals stress communication system), and the HP-thyroid (HPT) axis.

LOW THYROID FUNCTION | 199

When thyroid hormones are low, the hypothalamus informs the pituitary gland, at the base of the brain. The pituitary then sends a messenger, called thyroid stimulating hormone (TSH), to the thyroid. TSH tells the thyroid to release more thyroid hormones, which come in two main types. Most of the thyroid hormone you make is T4. This needs to be converted to T3, the active thyroid hormone in order to get inside cells to work. The trouble is, you may not be making enough T4 or if you are, it may not be converting to T3 efficiently.

Having low thyroid function makes you less likely to ovulate each cycle (anovulation), which is why thyroid function is one of the first things doctors check when you go for fertility testing. In perimenopause, anovulation can make symptoms such as heavy periods worse.

The reason why so many women are diagnosed with low thyroid in midlife is because at the beginning of the perimenopause, the drop in progesterone can trigger the thyroid into becoming underactive. Having high levels of oestrogen, common at the beginning of the perimenopause and if you take HRT, can also affect thyroid function. It reduces the amount of thyroid hormones that can get into cells to do their work. That's why if someone is on thyroid medication, which replaces T4, and then they start taking HRT, their dosage often has to go up.

THE MAIN PLAYERS

TSH: *Thyroid-stimulating hormone is produced in the brain and stimulates the production of thyroid hormones.*

T4: *Most of the thyroid hormone you make is T4. It is inactive and needs to be converted to . . .*

T3: *The active thyroid hormone, that does the work.*

Reasons for low thyroid function

1. STRESS

The thyroid is very sensitive to stress. When the HP (the hypothalamus) part of the HPA axis is dysregulated by stress, this spills over into the HPT axis too. The body will always prioritise the HPA axis (which is in charge of survival) over the HPT axis. The result is that stress can reduce how much T3 and T4 you make and the amount of T4 that gets converted to active T3.

Stress can take the form of emotional and life stress (for example, work and family), but it can also be caused by your gut being inflamed and eating a poor quality diet. You could also be putting stress on your body unintentionally: eating a keto diet and fasting for long periods can do this, as can exercising too hard. And, finally, there's stress on the body from the changing hormones of perimenopause, too.

2. LIVER FUNCTION

Most of T4 is made into the active form, T3, in the gut or the liver. So if either are not functioning at their best, this conversion may not happen. The liver has approximately 500 jobs – just one of these, alongside processing toxins and excreting used-up sex hormones, is that it has to process thyroid hormones.

When the liver is working well, it makes plenty of bile, a multi-tasking substance that's stored in and released by the gall bladder. I call it the liver's liquid gold because it helps fat digestion, helps to absorb fat-soluble vitamins A, D, E and K, and also helps eliminate used-up hormones. When the liver gets overloaded – for example, if the gut isn't functioning well – bile flow becomes poor and used-up hormones are instead recycled around the body. If used-up thyroid hormones are still circulating in your body, the hypothalamus might sense there is enough and scale back production. Added to this, absorption of the fat-soluble vitamins is also very important for supporting hormones, including thyroid hormones.

You can help treat low thyroid symptoms in a few ways. This chapter explains how to support your gut and liver function with nutrition, and the specific nutrients that the thyroid needs to work well, in particular to convert T4 to T3. The watchword is nourishment here: the thyroid is delicate and it doesn't respond well to lack or deprivation. And what's equally important is learning to rest properly too, so you reduce your stress levels.

> ### SHOULD I HAVE A BLOOD TEST?
>
> *If you have some of the low thyroid symptoms listed above, see your GP for a blood test. You're likely to be offered one that measures levels of TSH and T4. If these are outside the 'normal' range, the treatment is levothyroxine, which is T4.*
>
> *However, as I mentioned, in clinic, we see plenty of women whose tests show normal levels of TSH and T4 but who still have symptoms. In the blood test we run, we test additional markers, including T3. We often find that women with normal T4 and TSH have low T3, which suggests they aren't converting T4 to T3 very well. This means they won't have enough of the active form, T3, which explains their low thyroid symptoms. Our blood test also looks at thyroid antibodies to find out if your body is seeing your thyroid as foreign and attacking it. Plus it looks at whether T3 is getting into cells to do its work.*

Low thyroid function: what to eat

MAKE EACH MEAL WITH A LOW GLYCAEMIC LOAD (GL)

High GI foods such as white carbs and sugary foods can lead to insulin resistance (see chapter 12), which makes the symptoms of low thyroid worse. Build your plate from foods that keep your blood sugar stable, so that the total effect of your whole meal – its glycaemic load or GL – doesn't raise your blood sugar rapidly. Include protein and healthy fats, plus fibre in the form of vegetables and some slow-release carbs (see the next point, below).

EAT SOME CARBS (IN THE EVENING AT LEAST)

An underactive thyroid needs support to help it function – this is not the time to cut off its energy supply by doing a keto eating plan, following a very low calorie diet, skipping meals or fasting (although you can still stick to an overnight fast of 12 to 14 hours). Cutting carbs and fasting can slow the conversion of T4 to T3 even more, making symptoms worse. If you're trying to lose weight, stick to carbs in the evening only (see my previous book *Eat Right, Lose Weight* for more advice on this) and eat carbs such as butternut squash, parsnip, pumpkin, swede or sweet potato.

AVOID GLUTEN

As part of the Food Framework, you've already cut down or eliminated gluten and dairy as these two food types are the ones that people are most likely to have a reaction to. But there's even more reason to avoid gluten if your thyroid function is low as, for some people, gluten can make symptoms worse. So if you have symptoms of hypothyroidism, try cutting out gluten altogether.

FURTHER COOKING AND EATING ADVICE

- Lightly steam your cruciferous vegetables. Cooking and fermenting deactivate compounds that interfere with thyroid function. N.B. You can eat broccoli sprouts raw.

- Eat gut-friendly foods, including fermented foods such as sauerkraut, kimchi, miso, coconut yoghurt and kefir, and olives in brine.

- Beetroot, artichokes, nuts and seeds, oily fish, berries and turmeric are all liver supporting foods.

KEY THYROID NUTRIENTS TO INCLUDE IN YOUR DIET

- **Iodine and selenium:** Iodine is a key part of T3 and T4, while selenium is necessary to convert T4 to T3 and needed to make glutathione, an important antioxidant in the thyroid. Fish, seafood and seaweed are good sources of both iodine and selenium, as is egg yolk. All meats and poultry provide good levels of selenium. Mushrooms are a good vegan source of selenium, as are sunflower seeds, chia seeds, flaxseeds and Brazil nuts.

- **Vitamin D:** Essential for the activation of thyroid hormone in the cell. Find vitamin D in liver, oily fish, egg yolks and some mushrooms. However, the best way to get vitamin D is exposure to 20 minutes of sunshine a day on your limbs with no sunscreen. (N.B. In summer months, avoid 12pm to 3pm.)

- **Zinc:** Needed for T3 production, zinc is found in meat, seafood, pumpkin seeds and other seeds, pulses and beans, eggs and liver.

- **Vitamin B12:** Half of people with thyroid issues have low levels of B12, which is found in its highest quantities in red meat and organ meats. If you're veggie or vegan, you may need a supplement.

- **Vitamin A:** Having low thyroid function can affect the conversion of carotenoids in plant sources (apricots, carrots, squash) to the active form of vitamin A, retinol. You can get retinol directly from eggs, oily fish and liver.

- **Choline:** As it's essential to make flexible cell membranes, a good level of choline is needed if T3 is to get into cells. Eat eggs, fish, meat, soy, fish roe, nuts, beans and liver.

- **Omega-3 rich foods:** This fatty acid is also key to making flexible cell membranes. Eat fatty fish, such as salmon, sardines, mackerel, trout and herring. Veggie sources include chia seeds, pumpkin seeds and walnuts.

- **Iron:** Vital for converting T4 to active T3, good sources are lean meat, liver, eggs, oily fish, game and the darker meat from poultry. If you're vegetarian or vegan, you can get iron from beans, pulses and green leafy vegetables.

Low thyroid: lifestyle guidelines

KEEP MOVING

When you feel tired, exercise is the last thing you want to do! But honestly, it's really worth planning it into your day. A DUTCH study showed only a sixth of women diagnosed with hypothyroidism do even the minimum of exercise. In another study, women diagnosed with subclinical (mild) low thyroid were put on a programme of an hour on an exercise bike or treadmill three times a week. In the study authors said that after four months, they showed 'remarkable improvements' in their general fitness and physical and emotional health too.

There's a lot of evidence to indicate that aerobic exercise, strength training and a combination of the two have positive effects on thyroid hormones – although including some resistance exercise seems to give the edge. A study of women who were overweight due to being hypothyroid showed combining aerobic and resistance exercise was effective for weight loss too.

You could also try yoga: there's an ongoing study looking at whether specific yoga poses that work on the throat can help support the thyroid too. The theory is that a lot of yoga poses, which involve moving the neck release tension in the area, are helping increase blood flow to the thyroid.

Whatever you choose, exercise is about finding a balance; start moderately and keep monitoring how you feel.

AVOID THYROID-DISRUPTING CHEMICALS.

The thyroid is delicate and a lot of the endocrine-disrupting chemicals that we met in chapter four are known to interfere with the normal regulation of thyroid hormones, including BPA in plastics. If your thyroid isn't working properly, there are some specific chemicals to avoid too, such as chlorine and fluoride. Historically, fluoride was given medically in order to lower thyroid hormone levels. Avoid fluoride in toothpaste. And if you swim regularly in a chlorinated pool, reduce the amount of chlorine you absorb by showering and washing your hair both before and after swimming (before because wet hair will absorb less chlorinated pool water). Also filter your drinking water.

GET BETTER SLEEP

When you don't sleep enough, it affects your thyroid even more. If you feel exhausted during the day, it's fine to take a 10- to 30-minute nap, ideally after lunch. Research suggests that if you have low thyroid function, you're more likely get poor sleep at night, in particular less slow-wave deep sleep. Follow the sleep advice in chapter four.

If you snore, a friend or partner may have noticed that, during snoring, your breathing stops, which is called sleep apnoea (see page 78). This is more common if you have a thyroid condition. If this is the case, see your GP.

WORK ON YOUR STRESS

Because stress is a major underlying cause for underactive thyroid, it's really important to create your personal relaxation toolkit, as suggested in chapter four.

Treat your symptoms

1. FEELING TIRED OR SLUGGISH

When your thyroid gland doesn't produce enough hormones, it slows down your body's metabolic processes, which includes your production and use of energy. This is the core symptom of low thyroid function: a constant, nagging sense of fatigue. Sometimes women say they don't feel tired because they've felt tired for so long that they've got used to it. As this is the core symptom of low thyroid, follow all the advice for diet and lifestyle as above.

Suggested supplements: Iodine, selenium and zinc. These three minerals are absolutely integral to good thyroid function and people with low thyroid are very often lacking in them (PCH Meta-Boost contains all three key minerals as well as cayenne – see opposite).

2. FEELING COLD

You likely feel the cold, especially your hands and feet, even while others around you feel fine. This is because the slowdown in your metabolism includes your body's ability to generate heat.

Food: Make tea with the warming spices turmeric, ginger and/or cinnamon. Also use them in cooking, along with cayenne and chillies. Cayenne in particular is recommended for its thermogenic effect on metabolism, i.e. it improves it.

Lifestyle: Deep breathing exercises (see chapter four) can make you feel warmer. And this may sound obvious, but wrap up and keep moving. Around three quarters of the energy used in exercise comes out as heat, which is why moving makes you feel warm.

3. WEIGHT GAIN

A slow metabolic rate due to a low thyroid makes it easier for you to gain weight even when you are consistently eating a good diet. Follow the advice for eating and lifestyle above to support your thyroid function, plus:

Suggested supplement: Chromium can help with appetite regulation and to suppress cravings (in PCH Meta-Boost).

4. CONSTIPATION

Low thyroid slows the muscles that move food through the digestive tract, which means constipation along with bloating, discomfort and a sluggish feeling.

Food: Fibre provides bulk that helps food keep moving, so eat plenty of wholegrains, fruits, vegetables and legumes. Probiotic-rich foods, such as coconut, sheep or goat milk yoghurt, coconut kefir, sauerkraut, kimchi, olives in brine and apple cider vinegar, help keep digestion regulated too.

Lifestyle: Stay hydrated and exercise regularly, as it speeds up digestive transit time.

Suggested supplements: Magnesium has a mild laxative effect (in PCH Magnesium Complex) and supplementing with probiotics can promote regular digestion. Choose one that's broad spectrum and high potency (PCH Repopulate Probiotic). Aloe vera juice can also increase transit time (PCH Just Aloe Vera).

5. THINNING AND SHEDDING HAIR

Hypothyroidism can lead to shedding from all over the scalp because it puts more hair follicles into resting rather than growth phase.

Food: Make sure you're eating enough protein, as hair itself is made from protein, and that your diet includes nutrient-dense foods with plenty of leafy greens, nuts, seeds and fatty fish.

Lifestyle: Chronic stress can contribute to hair loss (as well as to hypothyroidism), so focus on your relaxation toolkit (see chapter four).

Suggested supplements: If your hair loss is caused by low thyroid function, following the advice in this chapter should help. But it may be worth looking at other possible reasons for losing your hair. Being anaemic or low in vitamin D can lead to hair loss – both deficiencies are very common, so ideally get a blood test for vitamin D, iron and ferritin. Finally, selenium and zinc have been shown to help improve hair growth in people who have low thyroid.

6. LOSS OF OUTER THIRD OF BROWS

Losing this section of your eyebrows can be a key sign your thyroid is underactive. Why it's this particular hair that disappears isn't known, but it's thought to be a similar mechanism to hair loss on the head. Follow the advice for hair loss above.

7. INDIGESTION AFTER FATTY FOOD

In order to digest fat in your food, you need bile, a fluid that's made and released by your gall bladder. But your gall bladder will struggle to contract and release the right amount of bile without a good level of thyroid hormones.

Food: Limit your intake of rich or fatty foods (for the time being), as these foods will make symptoms worse. Eat bitter foods to stimulate bile flow, in particular chicory, rocket, watercress, dandelion, radishes, mustard greens, artichokes, turnip greens and the spices fenugreek and turmeric. Dandelion root tea is a traditional remedy for indigestion.

Lifestyle: Eat slowly and chew your food thoroughly, and aim to stop eating before you become overly full.

Suggested supplements: Digestive enzymes such as lipase can help your body break down dietary fats (found in PCH Digest). Ox bile contains bile acids. This is a very good supplement if you've had your gall bladder removed.

8. HIGH LDL CHOLESTEROL.

When thyroid levels are low, it slows down liver function, including the processing of lipids in the blood. This can lead to high LDL (low-density lipoprotein) cholesterol, often referred to as 'bad' cholesterol.

Food: While you manage your thyroid issue, work on reducing your LDL levels. Eat a heart-healthy diet based on fruits, vegetables, whole grains and lean proteins with lots of garlic, as well as soluble fibre such as oats and legumes. Limit saturated fat (in meat and animal products) and trans fats (in baked goods and processed foods).

Lifestyle: Regular exercise will raise HDL (high-density lipoprotein) cholesterol, often referred to as 'good' cholesterol, and lower LDL cholesterol. Aim for at least 150 minutes of moderate-intensity aerobic exercise per week. Plus, managing stress is key too; chronic stress can impact cholesterol levels.

Suggested supplements: Plant sterols and stanols can help lower LDL cholesterol.

> ### EASY WIN: FOUR BRAZIL NUTS A DAY
>
> *Brazil nuts are high in selenium. This is a simple way to make sure you're getting a daily dose to support your thyroid function.*

Shirley's story

I had just turned 50 when I joined Pippa's Female Food Club (FFC) in 2022. I was really struggling with heavy periods and with PMS symptoms in the week leading up to my period. I was very teary and emotional, with a constant background level of anxiety. Even on holiday, where normally I'd feel relaxed, I'd feel tense and anxious. I could also get angry instantly, out of the blue, which would surprise me as much as my family or colleagues. If I wasn't premenstrual I would have been able to laugh off the things that upset me, but at that moment it felt like the end of the world. I've always had heavy periods but they'd got much worse. So much so that for two or three days a month, I'd struggle to leave the house.

However, I didn't join FFC for my hormones but because I wanted to lose weight. I didn't realise how much of an impact my hormones were having, and blamed the anxiety and tension on my job, which is pretty stressful. I have always needed time on my own to recharge my batteries, so I just thought I needed more of that, but I ended up not wanting to go out very much at all.

Having always struggled with my weight, I had put on quite a lot during my late forties. I found that, whatever I did, I couldn't lose it. My happy size is around a size 10 but by the time I joined FFC, I was a size 14 to 16.

What I learnt at FFC made me see that weight wasn't the issue. It showed me the bigger picture: that if I could focus on my health and learn to manage my hormonal symptoms, the weight would fix itself.

In FFC, we have online talks with Pippa, where we can ask questions too. During one of them, I asked Pippa about my PMS symptoms. She said it sounded as if I might have oestrogen dominance and low progesterone. Pippa suggested that I start seed cycling and taking Vitex agnus castus. I also focused on helping my body process used-up oestrogen. I upped the amount of cruciferous vegetables I was eating – in fact, all vegetables – and the amount of protein too.

In FFC, Pippa talked about the different personalities people have around food and lifestyle. Historically, I would have been a 'Cold Turkey Caroline' who has to give things up in order to stay off them. But I would then fall off the wagon. So I resolved to be a 'Moderation Mary', who gets healthy by going slow and steady, having a little of what you want. I wanted to make my good habits stick.

My next big shift happened while reading Pippa's first book, *Eat Right, Lose Weight*. I began to leave a gap of four to five hours between meals, and eat all my meals within a 12- to 13-hour window. The book also made me think my thyroid and cortisol levels might be impacting my weight. I started to see a real change in my weight, but also in how I was feeling and in my PMS symptoms.

After around a year of FFC, I noticed my PMS symptoms coming back. I decided to get some personalised help and booked in to see one of Pippa's nutritionists. She explained that our hormones are in flux at this time of our lives, so we do need to keep building on what we do to help ourselves.

I had a DUTCH hormone test and the results showed, as predicted, that my oestrogen was sky high. Pippa put me on a supplement called DIM, plus calcium D-glucarate, to help detox oestrogen. The test results also showed my cortisol as very low. And a thyroid function blood test showed that my thyroid was slightly low, so I had another reason for my difficulty in losing weight.

During this time, I was also seeing my GP. I asked for HRT and before prescribing it, my GP referred me for a scan to investigate my heavy periods. This showed I had adenomyosis, which is similar to endometriosis but the rogue cells that overgrow are inside the womb wall rather than outside. That was what was causing my heavy periods. Adenomyosis is a high oestrogen condition too, so detoxing my oestrogen levels was an important part of reducing symptoms.

I had to argue with my GP in order to be prescribed the HRT I wanted. I knew I needed body identical progesterone, Utrogestan. I was reluctant to take oestrogen because I was sure, even before my DUTCH test results, that I had high oestrogen levels.

My weight loss has been slow but sustained. I have achieved it through tweaking, not transforming. Each time I make a change I'll see an impact, then I'll plateau, then I'll make another change. In two years, I've lost around 1 to 1.5 pounds a month, which has added up to 1st 9lb. I'm now a size 12. I have more to lose but I know it will happen.

I start the day with a protein smoothie, adding seeds for that part of the month as per the seed cycling system, plus PCH Super Greens and some berries. For lunch, I tend to have salad with lots of leafy greens, colourful veg, plus some cheese, salmon or chicken and a sauce, or soup with bone broth as a base plus some nuts. I'll usually have dinner (protein plus cruciferous vegetables) by 6.30pm or 7pm. Before joining the FFC, I tried to avoid carbs but now I have a small portion of quinoa, rice or potatoes. That evening portion really helps my stress and sleep and supports my thyroid.

My exercise is a work in progress. Because of my thyroid and cortisol, I avoid exercise that will stress my body too much. I try to do 10,000 steps each day, plus I've started a weekly Pilates class and strength training two to three times a week. I'm also doing daily breathwork and mindfulness.

My hormonal symptoms aren't perfect but they are much improved. My periods are still heavy but manageable. And although I do sometimes feel quite anxious in the last week of my cycle, it's so much better now I can put a label on it and know that it's my hormones.

Although I'm losing weight, I don't feel as if I'm restricting. When I want to have food that's not in the Food Framework – say at the weekend or on holiday – I have what I want and enjoy it and get back on track the next day. I can make considered choices around food and not have a huge blowout. Sometimes I feel as if I'm not doing enough then I look back and see it's now become natural to make these choices and think about how good I feel.

CHAPTER 12

Blood Sugar Dysregulation

- Hanger. Do you feel both hungry and angry when you haven't eaten for a while?
- Fatigue after eating. Does it feel as if you go into a 'food coma' after meals, so that you could fall asleep?
- Waking at night. Do you often wake up during the night, in particular before 3am?
- Brain fog. Do you find it especially hard to focus either before eating or afterwards?
- Weight gain. Are you carrying weight around the middle? In particular, is your waist over 35 inches (89cm)?
- Sweet or carby cravings. Do you feel hungry even after eating? Do you crave sweets or carbs but when you eat them, you don't feel better?

> **THE MAIN PLAYERS**
>
> **Blood glucose or sugar:** *Glucose, from the food you eat, is your body's main energy supply.*
>
> **Insulin:** *The hormone that pushes glucose into the body's cells. High levels encourage fat storage.*
>
> **Cortisol:** *A hormone you produce in response to stress.*

When your blood sugar control is out of whack, it has knock-on effects on all your hormones. It makes the stress hormone cortisol go up, which can affect your production of oestrogen and especially progesterone. Fluctuating blood sugar levels can lead to erratic energy spikes and crashes, affecting your mood, vitality and mental clarity, compounding the emotional ups and downs of perimenopause.

One way to know your blood sugar mechanism is working properly is how you feel before and after eating. If I suspect a client has dysregulated blood sugar, I'll ask them these two key questions: 1) How do you feel if you go four to five hours without food? and 2) How do you feel after you eat?

People who have low blood sugar find it too hard to leave four to five hours between meals. They might feel shaky, tired, dizzy, weak and/or have brain fog. This is your body's hunger alarm system kicking in, telling you that you need to eat. If you have low blood sugar you're likely to feel super energised when you eat, as the energy from the food floods into your cells. If your blood sugar is functioning well, you won't feel transformed after eating; rather, you'll feel just right.

You're most likely to get low blood sugar symptoms – shakiness or hunger – an hour or two after eating high-carb or sugary foods. Your pancreas produces a hormone called insulin, whose job it is to push glucose into cells for energy, then store any spare glucose in the body. But sugary carbs cause a quick peak in blood sugar levels, which signals the pancreas to release a burst of insulin which quickly mops up all that glucose, and your blood sugar levels drop fast, setting off your hunger alarm.

THE DEVELOPMENT OF INSULIN RESISTANCE

Your blood sugar can also be dysregulated by being too high. The signs of high blood sugar tend to be less obvious than the signs of low blood sugar because the human body evolved in conditions of scarcity, when people didn't have an excess of fuel, so it didn't develop an emergency response to this. However, in the long term, having high blood sugar can cause inflammation and damage to the body.

If you have high blood sugar, you're more likely to feel really tired after eating, as if you could fall asleep. Clients with high blood sugar often like fasting for this reason and end up eating just one meal a day. However, I don't recommend skipping meals during perimenopause, as it's an extra stressor on top of a body that's already stressed. When you don't eat, blood sugar can become even more dysregulated and fasting can raise cortisol levels, which can have a knock-on effect on oestrogen and progesterone. It's better to eat meals at regular times with a 12 to 14 hour overnight fast.

Having high blood sugar levels can be the result of eating a lot of sugary foods or quick-release white carbs. In the long term, this forces the pancreas to keep having to work harder and harder, to produce lots of insulin to mop up all the glucose in the blood, then to push it into cells to be used or stored. But cells aren't programmed to take in energy all the time. If there's too much glucose in the body too much of the time, the cells begin to shut their doors to it. This is called insulin resistance.

All the spare sugar sloshing around the blood signals to the pancreas that it needs to produce more insulin to get the sugar into cells. The pancreas initially keeps up with this increased demand but over time, this can take it beyond its capacity, so that blood sugar stays high. Research shows that this can be a slow process: insulin can be rising for eight to ten years before it has an impact on blood sugar levels. And as another of insulin's roles is to promote fat storage, the spare sugar can get stored as fat. After years of this, the pancreas can get worn out from producing so much insulin and slow down the amount it produces. This leaves you with low insulin levels, high blood sugar and on the pathway that leads to insulin resistance and type 2 diabetes.

This is the key underlying mechanism of midlife weight gain: the change in the way your body processes food. And it's more likely to happen in perimenopause because as oestrogen falls, your body naturally becomes less responsive to insulin.

It's shocking how quickly this can happen. In one study, healthy men were given 6,000 calories a day of the standard American diet, which is admittedly a lot. They put on 3.5kg on average after a week of eating like this, which wasn't that surprising. What was eye opening is that after two to three days, they developed insulin resistance.

Of course, what you eat and how much you move matters as well as stress and sleep, but that hormonal change in insulin is the absolute game-changer. It's why I see women in clinic every week who've put on weight but their old tried-and tested methods of losing it no longer work.

Being obese – having a BMI over 25 – significantly increases your risk of developing insulin resistance and diabetes. However, research shows that losing between 5 and 10 per cent of your total weight is enough to improve insulin sensitivity. If you want to lose weight, there are guidelines for portion sizes in my previous book, *Eat Right, Lose Weight*.

You can be thin but still develop insulin resistance. This is due to a specific type of fat called visceral fat that is around your organs. This is why you might have noticed your waist thickening or your stomach sticking out more, even while the rest of you is slim.

Insulin resistance contributes to a higher risk of diabetes and of cardiovascular disease too. It increases inflammation and cortisol, which have a knock-on effect on your sex hormones.

Key reasons for insulin resistance

1. NOT MOVING

Your body loves to move! When you eat carbs, the pancreas produces insulin, which stores any spare energy (glucose) in the liver and muscles in the form of glycogen. When the liver and muscles are full, it stores glucose in fat cells. When you move your muscles, they use up the glucose from these stores, which then refill with the glucose in your bloodstream from the food you have eaten. The harder you exercise, the more glucose you use up. In addition, exercise increases insulin sensitivity – that is, how effectively your body stores and uses glucose.

The opposite is true too: not moving can decrease insulin sensitivity. In one study, just three days of bed rest – i.e. not moving much – was enough to bring on insulin resistance.

2. STRESS

The stress reaction raises blood sugar in order to give you instant energy to fight back or take flight. However, when stress is long term, cortisol becomes dysregulated, making it harder for insulin to work properly to bring down blood sugar. For example, research has established a connection between people who report that their jobs are stressful and the development of insulin resistance.

3. DISRUPTED SLEEP

Not getting enough sleep or broken sleep activates the body's stress response, elevating blood sugar levels and, over time, inducing insulin resistance. It also disrupts satiety hormones so you feel less full after eating and generally hungrier, and more likely to eat carbs and sugary foods. And the more of those you eat, the more likely you are, over time, to become insulin resistant.

This chapter shows you how to bring your blood sugar back into balance holistically. By doing this, you'll not only improve your health for the long term but help balance your hormones and feel better too.

Blood sugar dysregulation: what to eat

The advice in this section is for people who have low and high blood sugar, as it's about improving insulin sensitivity.

At mealtimes, each plate should contain protein, healthy fats and vegetables. If you include carbs, choose those that release their energy slowly, called slow release or low glycaemic index (GI) carbs, as low GI carbs are generally high in fibre, which makes them harder for the body to break down into glucose and so slows the rate that glucose hits the bloodstream. Think unprocessed rather than processed, whole rather than white, unpeeled rather than peeled. Choose from:

- Whole grains such as quinoa and buckwheat. These also contain nutrients including magnesium and chromium which help improve insulin sensitivity.
- Foods high in resistant starch. This is starch that doesn't turn to glucose quickly, so that it leads to a more gradual release of glucose into the bloodstream. Choose underripe

bananas rather than ripe ones, for example. Some starches, such as basmati rice and potatoes, become more resistant when they are cooked then cooled.
- Legumes including lentils, beans and chickpeas are not only sources of low GI carbs but contain protein too.
- Where you can, keep the skin of root vegetables on for maximum fibre.

BLOOD SUGAR-FRIENDLY FATS

Avocados are high in fibre and packed with monounsaturated fats that slow down the release of sugars into the bloodstream, while nuts are rich in fibre and healthy fats, which help lower the GI of a meal.

QUALITY PROTEIN

The best kind of protein has a high biological value (HBV) – that is, chicken, meat, fish, eggs and tofu. HBV proteins contain the widest variety of essential amino acids at the highest volume too. While quinoa has all the essential amino acids, it doesn't have the highest amount. A lot of veggie proteins – beans and pulses for example – don't have the widest variety. That's why a lot of clients say that when they have chickpeas or lentils for lunch, they're hungry and shaky two hours later. But when they have a piece of chicken, they feel fine. Also choose good quality protein powder (see page 51 for more).

BE AWARE OF PORTION SIZE

The more you have of any carb, the more your blood sugar level will go up. Women are often surprised when they see the amount of food they really need compared to the big plates of food that, culturally, we've become used to. If you are at an unhealthy body weight, reducing portion size is key (for a guide, see my previous book, *Eat Right, Lose Weight*).

STAY WELL HYDRATED

Drinking enough water allows the kidneys to flush out excess sugar via the urine and is essential for proper insulin function. Aim for two litres a day.

FOODS TO SUPPORT INSULIN SENSITIVITY

- Berries are the lowest GI fruits. Plus, they are high in antioxidants which combat the oxidative stress (damage) that's associated with high blood sugar.
- Some small studies on cinnamon show that it helps insulin sensitivity. Research suggests that ginger can improve insulin control too.
- Green tea is high in the antioxidant epigallocatechin gallate (EGCG), which improves insulin sensitivity.
- Broccoli sprouts are high in sulforaphane, which is not only helpful for the liver but can improve insulin sensitivity. They are also rich in antioxidants, are anti-inflammatory and can help reduce oxidative stress.
- Cocoa contains compounds that enhance insulin sensitivity and are antioxidant. Pick a dark chocolate that's over 75 per cent cocoa.
- Research shows that replacing vegetable oils with extra virgin olive oil can help reduce blood sugar spikes and improve insulin resistance.
- Flaxseeds are a rich source of lignans and omega-3 fatty acids, which have been shown to improve insulin sensitivity.

The high fibre content in flaxseeds also aids in blood sugar regulation.

- The body converts beta carotene (found in carrots, sweet potatoes and squash, among others) to vitamin A, which supports overall pancreatic health.

If you have low blood sugar – i.e. you feel weak and shaky between meals – ideally you should eat breakfast within 60 minutes of waking. Clients with blood sugar issues often say that when they eat porridge or toast for breakfast, they're hungry a couple of hours later, and have blood sugar symptoms for the rest of the day. It's better to have a protein-based breakfast. If you want porridge, add a scoop of protein powder.

You may also find that you can't initially go four to five hours between meals (as advised in the 5 Foundations). If you get too tired, shaky or hangry, then have a small snack, such as a handful of nuts or a boiled egg.

Blood sugar dysregulation: lifestyle guidelines

BETTER SLEEP

If your sleep tends to be broken or short, it's more likely that you'll develop insulin resistance. One reason is that lack of sleep raises levels of the stress hormone cortisol and increases inflammation, which can in turn raise blood sugar levels. It also increases appetite and the likelihood of being overweight, and so increases insulin resistance via these mechanisms too. See the sleep advice in chapter four for more.

Studies suggest that having at least seven hours of uninterrupted sleep each night is best for insulin function.

GET MORE ACTIVE

Moving stimulates muscles to take up glucose for energy, lowering blood sugar levels as well as increasing the efficiency of insulin. Find ways to be more active in your everyday life as well as regular workouts.

- Get up often (and sit down less). Sitting down for long periods leads to higher blood sugar levels after meals. One study showed that doing three-minute exercise 'snacks' – for example jumping jacks, stairs, squats – every 30 minutes helped to improve blood sugar control. Another study showed that 170 minutes of exercise a week – 20 minutes more than NHS guidelines – increases insulin sensitivity more than doing 115 minutes a week. Don't forget, you can break it up into short chunks that suit your schedule.

- Do a combination of aerobic and resistance exercise. Aerobic exercise improves insulin sensitivity and resistance training increases muscle mass, which means a greater uptake of glucose from the blood. This is especially important in midlife because as we age, we lose muscle (for more on strength training, see chapter four).

- Do HIIT. Research suggests that HIIT is effective at lowering blood glucose and even more so when you do it in the afternoon rather than the morning.

FIND YOUR PERSONAL STRESS TOOLKIT

People who are stressed are more likely to develop insulin resistance and diabetes. One reason is that chronic stress raises cortisol, which in turn may prevent insulin-producing cells in the pancreas from working properly.

GIVE UP SMOKING

It impairs the body's ability to use insulin. Once you quit, your insulin sensitivity will improve, reducing your risk of type 2 diabetes (and, of course, many other health conditions).

MINDFUL EATING

Focusing on savouring your food (and not on a screen!) is good for blood sugar control. That's because it teaches you to eat slowly, allowing you to notice when you start to feel full. The theory is, you'll then eat the amount your body needs, not clean your plate. Also, avoid eating close to bedtime. Eating late at night, especially high-carb or sugary snacks or large meals, can lead to blood sugar fluctuations.

CLEAN UP YOUR PERSONAL ENVIRONMENT

Studies show that people exposed to some pollutants including certain pesticides and plastics are more likely to develop insulin resistance and diabetes. See page 80 for more on endocrine disruptors.

> ### *EASY WIN: A DAILY TABLESPOON OF APPLE CIDER VINEGAR (ACV)*
>
> *Having a tablespoon of apple cider vinegar before or during eating helps keep blood sugar spikes to a minimum by helping more glucose get into your muscles to be used as fuel. Make salad dressings with ACV (see page 301 for a recipe) or add a tablespoon to a large glass of water to drink before eating (drink through a straw to protect your teeth).*

Treating symptoms

1. HANGER

This is a physiological response to blood glucose levels dropping too low (hypoglycaemia). When the body senses a shortage of its primary energy source, glucose, it releases cortisol and adrenaline to tell the liver to release more glucose into the bloodstream. This hormonal surge can bring on irritability and anger along with hunger.

Food: As described on page 222, your focus should be on low GI foods. Don't skip meals – make sure you eat nutrient-dense meals regularly every four to five hours. You may need to eat more at mealtimes so you don't get hungry in between. Try to notice your first signs of hunger. If you get too hungry you may eat too much, which can lead to blood sugar levels that go very high and low again. Carry a protein snack.

Lifestyle: Stress-reduction techniques such as deep breathing may help you in the moment as well as long term (see page 67 for more).

Suggested supplements: Chromium picolinate enhances the action of insulin, while B vitamins help balance blood sugar (PCH B-Complex).

2. FATIGUE AFTER EATING

If you have insulin resistance, you don't have enough glucose (energy) going into your cells, despite high blood sugar levels. Because the body isn't converting food into energy efficiently, you feel tired.

Food: Magnesium plays a critical role in energy production by improving insulin's ability to transport glucose into the cells. Eat: magnesium-rich foods such as leafy greens, nuts, seeds and whole grains.

Lifestyle: Exercising consistently improves insulin sensitivity. If you can't manage a workout, start by doing daily walking, swimming and/or cycling to encourage muscles to use glucose more efficiently.

Suggested supplements: Magnesium supports numerous

enzymatic reactions vital for energy production and insulin function (PCH Magnesium Complex).

3. WAKING AT NIGHT

If you wake in the night, particularly if it's before 3am, it's likely to be because your blood sugar has dropped. This sets off an internal alarm that you're running short of energy; your body pumps out the stress hormone cortisol, which is what wakes you up. Also, people who have insulin resistance are more likely to have sleep apnoea (when snoring wakes you) and restless leg syndrome (when movement wakes you).

Food: Make sure your evening meal in particular contains HBV protein (see page 221), fibre from vegetables and low GI carbs, plus healthy fats. Include foods rich in tryptophan (turkey, chicken, beef, salmon, pumpkin seeds), as they can help your body make the sleepy hormone melatonin. If this doesn't work, you may not be eating enough: try increasing the size of your meal. And if that doesn't work, have a very small snack – such as almond butter on a small cracker – before bed.

Lifestyle: Ensure you have a regular bedtime, a calming bedtime routine and a sleep-happy environment that's dark cool and quiet (see chapter four for more).

Suggested supplements: Magnesium. This can help both relaxation and regulating sleep cycles. 5-HTP is the precursor for serotonin, which converts to melatonin (in PCH Mood & Sleep). N.B. Don't take 5-HTP with SSRI antidepressants.

4. BRAIN FOG

When the brain doesn't receive a steady supply of glucose – its energy source – this affects memory, concentration and decision-making. The brain can also become insulin resistant, which has been linked to dementia and cognitive decline, as well as your ability to keep your weight stable.

Food: As above, eat low-GI meals. Include foods rich in omega-3 fatty acids, such as fatty fish (salmon, mackerel) and flaxseeds to stabilise blood sugar and support brain health.

Lifestyle: Not only does exercise increase insulin sensitivity but also blood flow to the brain. In an eight-week study of overweight non-exercisers who started to work out regularly, their brain insulin sensitivity improved until it was the level of someone at a healthy weight.

Suggested supplements: Chromium picolinate and magnesium can help insulin sensitivity and management of blood sugar levels (PCH Meta-Boost and PCH Magnesium Complex). Phosphatidylcholine helps to support acetylcholine, a neurotransmitter (brain chemical) that regulates sleep but also learning, attention and memory (BodyBio PC).

5. WEIGHT GAIN

High levels of insulin encourage the body to store fat, especially visceral 'hidden' fat around your organs, so around your waistline and stomach. Visceral fat is more harmful to health than subcutaneous (under-the-skin) fat because it's metabolically active, releasing inflammatory substances that make weight gain more likely. Research shows if your waist measures 35 inches or more (40 inches for men), your risk of type 2 diabetes and heart disease increases.

Food: Focus on low-fat protein and fibre (veg, legumes and whole grains). Even if you're trying to lose weight, make sure you get healthy fats from avocados, nuts, seeds and olive oil, as they reduce inflammation and improve insulin sensitivity. Limit oil to one tablespoon per day. For more on portions for weight loss, see my book *Eat Right, Lose Weight*. Drink green tea as it has multiple beneficial effects on the metabolism.

Lifestyle: For best results, do both aerobic and resistance training. It's also key to manage your stress and sleep (see chapter four).

Suggested supplements: Chromium and cayenne have been shown to support weight management (in PCH Meta Boost).

6. SWEET OR CARBY CRAVINGS

When you eat high GI and/or sugary foods, blood sugar levels go high then plummet rapidly. Your body then asks for a quick energy fix (very often sweet). If you are insulin resistant, the energy or glucose from food doesn't get into muscles, so your body will keep asking for more energy with hunger signals.

Food: As you're getting your blood sugar into balance, try to avoid eating sweet foods. But if you're the type of person who doesn't do well with strict rules, eat low GI fruits (berries, an apple, a pear), preferably after meals.

Lifestyle: Regular exercise is key to help regulate blood sugar levels. Plus, mindful eating practices – eating slowly and without distractions – can also enhance your body's satiety cues, helping you to recognise when you're full.

Suggested supplements: Chromium picolinate and magnesium can help insulin sensitivity and management of blood sugar levels.

SHOULD I TRY A BLOOD GLUCOSE MONITOR?

You may have seen people wearing a continuous glucose monitor (CGM), which looks like a white plastic circle stuck to their upper arm. These were developed for diabetics but can be really useful to discover how much your blood sugar levels go up in response to what you eat, as different people can have varying responses to the same foods. You can become your own personal experiment. For example, you may find that upping your protein at lunchtime keeps your levels more stable. Or a CGM may reveal, for example, that you're waking up in the night because your blood sugar levels have gone very low. I've seen results from these shock clients into not eating, for example, toast for breakfast or biscuits or chocolate mid-morning. Once they see in black and white how these kinds of foods put them on a blood-sugar rollercoaster and make them hungry for the rest of the day.

DO I NEED A BLOOD TEST?

If you are worried about blood sugar symptoms, ask your GP for a blood test. The NHS will generally measure fasting blood glucose and HbA1C, which shows if your blood glucose levels have been high for a while. You could also ask for your fasting insulin to be included in the test, although this isn't automatically offered on the NHS. But it's a very useful indicator: research shows that insulin levels can be rising eight to ten years before blood glucose shows changes on tests.

Sally's story

Four years ago, when I turned 50, I decided to treat myself to a health overhaul at Pippa's clinic. I thought it would be a good present to myself.

I've always had a lot of liver health issues. When I was 23, I had my gall bladder removed, due to having a small bile duct that gave me painful gallstones. Since then, I've always had bloating and indigestion and found it hard to digest some foods.

Three years later, I developed pancreatitis, an inflamed pancreas. I was very ill and spent three weeks in hospital on a liver ward. When I had my daughter, aged 42, I developed obstetric cholestasis, a liver problem where you become really itchy and which is a threat to the baby's life. After my daughter was born, it took ages for my liver function tests to go within the range that's considered normal. Fifteen years ago, I also had a hernia that was repaired with mesh, and that has left me with constant pain.

I worked as airline cabin crew for 28 years and I loved my job. That is, until the menopause came along. From the age of 46, I started to really struggle. I had terrible hot flushes to the point where my face would get sweaty and wet looking. I'd wake up throughout the night. I had bad anxiety – so much so that I'd stress about going to work, even though, at that point, I'd been doing the job for 27 years. I'd worry about my brain fog, anxious that when I did an announcement my words would come out in the wrong order. I put on a stone, so all my clothes felt tight. I just didn't feel like me any more; it was as if I was going around in a trance. And there wasn't a lot of support available at work. By the beginning of the pandemic, I was struggling. That was the main reason why when I was offered redundancy, I took it. That's when I went to Pippa's clinic.

Pippa advised me that if you have no gall bladder, taking ox bile salts will replace your own bile salts and help with digestion. It did help straight away. She said some of the bloating was due to my liver function and some was likely due to anxiety caused by hormonal changes.

I had a DNA test that showed that I didn't process caffeine well. At the time, I was drinking eight cups of builder's tea a day and I stopped straight away. I also did a DUTCH test, which showed my cortisol was high and that I was in menopause. Pippa advised me to drink holy basil tea to wind down in the evening.

Cutting out sugar and caffeine definitely helped with my anxiety. Claire, a nutritionist at Pippa's clinic, sent me more ideas to bring down my cortisol, like meditation and journaling. She told me to make time for me and not rush around after everyone else. So now I take ten minutes a day to write a journal, plus I'll meditate and do yoga twice a week. I also go to sound baths, which is incredibly relaxing.

Pippa sent me lists of good foods to eat and I started by cutting out sugar as much as possible. My aim was to eat zero processed ingredients, just good, fresh foods. I adopted the changes slowly, so that I would be more likely to stick to them.

Then, when Pippa's first book, *Eat Right, Lose Weight*, came out, I followed the 21-day eating plan. I started to leave a gap of four hours between meals. That also stopped me nibbling in the evenings, which was my bad habit. From the book, I often make a bowl for dinner, with a protein source plus veggies and homemade hummus, topped with one of Pippa's dressings – either lemon gremolata, avocado or tahini.

Eating well reduced the number of hot flushes I was getting, as well as helping me to lose weight. Now, I make sure all my meals are good food rather than eating rubbish that doesn't fill me up. I do eat some bread, but only natural bread such as sourdough and rye. If I go out at the weekend and eat and drink more than usual, then I just go back to the Food Framework on Monday. I've noticed that if I eat a big pudding when I'm out, I get a bad sugar rush and hot sweats lasting a few days, so I've decided that these kinds of foods are not worth eating.

I have lost weight and I don't feel as bloated. Recently, I decided to start taking HRT. My GP was unhelpful when I asked for it, but I've managed to get it via a private doctor. The hot flushes have practically disappeared, although I'll get the odd night sweat. It's also helped me get to sleep more easily and to sleep through the night.

Now, I don't know how I ate any differently before. I'd never go back to it. My energy is better, I don't feel bloated and I'm back to my happy weight. This way of eating is my way of life, not a diet.

Part 4

The PCM Hormone Balance Recipes

I'm a passionate foodie, and my biggest wish is for all our clients to enjoy food while doing their bodies and minds good, too. This section is a collection of the recipes I've created that are suited to women in midlife but also work for the whole family. I've focused on the ingredients and nutrients that are most helpful at this time of life: protein, fibre, good fats, the widest range of colourful plants and plenty of herbs and spices.

With my 80:20 approach, you will eat what's good for your hormones and health most of the time, along with some more indulgent foods. I'm very proud of the sweet recipes, as it took me a long time to get some of them right. They may not be for every day, but my version of these desserts won't raise blood sugar and they've got real nutritional value too. I hope these recipes make it easier for you to make the Food Framework part of your life, and give you ideas of how to adapt your own recipes or end up on your regular recipe rotation. You deserve to eat delicious, nutritious food – and every bite you take is a chance to feel better.

BREAKFAST

My clients say the protein shake is a life changer, as they can make it the night before or first thing and take it with them. So it's ideal if you're someone who is short of time. If you make one of the breakfast recipes that has less protein – for example, the granola – you can ramp up the protein content by including a scoop of protein powder, or having a couple of boiled eggs or any other protein you fancy on the side.

Chocolate Orange Tofu Bowl

As well as tofu being a complete protein – meaning it contains all the essential amino acids – it contains isoflavones. These are the most-researched type of phytoestrogen and evidence suggests that they do help balance the hormonal fluctuations of perimenopause.

Serves 1

1 orange
80g silken tofu
2 tsp cocoa powder
1 tbsp grain-free granola (see page 243), optional

1. Zest the orange and blend the zest together with the tofu and cocoa powder until smooth.
2. Use a sharp knife to remove the remaining peel and pith from the orange then slice the flesh.
3. Pour the chocolate tofu into a serving bowl and top with the orange and granola, if using.

My Go-to Breakfast Protein Shake

This is a typical shake for me on weekdays. It is quick and easy to make, and I can pile in lots of nutrients. It provides 20g to 30g of protein along with some healthy fats and keeps me going until lunchtime.

Serves 1

- 100–200ml non-dairy milk (depending on how thin or thick you like it)
- 1 serving of pea or whey protein powder (see my 'Pippa Loves' on my website for brands)
- 1 small handful blueberries
- 1 small handful rocket (or whatever greens you have in the fridge)
- 1 tbsp each ground seeds (depending on my menstrual cycle – see page 58 for seed cycling)
- 1 tbsp walnut butter (or other nut butter)
- 1 scoop PCH Marine Collagen (optional)
- 1 scoop PCH Super Greens (optional)
- 1 tsp maca (optional)

Put all the ingredients in a blender with some ice and blitz into a smoothie.

Flaxseed Bread

Flaxseeds really are a perimenopause superfood. They're rich in lignans, a type of phytoestrogen, so can reduce symptoms including hot flushes and mood swings by helping to balance fluctuating oestrogen levels. They're also rich in soluble and insoluble fibre, which is great for the gut microbiome and lowering bad (LDL) cholesterol. You can buy psyllium husks, a source of soluble fibre, in health food shops.

Makes 1 small loaf

240g whole golden flaxseeds
40g psyllium husk powder
2 tsp baking powder
½ tsp fine salt

320ml hot water
1 tbsp olive oil
Extra flaxseeds and flaked salt (optional)

1. Preheat the oven to 180°C. You will need a 1lb loaf tin for baking.
2. Blend the flaxseeds in a spice grinder until they are a fine flour. Sift the flour into a bowl to remove any whole seeds or husks then blend these again.
3. Whisk the ground flaxseeds, psyllium husk powder, baking powder and fine salt together in a mixing bowl, then add the water and olive oil. Stir together into a rough dough then use your hands to gently knead it, ensuring that the dry ingredients are fully incorporated. Shape the dough into a log shape roughly the size of your loaf tin and place it into the tin.
4. Mist the top of the loaf with water and sprinkle over a few extra flaxseeds and a little flaked salt if you want to. Bake for 65 minutes or until risen and golden. Allow to cool in the tin for 10 minutes before transferring to a wire rack to cool completely.

Optional sesame seasoning:

2 tsp poppy seeds	1 tsp dried minced garlic
1 tsp white sesame seeds	1 tsp dried minced onion
1 tsp black sesame seeds	1 tsp flaked sea salt

Mix together all ingredients and blend 1½ tbsp of the seasoning into the bread dough. Shape the dough and top with the remaining seasoning. Bake as above. (N.B. If using the seasoning, omit the fine salt from the main recipe.)

Flaxseed Porridge with Apple and Coconut

A low-GI, high-fibre alternative for porridge lovers, this version will keep you feeling full until lunchtime. The hazelnuts give it a satisfying crunch and are a great source of heart-healthy monounsaturated fats and skin-plumping vitamin E.

Serves 1

2 tbsp whole hazelnuts
1½ tbsp golden flaxseeds
250ml plant-based milk

1½ tbsp desiccated coconut
1 small apple, coarsely grated
Cinnamon to serve

1. Grind the hazelnuts in a spice grinder or blender into a fine meal then tip into a saucepan. Grind the flaxseeds in the same way and add to the pan.
2. Pour the milk into the saucepan along with the coconut and three quarters of the grated apple. Stir over a low heat for 4–5 minutes or until starting to thicken. The porridge will continue to thicken as it cools in the bowl.
3. Serve the porridge topped with the remaining apple and a sprinkle of cinnamon.

French Toast

You will not get hungry before lunchtime if you eat this for breakfast, it's so filling! It's packed with fibre and the cinnamon gives a natural sweetness while helping to keep blood sugar levels even.

Serves 2

100ml plant-based milk
1 medium free-range egg
1 tsp vanilla extract
1 tsp cinnamon
4 slices flaxseed bread
   (see page 239)
3–4 tsp coconut oil
Coconut yoghurt and berries
   to serve

1. Whisk the milk with the egg, vanilla and cinnamon and pour into a dish large enough to lay your bread in flat.
2. Dip the bread into the egg mixture, leaving it to soak for one minute on each side.
3. Heat a frying pan over a medium heat and add 1 tsp coconut oil.
4. Carefully lift up the bread, allowing any excess liquid to drain off, then fry for 4–5 minutes or until golden and crisp, then flip over and cook the other side.
5. Repeat for the remaining slices of bread, adding oil to the pan as necessary.
6. Serve with a spoonful of coconut yoghurt, berries and an extra sprinkling of cinnamon.

Grain-free Granola

The great thing about making your own granola is that you can adapt it to make it hormone friendly. This one is a nutrient powerhouse, packed with good fats, magnesium, zinc, vitamin E. It's also high in gut-friendly fibre and low GI.

Batch recipe

50g pecans
30g hazelnuts
35g flaked coconut
20g pumpkin seeds
15g sunflower seeds

2 tbsp chia seeds
2 tbsp milled flax seed
1 tbsp coconut oil, melted
1½ tbsp maple syrup

1. Preheat the oven to 150°C.
2. Mix all of the dry ingredients in a large bowl then pour over the melted coconut oil and maple syrup. Stir until everything is evenly coated.
3. Tip onto a baking tray and bake for 25–30 minutes, stirring every 10 minutes, until golden. Leave to cool then store in an airtight container. Serve with sheep, goat or coconut yogurt.

Homemade Baked Beans

Our gut microbiome just loves beans! They're full of fibre that feeds the good bugs and helps stabilise blood sugar levels. Make a batch the night before, so it's ready to heat and eat at breakfast time.

Serves 2

- 1 tbsp olive oil
- ½ red onion, finely chopped
- 2 cloves garlic, minced
- 1 tsp dried oregano
- ½ tsp smoked paprika
- 400g tin cannellini beans, drained and rinsed
- 250g passata
- 100ml water
- 1 tbsp tomato puree
- 1 tbsp Worcestershire sauce (or soy sauce if vegan)
- 2 tsp maple syrup
- Salt and pepper

1. Heat the olive oil in a saucepan over a medium/low heat and gently fry the onion with a pinch of salt for 4–5 minutes until softened.
2. Add the garlic, dried oregano, smoked paprika and beans and cook for a further two minutes.
3. Now add the passata, water, tomato puree, Worcestershire sauce and maple syrup. Stir well and simmer for 15–20 minutes or until thickened to your liking. Season with salt and pepper to taste.

Protein Pancakes

Back when I was making pancakes with flour, I found that they didn't balance my blood sugar very well and I'd be hungry mid-morning. By making them with protein powder, they will balance your blood sugar and keep you feeling satiated for longer. Coconut oil contains medium-chain fatty acids (MCFAs), which are easily metabolised by the body for immediate energy.

Serves 1

- 1 medium free-range egg
- 65ml almond milk or plant-based milk of choice
- ½ tsp vanilla paste or extract
- 1 tsp coconut oil, melted
- 20g coconut flour
- 10g whey or pea protein powder
- ½ tsp baking powder
- ½ tsp cinnamon
- Coconut oil for cooking
- Coconut yoghurt, fruit and cinnamon to serve

1. Beat the egg with the almond milk, vanilla and coconut oil.
2. In a separate bowl, whisk together the coconut flour, protein powder, baking powder and cinnamon.
3. Heat a frying pan over a medium/low heat and add 1 tsp coconut oil. Once the pan is hot, carefully wipe away the oil with some kitchen paper so only a thin film remains.
4. Whisk the wet ingredients into the dry ingredients then, one by one, spoon into the pan to make three pancakes.
5. Cook for 3–4 minutes or until golden on the underside and the top looks matte. Carefully flip the pancakes and cook for a further 3–4 minutes.
6. Serve with coconut yoghurt, your choice of fruit and an extra sprinkling of cinnamon.

Seeded Red Lentil Rolls

These are so easy – in fact, I am obsessed with them. Packed with protein, it's hard to believe these rolls are made from lentils. Not many supermarkets sell whole psyllium husk rather than ground, but it's easy to find online. These go with anything: with eggs for breakfast, to make a sandwich, to go with dips and soup.

Makes 4

200g red lentils, rinsed and soaked for at least 3 hours, ideally overnight
20g whole psyllium husk
60ml water
1½ tbsp olive oil
½ tsp fine salt
½ tsp bicarbonate of soda
½ tbsp apple cider vinegar
1½ tsp white sesame seeds
1½ tsp poppy seeds
Extra seeds as topping (optional)

1. Preheat the oven to 180°C and line a baking tray with non-stick baking parchment.
2. Drain the soaked red lentils and tip into a food processor along with the psyllium husk, water, olive oil, salt, bicarbonate of soda and apple cider vinegar. Blend into a soft dough.
3. Add the sesame and poppy seeds to the processor and pulse until combined.
4. Tip the dough onto the work surface and divide into four. Wet your hands then shape each piece into a ball. If you want to top the rolls with seeds, tip the seeds onto a plate and press the top of the roll gently into them. Transfer to the lined baking tray and bake for 25–30 minutes or until crisp and golden brown.

Shiitake Mushrooms and Spinach on Toast

All mushrooms contain fibre and some protein, but I particularly like the taste of shiitake mushrooms. They're rich in B vitamins, including B2 (riboflavin), B3 (niacin) and B5 (pantothenic acid), as well as beta-glucans, which support immune function. You can sub them out for other mushrooms in this recipe, too.

Serves 1

½ tbsp pine nuts
1 tbsp extra virgin olive oil
80g shiitake mushrooms, halved if large
120g spinach
1 clove garlic, thinly sliced
Salt and pepper
1 lentil roll (see page 246) or 1 slice of flaxseed bread (see page 239)

1. Toast the pine nuts in a dry pan on a medium heat for a minute or two – keep watching so they don't burn!
2. Heat the olive oil in a frying pan over a medium/high heat then add the mushrooms. Cook for 4–5 minutes, stirring regularly, until the mushrooms have browned.
3. Add the spinach and garlic and cook for a further 2–3 minutes until the spinach has wilted and any liquid has evaporated. Season to taste.
4. Meanwhile, toast your bread and serve the mushrooms and spinach on top. Scatter over the pine nuts.

Spinach and Pepper Egg Muffins

A savoury and portable breakfast that works for all the family, and for lunch boxes too. They will keep in the fridge for a couple of days (by the third day they aren't as nice). It's an easy way to get in some green leaves early in the day, too. Spinach is high in magnesium, good for sleep and mood, plus it's an excellent source of iron, vitamin K, vitamin A and folate.

Makes 6

1 tbsp olive oil
½ red or orange pepper, diced
80g spinach, chopped
3 spring onions, sliced
5 medium free-range eggs
1 tsp smoked paprika
Salt and pepper
30g feta, crumbled

1. Preheat the oven to 180°C.
2. Heat a pan over a medium heat and add the oil. Once hot, add the pepper and cook gently for 4–5 minutes until softened.
3. Add the spinach and spring onions to the pan and cook until the spinach has wilted and any liquid has evaporated.
4. Whisk the eggs with the paprika and salt and pepper.
5. Grease six holes of a muffin tin and divide the vegetable mixture between them. Pour over the egg then top with the crumbled feta.
6. Bake for 15–20 minutes until risen and cooked through.

Stewed Apples with Yoghurt and Almonds

This is a marriage made in heaven for the gut, with prebiotic fibre in the apple and probiotics in the yoghurt.

Serves 3

- 3 apples, peeled, cored and diced
- 60ml of water
- 2 tsp cinnamon
- 150g coconut, almond, sheep or goat yoghurt
- 1 tbsp toasted flaked almonds

1. Put apples, water and cinnamon into a heavy-based saucepan and cover with a lid.
2. Cook over a low heat, stirring occasionally, for 10 minutes or until the apples have broken down but still have some texture.
3. Spoon 50g yoghurt into a bowl per portion and top with a third of the stewed apple and a sprinkle of toasted almonds.

THE DIY BREAKFAST FORMULA

If you want to create your own, or if you've got ingredients to use up, follow this formula

Breakfast
Aim for 20–30g of protein (ideally 30g).
2–3 eggs (ideally 3), in an omelette, boiled, poached. Or 50–70g tofu. Or 50–70g smoked salmon or other protein. And 50g–70g vegetables and/or fruit.

OR
✣ *A smoothie: one portion of protein powder (20–30g protein – ideally 30g), a small handful leafy greens, two tablespoons of berries or a small pear, 1 tablespoon of chopped nuts or seeds, with non-dairy, goat or sheep milk.*

LUNCH

I've chosen these recipes as they can be made in advance and packed in a lunch box or flask, or made quickly if you're at home. And they include the lunches I often make for myself! If you're creating your own recipe or adapting one you already like, make sure your lunch (or dinner) is satisfying by including the following: 1 portion of protein (to give you 20 to 30g), varied vegetables and/or salad, a delicious dressing and, if you wish, an optional carb source, such as quinoa or a root veg.

Beetroot Hummus

Who doesn't love hummus? Making your own means you don't have to add oil and you can whizz it to the consistency you prefer. Beetroot is high in nitrates, which your body converts to nitric oxide. This helps improve blood flow, delivering nutrients and oxygen throughout the body, so it's good both for energy levels and cardiovascular health.

Serves 2

250g cooked beetroot
400g tin chickpeas, drained and rinsed
2 cloves garlic
2 tbsp tahini
Sprig of mint, leaves only
Salt and pepper
Crudites or seeded crackers (see page 263) to serve

Tip all ingredients into a blender and blend until smooth, then season to taste. Serve with crudites of your choice.

Caesar Salad

Crunchy, savoury and satisfying, this is a nutrient-, antioxidant- and fibre-boosted version of the Caesar salad that works as a side with leftover chicken, prawns or tofu. I was so pleased when I finally got the recipe for the 'parmesan' part right! It really adds a nice crunch. Watercress is a cruciferous vegetable, so it counts as one of your two portions a day, plus it's a good source of calcium, essential for bone health.

Serves 2

1 romaine lettuce, shredded
50g watercress

1 tsp capers
Salt and pepper

For the dressing:

65g cashews, soaked for at least 3 hours
3 tbsp water
1 clove garlic, peeled
Juice of ½ lemon
1 tsp Dijon mustard
2 tsp nutritional yeast

For the Brazil nut 'parmesan':

50g Brazil nuts, roughly chopped
10g flaxseeds
10g nutritional yeast
½ tsp garlic granules
½ tsp flaked sea salt

1. To make the dressing, drain the cashews then tip into the bowl of a mini blender and blend with the rest of the ingredients until smooth. Add water as needed to achieve a creamy consistency, then season to taste.
2. Blend the Brazil nuts, flaxseeds, nutritional yeast, garlic granules and salt together in a spice or coffee grinder into a texture similar to that of grated parmesan.
3. Toss the romaine lettuce and watercress together with a spoonful of dressing and divide between two serving plates.

Drizzle over a little extra dressing and finish with a generous sprinkle of 'parmesan'.
4. Serve with your choice of protein.

Store any extra dressing or Brazil nut 'parmesan' in an airtight container in the fridge for up to one week.

Carrot and Lentil Soup

An organic carrot a day keeps hormonal imbalance away! Carrots contain a specific type of fibre that can bind to excess, used-up oestrogen in the gut, helping to carry it out of the body. Eat your daily carrot straight up, raw in a salad (see page 261) or in this filling soup. The fibre is in the skin of the carrot, so wash it rather than peel it and buy organic if you can.

Serves 4

3 tbsp olive oil
600g carrots, washed and coarsely grated
2 onions, finely sliced
2 tsp turmeric
1 tsp cumin
1½ tbsp fresh grated ginger

200g red lentils, rinsed
1½ litres vegetable stock

For the topping:
1 tbsp pumpkin seeds
1 tbsp sunflower seeds

1. Heat the olive oil in a large saucepan and add the carrot and onions. Sweat the vegetables for 10 minutes until softened.
2. Add the spices and lentils. Stir well and cook for a further 2–3 minutes.
3. Pour in the stock, bring to the boil, then simmer for 20 minutes or until the lentils are tender.
4. Use a stick blender to puree the soup, adding boiling water as necessary to achieve your desired consistency; season to taste.
5. Toast the seeds in a dry frying pan over a medium heat until they start to pop. Serve on top of the soup with a crack of black pepper.

Tip: Seeded crackers (see page 263) also make a great topping when broken into small pieces.

Celeriac Soup with Toasted Walnuts and Crispy Sage

A single bowl of this creamy, filling soup racks up eight plant foods, including three veg, taking you a good way towards your goal of four different veg a day. Plus, the walnuts give you good fats and sage is a hormone-balancing herb.

Serves 4

- 1 tbsp olive oil
- 1 leek, finely sliced
- 1 sticks of celery, finely sliced
- 2 cloves garlic, minced
- 2 eating apples, diced
- 1 small celeriac (approx. 600g), peeled and diced
- 4–5 sage leaves, finely chopped
- 400g tin butter beans, drained and rinsed
- 1 litre vegetable stock

For the topping:
- Handful walnuts, roughly chopped
- Olive oil
- 8–10 sage leaves

1. Heat the olive oil in a large saucepan then add the leek and celery. Sweat gently for 10 minutes until softened.
2. Add the garlic, apples, celeriac and sage to the pan and cook for a further 5 minutes.
3. Stir in the butter beans and stock then bring to the boil. Turn down to a simmer and cook for 20–30 minutes or until the celeriac is tender.
4. Meanwhile, prepare the topping. Toast the walnuts in a small, dry frying pan until golden then tip onto a plate.
5. Return the pan to the heat and add 1 tbsp olive oil, or enough to cover the base of the pan. Once the oil is hot, add the sage

leaves; they should sizzle as they hit the pan. Cook for 30 seconds on each side or until deep green and crisp. Tip the sage onto kitchen paper to drain.

6. Use a stick blender to puree the soup, adding a little boiling water if necessary to reach your desired consistency. Season to taste.
7. Serve the soup topped with the toasted nuts, crispy sage and a crack of black pepper. Add your choice of protein – toasted tempeh would be lovely.

Crispy Artichoke and White Bean Salad

This is a quick and filling salad that works really well served with leftover salmon or chicken. Roasting the artichokes gives them a satisfying smoky flavour and chewy texture. Artichokes are one of the bitter foods that stimulate bile flow, which is good for fat digestion and helping move used-up hormones out of the body. Along with the beans in this recipe, they're high in prebiotics too – fibres that feed the beneficial bacteria in the gut.

Serves 2

160g marinated artichoke hearts in olive oil, quartered
400g tin cannellini beans, drained and rinsed
150g cherry tomatoes, halved
Handful of rocket
1 romaine lettuce

For the dressing:
2 tbsp extra virgin olive oil
Juice of ½ lemon
½ tsp fresh parsley, chopped
Salt and pepper

1. Preheat the oven to 200°C.
2. Spread the artichokes out onto a baking tray, taking some of their oil with them, and roast for 8 minutes. Turn them over then roast for a further 5–6 minutes or until golden and crispy. Drain any extra oil on kitchen paper.
3. Meanwhile, combine the rest of the salad ingredients in a bowl and whisk the dressing together.
4. Add the crispy artichokes to the bowl then toss with the dressing.

Fajita Bowls with Cauliflower Rice

An adaptable base for chicken, fish or toasted tempeh, this recipe is a feast for the liver, with a portion of cruciferous cauliflower plus sulphur-rich garlic. It's also high in vitamin C which is essential for your skin to make collagen, and the capsaicin in the cayenne helps rev up your metabolic rate.

Serves 4

- 1 medium cauliflower (approx. 750g)
- 2 tbsp olive oil
- 1 red pepper, sliced into 1cm slices
- 1 yellow pepper, sliced into 1cm slices
- 1 red onion, sliced into thin wedges
- 2 large flat mushrooms, sliced into 1cm slices
- 1 clove garlic, minced
- 1 tsp smoked paprika
- ½ tsp cayenne pepper
- ½ tsp ground coriander
- ½ tsp dried oregano
- Juice of 1 lime

For the guacamole:
- 1 large avocado
- 1 clove garlic, minced
- Juice of ½ lime
- Flaked sea salt
- Small handful coriander leaves, finely chopped (optional)

1. Begin by preparing the cauliflower rice. Remove the tough stalk and break the remaining cauliflower into florets. Pulse in a food processor into a rice-like consistency. Set aside.
2. To make the guacamole, mash the avocado together with the garlic and lime juice then season with salt to taste. Stir in coriander, if liked.
3. Heat 1 tbsp olive oil in a large frying pan over a medium heat and add the peppers to the pan. Fry for 5 minutes, tossing

occasionally, until starting to soften.
4. Add the onion, mushrooms, garlic, spices and lime juice, and cook for a further 4–5 minutes until the vegetables are tender.
5. Heat the remaining olive oil in a frying pan then tip in the cauliflower rice. Cook over a medium heat for 4–5 minutes, stirring regularly, until tender. Season with salt and pepper.
6. Divide the cauliflower rice between four plates and top with the spicy vegetables and a spoonful of guacamole. Add choice of protein, such as chicken, fish or toasted tempeh.

Prawn Lettuce Wraps

If you make the marinade in advance, this dish only takes a few minutes to put together. It's the ideal light lunch because it won't leave you feeling sleepy in the afternoon. It contains a lot of key Food Framework nutrients: omega-3 fatty acids, quality protein (you can swap out for tofu) and fibre.

Serves 2

165g raw king prawns (or tofu)
1 baby gem lettuce, leaves separated
1 avocado, sliced
Coriander and lime wedges to serve

For the marinade:

½–1 tsp cayenne (to taste)
½ tsp cumin
½ tsp dried fenugreek leaves
Juice of 1 lime
1 clove garlic, minced
2 tbsp extra virgin olive oil
½ tsp flaked sea salt

1. Whisk all the marinade ingredients together, adjusting the amount of cayenne to suit your taste. Add the prawns then leave to marinate for 30 minutes.
2. Heat a frying pan over medium heat then pour in the prawns along with the marinade. Cook for 2–3 minutes on each side or until pink and cooked through.
3. Lay the gem lettuce leaves onto a plate and top with the prawns and avocado. Garnish with fresh coriander and lime wedges.

Raw Carrot Salad

I recommend this salad to all my clients who have oestrogen dominance because the fibre in carrots is so good at binding used-up oestrogen in the digestive tract to carry it out of the body. But it's good for all hormone imbalances. Buy organic carrots where possible, as you'll be using the skin.

Serves 2

2 medium free-range eggs, room temperature
2 medium carrots
1 avocado
10–12cm piece of cucumber
Handful cashews
1 tbsp sunflower seeds

For the dressing:
½ tsp grated fresh ginger
½ tbsp tamari (gluten-free soy sauce)
Juice of ½ lime
1 tbsp sesame oil
½ tsp sesame seeds

1. Bring a small pan of water to the boil then slowly lower in the eggs. Boil for 7½ minutes. Meanwhile, fill a jug with cold water and add a few ice cubes. As soon as the eggs are cooked, plunge them into the iced water and leave for 3 minutes. Peel the eggs.
2. To make the salad, scrub the carrots if needed. Then use a vegetable peeler to cut the carrots into ribbons. Halve and slice the avocado.
3. Cut the cucumber in half lengthwise, use a teaspoon to remove the seeds, then slice. Add to a bowl with the carrots, cashews and sunflower seeds.
4. Whisk all of the dressing ingredients together until emulsified, then pour three quarters of it over the salad.
5. Divide the salad between two bowls and top with half an avocado each and a boiled egg, sliced in half. Finish with a drizzle of the remaining dressing and an extra sprinkle of sesame seeds.

Salmon and Broccoli Salad

Salmon is probably the easiest fish to cook, or you can buy it ready steamed. It contains anti-inflammatory omega-3 fatty acids, including EPA and DHA, which can help calm the joint pain and stiffness that's common during perimenopause. They also help to reduce the risk of heart disease.

Serves 2

150g tenderstem broccoli
110g French beans, trimmed
1 small bulb fennel, cut into thin wedges
2 tbsp olive oil
1 tsp sesame seeds
Salt and pepper
2 handfuls rocket
2 salmon fillets, cooked

For the dressing:
2 tbsp extra virgin olive oil
1 tbsp apple cider vinegar
1 tsp Dijon mustard
1 clove garlic, minced
Salt and pepper

1. Halve any thick broccoli stems lengthwise then tip into a bowl along with the French beans and fennel. Drizzle over the olive oil then add the sesame seeds and season well with salt and pepper.
2. Heat a griddle pan over a high heat and cook the vegetables for 6–7 minutes, turning halfway through, until charred and just tender.
3. Whisk the dressing ingredients together then toss the vegetables and rocket. Serve with the cooked salmon fillets.

Seeded Crackers

This is another way to get in your daily dose of hormone-friendly flaxseeds, which, as you know by now, is my obsession for women in later perimenopause – and especially after the menopause. Four to five is roughly a portion, depending on how hungry you are.

Makes approx. 25 crackers

- 60g sunflower seeds
- 100g pumpkin seeds
- 20g sesame seeds
- 10g poppy seeds
- 60g flaxseeds
- 1 tbsp psyllium husk
- ½ tsp flaked sea salt
- 1 tsp dried oregano
- 375ml water

1. Mix all ingredients together then leave to stand for 15–20 minutes, or until thick and gelatinous.
2. Meanwhile, preheat the oven to 160°C and line a large baking tray (approx. 30cm x 40cm, or use two smaller tins) with baking paper.
3. Pour the seed mixture into the tin and spread into a very thin layer. Bake for 40 minutes or until golden and crisp.
4. Leave to cool in the tin for 10 minutes then carefully peel off the baking paper. Leave to cool completely, then break into pieces to serve.

N.B. If you would prefer more even, square crackers, remove from the oven after 20 minutes and use a pizza cutter to cut it into 25 pieces. Continue cooking as above.

Spiced Root Vegetable Soup

Root vegetables are my favourite kind of carbohydrate. They're low GI, which means they release glucose slowly into the bloodstream, leading to more stable blood sugar levels. They contain a good dose of fibre to feed the microbiome and help keep the digestive system moving. And they're packed with vitamins and minerals, including vitamin A, potassium, folate and manganese, plus antioxidants to help counter the oxidative stress that rises in times of hormonal flux.

Serves 4

2 tbsp olive oil
2 tbsp curry powder
2 white onions, diced
2 leeks, sliced
4 carrots, sliced
3 parsnips, sliced
2 litres vegetable stock

For the parsnip crisps:
1 parsnip
1 tbsp olive oil
Flaked sea salt

1. Heat the olive oil in a large stock pot then add the curry powder. Tip in the vegetables and gently fry for 10 minutes, stirring regularly.
2. Pour in the stock, bring to the boil then turn the heat down and simmer for 30 minutes or until the vegetables are tender.
3. Meanwhile, make the parsnip crisps. Preheat the oven to 180°C. Use a vegetable peeler to cut the parsnips into thin ribbons then toss with the oil and salt.
4. Spread the parsnip ribbons out onto a large baking sheet, making sure they're not overlapping, then bake for 8–10 minutes until starting to brown. Flip them over then bake for a

further 3–4 minutes or until golden and crisp. Tip onto kitchen paper to drain.
5. Puree the soup and season to taste. Add a little more stock or water if needed for your desired consistency.
6. Serve the soup topped with the parsnip crisps and fresh black pepper. Add a choice of protein.

DINNER

Beef Bolognese

If you're not a fan of liver, this is how to sneak it into your diet – and that of your loved ones – without any fuss. Adding it to the bolognese just makes the taste a little richer. Liver is the original superfood, with vitamin B12 for energy, plus vitamin A and lots of iron – particularly important if your periods have got heavier during perimenopause. Both the liver and the beef in this recipe provide haem iron, which is more easily absorbed than plant sources of iron.

Serves 6

1 tbsp olive oil
500g beef mince
150g chicken livers, pureed
1 onion, finely chopped
1 carrot, finely chopped
1 stick celery, finely chopped

1 clove garlic, minced
250 ml beef stock
700g passata
2 tsp dried oregano

1. Heat the oil in a heavy-bottomed pan and fry the beef over a high heat for 3–4 minutes until sealed.
2. Add the pureed chicken livers and cook for 5 minutes until the beef is well browned.

3. Transfer the meat to a plate then turn the heat down to low. Sweat the onion, carrot, celery and garlic for 10 minutes until softened then return the beef to the pan.
4. Pour in the stock and passata and add the oregano. Season with salt and pepper.
5. Bring to the boil then simmer for 45 minutes or until reduced by half and you have a thick ragu. Serve with buckwheat or chickpea pasta or rice.

Chicken Fajitas with Chickpea Tortillas and Sweet Pepper Chilli Sauce

I absolutely love this chilli sauce – and my family do too, so it never lasts long! If there's ever any left, I think it's wonderful with leftover roast chicken. The chilli and cayenne heat you up and give a little kick to the metabolism. The tortillas aren't instant like the ones that come from packets but they're so worth the time and effort to make.

Serves 2

1 tsp smoked paprika
1 tsp cumin
½ tsp dried garlic
½ tsp cayenne
Juice of ½ lime
2 tbsp coconut oil, melted
250g chicken breast, cut into thin strips
1 red pepper, sliced
1 small pepper, sliced
1 red onion, sliced
3 tbsp plant-based, goat or sheep yoghurt
1 avocado, sliced
2 spring onions, finely sliced
Lime wedges to serve

For the tortillas:
2 tbsp milled flaxseed
90g chickpea flour (gram flour)
½ tsp smoked paprika
Pinch of salt
Coconut oil for cooking

For the sweet pepper chilli sauce (optional):
1 long red chilli
2 red peppers, seeded and chopped
1cm fresh ginger, grated
4 fresh pitted dates
1cm fresh turmeric or ½ tsp ground
Juice of 1 lime
1 tsp olive oil
Small handful fresh coriander or basil (optional)
Salt and pepper to taste

Directions for the sauce:

The easiest way is to put all the ingredients in a food processor and blend until smooth. However, this sauce is even better if you roast the peppers in a hot oven for 30 minutes first. Remove the blackened skins and use the flesh in the sauce. Add more chilli if you dare!

Directions for the chicken tortillas:

1. First prepare the tortillas. Mix the flaxseed with 2 tbsp warm water and set aside for 5 minutes to thicken.
2. Add the chickpea flour, paprika, salt and 220ml water. Mix together into a soft dough.
3. Divide the dough into four pieces and roll each piece out between two pieces of baking paper into a circle as thin as possible.
4. Heat ½ tsp coconut oil in a large frying pan over a medium heat. Remove the top piece of baking paper from the tortilla, slide your hand under the bottom piece of paper and flip into the pan. Remove the paper and cook for 3–4 minutes on each side until golden. Transfer to a cooling rack then repeat with the remaining dough, adding oil to the pan as necessary.
5. Now prepare the fajita filling. Mix the spices with the lime juice and coconut oil in a large bowl then tip in the chicken and vegetables and toss to coat evenly.
6. Heat a large frying pan over a medium/high heat then cook the chicken and vegetables for 5–6 minutes, stirring regularly, until the chicken is cooked through.
7. To serve, divide the yoghurt between the tortillas and spread down the centre of each one. Top with the fajita mix and sliced avocado. Sprinkle over the spring onions and serve with lime wedges and the chilli sauce, if using.

Chicken Noodle Soup

Ginger and turmeric are a power spice combo for perimenopause. They're packed with antioxidants, anti-inflammatory compounds and other plant chemicals that can help with digestion, menstrual cramps, mood shifts and brain fog.

Serves 2

½ tbsp olive oil
1 small onion, finely chopped
3 cloves garlic, minced
1 tbsp fresh ginger, grated
½ tsp turmeric
Juice and zest of ½ lemon
1 litre chicken stock
200g chicken breast, cut lengthwise into 4 strips
½ head broccoli, cut into small florets
75g buckwheat noodles
½ bunch fresh parsley, finely chopped

1. Heat the oil in a large saucepan over a low heat and fry the onion for 3–4 minutes until translucent.
2. Add the garlic, ginger, turmeric and lemon juice and zest. Cook for a further 2–3 minutes then pour in the stock.
3. Bring to the boil then add the chicken to the pan. Simmer for 10 minutes.
4. Add the broccoli and cook for a further 5 minutes or until the chicken is cooked through.
5. Remove the chicken from the pan and use a fork to shred it into bite-sized pieces.
6. Cook the noodles in the broth for 3–4 minutes or until cooked. Return the chicken to the pan and stir in the parsley before serving.

Coconut Chicken Noodles

If I'm feeling a bit under the weather, this is the noodle dish that comforts me. It's also another way to cook chicken, which is such a good source of high-quality protein. And protein is the watchword for perimenopause: it helps maintain muscle, manage your appetite and weight, and provides the building blocks for neurotransmitters and hormones.

Serves 2

For the sauce:

200ml coconut milk
1 tsp fresh ginger, grated
1 garlic clove, minced
1 tbsp tamari
½ tsp turmeric
Juice of 1 lime
1 tsp fish sauce
½ red chilli, finely chopped

1 tbsp coconut oil
300g chicken breast, cut into thin strips
1 yellow pepper, sliced
80g mange tout
200g buckwheat noodles
70g spring greens, shredded
125g cherry tomatoes, halved

1. Mix together all the ingredients for the sauce.
2. Heat the oil in a large frying pan or wok then add the chicken. Stir fry for 4–5 minutes until golden on all sides.
3. Add the pepper and mange tout and cook for 5 minutes or until veg are just tender.
4. Meanwhile, cook the noodles according to the package instructions.
5. Pour the sauce into the pan and add the spring greens and tomatoes. Turn down the heat then continue cooking until the spring greens are wilted. Add the cooked noodles and mix well.

'Fakeaway' Curry with Coconut Rice

This may just become your new Friday night takeaway – and it's one the whole family will love. I call it a fakeaway but really it's the opposite, as it's 100 per cent from scratch and not a packet. This curry is packed with health-boosting spices, including turmeric, fenugreek, garlic, ginger and chilli. Choose from chicken or chickpea, and make a large batch and freeze for those Friday nights when you just cannot be bothered to cook.

Serves 4

For the coconut rice:
200g basmati rice
100ml coconut milk

For the curry:
2 tbsp coconut oil
500g chicken breast, diced *or* 400g chickpeas plus 350g cauliflower florets
1½ tsp cumin
1 tsp turmeric
1 tsp fenugreek seeds
1 tsp sumac
2 onions, finely sliced
2 cloves garlic, minced
Thumb-sized piece of ginger, peeled and minced
1 red chilli, finely sliced
300ml coconut milk
400g tinned plum tomatoes
Fresh coriander to serve (optional)

1. Heat a casserole dish or large saucepan over a medium/high heat and add 1 tbsp coconut oil. Once hot, fry the chicken for 3 minutes on each side, then remove from the pan onto a plate. (Skip this step if making a chickpea curry, just heat the oil.)
2. Tip the spices into the pan and toast for 1 minute or until fragrant.
3. Turn the heat down to low and add 1 tbsp coconut oil to the pan. Add the onion, garlic, ginger and chilli and cook for

5–10 minutes, or until the onion has softened but not coloured.

4. Stir in the coconut milk and plum tomatoes, then fill up the tomato tin with water and add to the pan. Break the tomatoes up with the back of a spoon then turn up the heat to bring to the boil. Turn down the heat and leave to simmer gently for 15–20 minutes, stirring occasionally, until starting to thicken.
5. Return the chicken to the pan and simmer for a further 15 minutes, lid on, or until the chicken is cooked through. Or, add the chickpeas and cauliflower and cook until the cauliflower is tender.
6. Meanwhile, prepare the rice. Rinse the rice thoroughly then pour into a saucepan with the coconut milk and a generous pinch of salt. Add enough cold water so that there is 1.5cm of water above the level of rice. Cook for 10 minutes over a medium/low heat, with the lid off, stirring occasionally, until the rice is cooked and the water has been absorbed. Leave the rice to steam with the lid on for 5 minutes then fluff up with a fork and taste for seasoning, adding salt as needed.
7. Serve the curry with the rice and top with fresh coriander if you like.

Roasted Butternut Squash Dhal

When I'm on my own in the evening, this is my go-to cosy bowl of food. I usually have some portions in the freezer so I can have dinner ready to eat with zero effort. I top it with chopped coriander and a pinch of good sea salt. If my husband is eating with me, he has a portion of a protein on the side.

Serves 4

1 butternut squash, peeled and diced (approximately 480g)
2 tbsp coconut oil
1 tsp cumin
1 tsp turmeric
1 tsp garam masala
½ tsp cayenne
Pinch of fenugreek seeds
1 red onion, finely chopped
2 cloves garlic, minced
3 tomatoes, chopped
200g red lentils, rinsed
500ml vegetable stock
75g spinach
Fresh coriander, to serve

1. Preheat the oven to 200°C.
2. Toss the butternut squash with 1 tbsp coconut oil and the cumin. Spread out onto a baking tray and roast for 25–30 minutes, turning halfway through.
3. Meanwhile, toast the remaining spices in a dry casserole dish for 30 seconds until fragrant.
4. Add 1 tbsp coconut oil to the pan. Once hot, add the onion and garlic and fry gently for 5 minutes until softened. Add the tomatoes and cook for 3 minutes more.
5. Tip the lentils into the pan and pour over the stock. Mix well and cook for 15 minutes or until the lentils are soft.
6. Add the spinach and cook until wilted, then stir through the roasted squash and serve. Top with fresh coriander.

Monkfish Curry

Another option for Friday nights – although this curry is lovely on any night of the week. Making your own curry paste means you get the flavour and health benefits of the spices being fresh.

Serves 2

For the curry paste:
- 1 tsp cumin seeds
- 1 lemongrass stalk, tough outer layer removed then roughly chopped
- Juice of 2 limes
- 4 green chillies
- 3 garlic cloves, peeled and roughly chopped
- Thumb-sized piece of ginger, peeled and roughly chopped
- 3 dried lime leaves
- 1 tbsp fish sauce
- 15g fresh coriander
- 3 tbsp coconut oil

For the curry:
- 300g monkfish (or other firm white fish), cut into bitesize pieces
- ½ tsp turmeric
- 1 tbsp coconut oil
- 5 tbsp curry paste
- 2 cloves garlic, minced
- 1 tsp fresh ginger, grated
- 400ml coconut milk
- 150ml fish stock
- 100g mange tout
- 100g tenderstem broccoli, larger stalks halved lengthwise
- Handful Thai basil, roughly chopped
- Half a lime, cut into wedges (to serve)

1. Begin by making the curry paste. Toast the cumin seeds in a dry frying pan for 1–2 minutes or until fragrant, then tip into a blender with the rest of the curry paste ingredients. Blend until smooth.

2. Sprinkle the fish with the turmeric and a large pinch of salt, toss to coat then set aside.
3. Heat the oil in a deep frying pan or casserole dish over a low heat then add the curry paste, ginger and garlic. Fry for 2–3 minutes, stirring frequently.
4. Pour in the coconut milk and fish stock. Turn up the heat to bring to the boil then turn down to a simmer and cook for 15 minutes.
5. Add the mange tout, broccoli and fish to the sauce and simmer for 4–5 minutes or until the vegetable are tender and the fish is cooked through.
6. Stir through the Thai basil, reserving a few leaves for garnish, and serve with lime wedges on the side. Serve with rice.

Tip: Extra curry paste can be frozen in ice cube trays for later use.

Lemon and Herb Chicken Casserole

This is a complete meal in a single pot – just what you need at the end of a busy day. Lemon is high in vitamin C – an antioxidant that supports the immune system and skin health, both of which can be affected by hormonal changes during perimenopause.

Serves 2

4 skinless, boneless chicken thighs
1 tbsp coconut oil
1 bulb fennel, sliced
2 shallots, sliced
1 garlic clove, finely sliced
300ml chicken stock
Zest and juice of 1 lemon
150g baby new potatoes, halved
85g French beans
50g kale, roughly chopped
½ bunch parsley, chopped

1. Season the chicken with salt and pepper then heat the oil in a casserole dish over a medium/high heat. Fry the chicken for 5 minutes on each side until golden, then remove from the pan and onto a plate.
2. Add the fennel and shallots to the pan with a splash of water and cook for 2–3 minutes. Add the garlic and cook for a few more minutes until the fennel has softened.
3. Pour in the stock and lemon juice and zest, then return the chicken to the pan along with any resting juices. Add the potatoes and green beans then cover the pan and simmer for 5 minutes. Add the kale and continue cooking for 10 more minutes, or until the chicken is cooked through and the potatoes and green beans are tender.
4. Season to taste then stir through the parsley and serve.

Lime Chicken Thighs with Super Green Cauliflower Rice

The double veg rice gives you two kinds of cruciferous vegetables in one hit! Made as it is below, it's a low-carb option. If you want to add some carbs, stir through some cooked rice or quinoa.

Serves 2

4 chicken thighs
1 tbsp coconut oil

For the marinade:
6 spring onions
15g coriander, tough stalks removed
2 cloves garlic
Zest and juice of 2 limes

1½ tbsp tamari
2 tbsp olive oil
½ tsp flaked salt

For the super green cauliflower rice:
200g cauliflower
200g broccoli
Large handful spinach

1. Set aside one spring onion then roughly chop the remaining five. Pulse together in a food processor with the rest of the marinade ingredients into a coarse puree.
2. Reserve a quarter of the marinade then pour the rest into a bowl. Add the chicken thighs and toss around in the marinade. Leave to marinate at room temperature for 30 minutes.
3. Preheat the oven to 180°C.
4. Heat the coconut oil in a frying pan over a high heat and fry the chicken thighs, skin side down, for 5 minutes or until the skin is crisp and golden. Place the chicken thighs onto a baking tray and pour over the marinade from the bowl. Roast for 30 minutes or until cooked through.

5. Meanwhile, prepare the rice. Blitz the cauliflower, broccoli and spinach together in a food processor into a rice-like consistency. Heat the reserved marinade in a large frying pan and cook for 2–3 minutes. Add the blitzed vegetables with a splash of water and cook for 5 minutes, stirring occasionally until tender.
6. Slice the remaining spring onion. Serve the vegetable rice topped with the chicken thighs and spring onion.

Mackerel and Watermelon Noodle Salad

If you prepare the dressing in advance, this whole meal can take 15 minutes from fridge to table. This is fast food but the kind you do need in your life! Mackerel is a great protein as it's full of anti-inflammatory omega-3 good fats and high in vitamin D and calcium.

Serves 2

150g buckwheat noodles
2 smoked mackerel fillets
10cm piece cucumber, deseeded and sliced
200g watermelon, diced
3 spring onions, finely sliced
25g cashews, chopped
1 tsp black sesame seeds
Handful mint leaves

For the dressing:
Juice and zest of 1 lime
1 tsp fresh ginger, grated
3 tsp tamari
2 tsp rice wine vinegar
2 tbsp sesame oil
1 tsp maple syrup
Pinch of chilli flakes

1. Cook the noodles according to the package instructions, rinse with cold water then toss with a little sesame oil.
2. Make the dressing by mixing all the ingredients together.
3. Heat a griddle pan over a medium heat then cook the mackerel fillets for 2 minutes on each side. Remove the skin and flake the flesh.
4. Mix the cucumber, watermelon and spring onions with the mackerel and noodles, then pour over the dressing, tossing together to combine.
5. Serve the salad topped with the cashews, sesame seeds and mint leaves.

Chargrilled Pork Satay Salad

This uses a really lean cut of pork, although you can also make it with tofu. It works brilliantly cooked on a barbecue in summer – or in the oven for the 50 weeks of the year when it's not warm enough to cook outside! The salad gives your gut bugs a whole lot of fibre to feed on.

Serves 2

300g pork fillet, diced
1 carrot, julienned
½ red pepper, julienned
2 spring onions, thinly sliced
⅛ red cabbage, thinly shredded
1 tbsp coriander, chopped

For the marinade:
2 tbsp tamari
1 tsp curry powder
½ tsp turmeric
1 tsp grated fresh ginger

1 clove garlic, minced
Juice and zest of 1 lime
2 tbsp coconut oil

For the satay sauce:
1½ tbsp peanut butter
½ tbsp tamari
Juice of ½ lime
½ tsp maple syrup
1 small garlic clove, crushed
1 tsp fresh grated ginger

1. Mix together the marinade ingredients, pour over the pork and leave to marinate in the fridge for at least 2 hours, ideally overnight.
2. Remove the pork from the fridge 60 minutes before cooking. Meanwhile, make the satay sauce by mixing all the ingredients together, adding hot water as needed to reach a drizzling consistency.
3. When ready to cook, thread the marinated pork pieces onto skewers and heat a griddle pan over a high heat. Cook for

10–12 minutes, turning regularly, or until cooked through and charred. Leave to rest for 15 minutes while you prepare the salad.

3. Tip the carrot, red pepper, spring onion, red cabbage and coriander into a mixing bowl. Add 1 tbsp of satay sauce and mix together to coat the vegetables. Divide the salad between two plates and serve with the pork skewers and the remaining satay sauce.

Pine Nut Crusted Salmon and Lentils

This dish ticks every box in the Food Framework: two types of protein, rocket providing the leafy greens (rocket is also cruciferous), good fats from the nuts and seeds, lots of fibre and a big boost of flavonoids from the pomegranate.

Serves 2

1 tbsp pine nuts
1 tbsp pumpkin seeds
2 salmon fillets
250g cooked puy lentils
6cm piece of cucumber
2 large handfuls rocket
3 tbsp pomegranate seeds

For the walnut pesto:
(Batch recipe)
30g walnuts
1 clove garlic
30g basil, leaves only
Juice of 1 lemon
½ tsp flaked sea salt
4 tbsp extra virgin olive oil

For the dressing:
2 tbsp extra virgin olive oil
Juice and zest of 1 lemon
Salt and pepper

1. Preheat the oven to 180°C.
2. For the pesto, add the walnuts, garlic, basil, lemon juice and salt to the food processor and blend until finely chopped. With the processor still going, slowly add the olive oil. Check for seasoning and adjust as needed.
3. Chop the pine nuts and pumpkin seeds into a coarse crumb then spread out on a plate.
4. Spread 1 tbsp pesto over the top of the salmon fillets then press into the nut crumb to coat the top. Store the rest of the pesto in a jar; it will keep for five days in the fridge.

5. Transfer to a baking tray lined with unbleached parchment paper and bake for 15 minutes or until cooked through.
6. Whisk the dressing ingredients together, season to taste, then toss with the rest of the salad ingredients.
7. Serve the salmon on top of the salad.

Roasted Cauliflower and Quinoa Salad with Romesco Sauce

The traditional recipe for romesco sauce is made with almonds, and you can use those instead of the hazelnuts in this recipe if you prefer them or that's what you have. Once clients are in the habit of eating cruciferous vegetables daily, they are always asking me for new cauliflower recipes because it's the most adaptable of the cruciferous veg. Steamed cauli reminds me of school, so I don't tend to eat it very often, but I do love it roasted. To make roasted cauli as a side for any dish, you can add your choice of spices; my favourites are garam masala, sumac or paprika, turmeric and chilli flakes.

Serves 2

100g quinoa
1 tsp cumin
½ tsp cayenne
1 tbsp olive oil
1 small head cauliflower, cut into small florets
1 red onion, cut into wedges
35g black olives, pitted
15g watercress
15g rocket
Handful hazelnuts, toasted and roughly chopped
Salt and pepper

For the romesco sauce:
Juice of ½ lemon
1½ tbsp olive oil
½ tsp chilli flakes
50g roasted red peppers (from a jar or make your own)
1 tomato
15g hazelnuts
1 small clove garlic
¼ tsp flaked sea salt
½ tsp smoked paprika

1. Preheat the oven to 180°C.
2. Cook the quinoa according to the package instructions.

3. Mix the spices and oil together then toss on a baking tray with the cauliflower and onion. Roast for 15–20 minutes or until tender and starting to brown.
4. Meanwhile, make the sauce by blending all the ingredients together.
5. Toss the roasted vegetables together with the quinoa, olives, watercress and rocket.
6. Serve topped with the chopped hazelnuts and drizzle with the romesco sauce.

Roasted Vegetable Pasta

Roasting the vegetables brings out the flavour of all the veg in the sauce – it's how the Italians do it. Make sure you use all the garlicky olive oil juices from the roasting tin. If you serve this with lentil or chickpea pasta, you're upping the protein content and making it more filling. Also, did you know that, gram for gram, peppers have more vitamin C than oranges? If you want added protein, crumble over soft goat or feta cheese.

Serves 4

1 red pepper, chopped
1 yellow pepper, chopped
1 courgette, halved lengthwise then sliced
1 red onion, chopped
2 cloves garlic, peeled
2 tbsp olive oil
1 tsp dried oregano

1 tsp smoked paprika
1 tbsp balsamic vinegar
150g cherry tomatoes, halved
250ml vegetable stock
500g gluten-free pasta (such as chickpea, lentil or buckwheat)

1. Preheat the oven to 180°C.
2. Tip the vegetables into a large baking tray and toss with the olive oil, oregano, paprika and balsamic vinegar.
3. Roast for 30 minutes or until starting to caramelise at the edges. Add the tomatoes and stock to the pan and stir everything together. Cook for a further 10 minutes.
4. Remove a third of the vegetables from the tin and puree the rest, seasoning to taste and adding extra stock or water if needed.
5. Meanwhile, cook the pasta for 3 minutes less than the packet instructs and drain.
6. Tip the sauce into a saucepan along with the reserved vegetables and heat through. Stir the pasta through the sauce until al dente.

Sardine Fish Cakes

You probably think of a tin of sardines as a quick lunch option but this recipe is a tasty way to turn sardines into a proper, filling dinner. Using butterbeans instead of mash adds fibre, and the flaxseed replaces an egg, to bind the fishcakes. It's good to get sardines in your regular recipe rotation because they are high in both calcium and vitamin D, crucial for maintaining bone health, as well as good omega-3 fats.

Serves 4

3 tbsp milled flaxseed
400g butterbeans, cooked (drained weight)
Zest and juice of 1 lemon
2 x 120g tins sardines in spring water, drained and finely chopped
4 spring onions, finely sliced
2 tbsp fresh parsley, finely chopped
1 tbsp fresh dill, finely chopped
200g cooked quinoa

For the herb yoghurt:
4 tbsp plant-based, goat or sheep milk yoghurt
2 tsp fresh parsley, finely chopped
2 tsp fresh dill, finely chopped
Juice of ½ lemon
Salt and pepper

1. Preheat the oven to 180°C.
2. Make a flax egg by mixing 1 tbsp milled flax seed with 2.5 tbsp warm water and set aside for 5 minutes until thickened.
3. Meanwhile, tip the butterbeans into the bowl of a food processor along with the lemon juice and zest. Blend until almost smooth.

4. Add the sardines, spring onions, parsley, dill and flax egg then pulse until combined.
5. Mix the remaining 2 tbsp milled flax seed with 5 tbsp warm water in a small bowl. Tip out the quinoa onto a plate.
6. Divide the fish mixture into eight. Roll each into a ball then gently flatten. Dip into the flax seed mixture then roll in the quinoa to coat all sides completely.
7. Lay the fishcakes onto a baking tray and cook for 30–35 minutes or until the quinoa is crisp and the fishcakes are piping hot through.
8. Meanwhile, make the herb yoghurt by mixing the yoghurt with the parsley, dill and lemon juice, then season to taste with salt and pepper.
9. Serve the fishcakes with salad leaves and a spoonful of yoghurt.

Sea Bass and Samphire Salad

I'm lucky enough to live in Jersey, and one of my favourite things is to go to the fish stall in the harbour in St Helier to buy wild sea bass and samphire, when it's in season. Everything from the sea – fish, seafood and sea vegetables – is high in iodine and selenium, minerals needed for thyroid function.

Serves 2

1 tbsp dried dulse red seaweed, crumbled
Juice of 1½ lemons, zest of 1
1 tsp chilli flakes
½ tsp flaked sea salt
¼ tsp coconut sugar
1 tbsp olive oil

2 fillets sea bass
90g samphire
80g watercress
6cm piece cucumber, deseeded and sliced
5 radishes, thinly sliced

1. Mix the seaweed with the juice and zest of 1 lemon, chilli flakes, salt, coconut sugar and oil. Pour into a Ziplock bag with the sea bass fillets and marinate for 30 minutes.
2. Meanwhile, preheat the grill to a medium/high heat. Line a baking tray with foil and place the fish on top, skin side up. Grill for 6–8 minutes or until cooked through and the skin is crisp.
3. Steam the samphire for 5 minutes then toss with the watercress, cucumber, radish and juice of half a lemon.
4. Divide the salad between two plates and top with the sea bass fillets. Sprinkle with a little extra seaweed to serve. Serve with a side of baked sweet potato.

Turkey Burgers with Tzatziki

Turkey isn't just for Christmas – it's a lean source of high-quality protein, good for maintaining muscle mass. It's rich in tryptophan, an amino acid that can help you make the good-mood brain chemical serotonin. Turkey thigh mince is the most versatile – you can use it to replace beef mince in most recipes.

Serves 4

- 1 small courgette, grated
- 1 small potato, peeled and grated
- 2 spring onions, finely sliced
- 1 clove garlic, minced
- 10g fresh mint, finely chopped
- 10g fresh parsley, finely chopped
- Zest of 1 lemon
- 1 egg, beaten (or flax egg)
- 40g ground almonds
- Pinch chilli flakes
- Salt and pepper
- 500g turkey thigh mince
- 1 tbsp coconut oil

For the tzatziki:
- 5cm piece cucumber, deseeded and grated
- 1 tsp fresh mint, finely chopped
- 4 tbsp plant-based yoghurt
- Salt and pepper

1. Squeeze the moisture from the courgette and potato then use your hands to mix it with all other ingredients except the coconut oil.
2. Divide the mixture into 12, shape each piece into a ball then gently flatten.
3. Heat the oil in a frying pan over a medium heat and fry the patties for 3–4 minutes on each side or until golden and cooked through.
4. Make the tzatziki by mixing all ingredients together, season to taste then serve with the burgers. Serve in a red lentil roll (see page 246).

Vegetable Chilli with Guacamole

Depending on the brand, a tin of mixed beans will give you three to six plant foods in one dish, and that's before you consider the onion, peppers, courgettes and tomatoes! There's loads of colour, texture and fibre in this recipe, plus flavonoids in the spices and good fats in the avocado.

Serves 4

1 tbsp coconut oil
1 onion, finely chopped
1 red pepper, finely chopped
1 yellow pepper, finely chopped
2 cloves garlic, minced
1 courgette, finely chopped
2 red chillies, finely chopped
2 tsp cumin
2 tsp smoked paprika
1 tsp dried oregano
2 x 400g tins mixed beans, drained and rinsed
2 x 400g tins plum tomatoes
1 tbsp tomato puree

For the guacamole:
2 avocados, peeled and destoned
1 small tomato, finely chopped
½ small red onion, finely chopped
1 small red chilli, finely chopped
Juice of 1 lime
1 tbsp fresh coriander, finely chopped

1. Heat the oil in a casserole dish over a low heat then gently cook the onion, peppers and garlic for 10 minutes until softened.
2. Add the courgette, chilli and spices and oregano and cook for a further 10 minutes.
3. Add the beans, tomatoes, puree and half a tin of water. Stir well, breaking up the tomatoes with the back of the spoon. Bring to the boil then simmer for 30–40 minutes, stirring occasionally, until thickened and reduced.
4. Meanwhile, make the guacamole. Mash the avocado and mix with the rest of the ingredients, then serve with the chilli.

SIDE DISHES

You can serve these with any of the main meals to bump up your vegetable portions. Or you can serve them alongside your choice of protein, such as grilled or poached fish, tempeh or tofu.

Cayenne Sauerkraut

This is a really brilliant budget recipe. It sounds like a lot of work but it makes a lot! You do need to be around to nurture the sauerkraut every day. I use cayenne not only because it's tasty but you also get a little kick for your metabolism to add to the goodness of this fermented food.

(Batch recipe)

1kg white cabbage, thinly shredded, 1 outer leaf reserved
1½ tbsp flaked sea salt
1 tsp pink peppercorns
1 tsp caraway seeds
⅛ tsp cayenne pepper

1. Tip the cabbage into a large mixing bowl, mix in the salt and leave to sit for 10 minutes.
2. Massage the salt into the cabbage for 10–15 minutes. At the end of this, the cabbage should be soft and reduced in volume by half. There should be a pool of brine in the bottom of the bowl.
3. Stir in the peppercorns, caraway seeds and cayenne, then

transfer the cabbage and brine to a large clean jar and pack tightly. Cut the reserved outer cabbage leaf to fit inside the jar and lay it over the top of the shredded cabbage.
4. Place a weight into the jar, such as a ramekin or egg cup, to press down the cabbage so it is covered in brine. Seal the jar tightly.
5. Leave to ferment in a cool dark place for seven days. Loosen the lid once a day to release any gases that have built up through the fermentation process. Give it a stir then reseal.
6. Taste the sauerkraut after seven days. Once the flavour is to your liking, transfer to smaller jars and store in the fridge to slow down the fermentation. Continue to ferment out of the fridge for up to four weeks for a stronger flavour.

Brussel Sprout Slaw

This slaw is for the days when you feel in need of some crunch and tanginess. It goes with any protein, particularly grilled meat or fish, and it also works as a good lunchbox filler.

(Batch recipe)

200g Brussels sprouts, finely shredded
60g radish, thinly sliced
120g carrot, grated
40g red onion, finely sliced

2 tbsp pumpkin seeds
3 tbsp extra virgin olive oil
2 tbsp apple cider vinegar
2 tsp wholegrain mustard
Salt

To prepare the slaw, mix the vegetables and pumpkin seeds. Whisk together the olive oil, vinegar, mustard and a pinch of salt (or to taste) until emulsified then tip over the slaw and mix to combine.

'Cheesy' Cauliflower Mash

The ultimate comfort food side – I could eat this by the bowlful. It also ticks off two of your daily veg categories: cauliflower for the cruciferous veg and spinach for leafy greens.

Serves 4

- 500g cauliflower, cut into small florets
- 2 tbsp nutritional yeast
- 3-4 tbsp plant-based milk
- 40g chopped spinach
- Salt and pepper

1. Put the cauliflower into a large saucepan along with 3 tbsp water and a pinch of salt. Cover with a lid and steam for 5 minutes or until the cauliflower is tender.
2. Tip the cooked cauliflower into a food processor and add the nutritional yeast. Blend until smooth, adding the milk gradually until you reach a creamy consistency.
3. Scoop the mash back into the saucepan and place over a low heat to heat back through, then add the spinach. Stir until wilted then taste for seasoning and adjust to taste.

Balsamic Braised Red Cabbage

When I cook a Sunday roast, I aim to make as many brightly coloured veg as I can to go on the plate. This dish is an absolute beauty. It does take around an hour to cook (plus prep) but on the upside, it's very little work.

Serves 4

1 tsp olive oil
400g red cabbage (approx. ½ cabbage), thinly sliced
80ml balsamic vinegar
Salt and pepper

1. Heat the oil in a large frying pan or casserole dish over medium heat. Once hot, add the cabbage and give it a good stir to coat in the oil. Turn the heat down to low and cook for 30 minutes, stirring occasionally.
2. Season the cabbage with salt and pepper, then add the balsamic vinegar and stir well.
3. Cook for a further 20–30 minutes, stirring occasionally as before, until the vinegar has absorbed and the cabbage is tender.

Sauteed Kale with Garlic and Chilli

Not everyone is a fan of kale – that is, until they try this dish! The key is in flavouring the oil before you add the kale.

Serves 2

- 1 tbsp olive oil
- 2 cloves garlic, thinly sliced
- ¼–½ red chilli, deseeded and finely chopped
- 160g shredded kale, tough stalks removed
- Juice of ½ lemon
- Salt and pepper

1. Heat the oil in a large frying pan over a medium heat and add the garlic and chilli. Cook for 2–3 minutes or until softened but not coloured.
2. Add the kale in batches, stirring to coat in the flavoured oil until all the kale is in the pan. Add a pinch of salt and 2 tbsp water and cook for 5 minutes or until the kale is tender.
3. Squeeze over the lemon juice and season to taste.

Lemon and Garlic Broccoli

Broccoli is the cruciferous veg that people often end up eating quite often. If you're bored of broccoli, this is a great way to add some flavour.

Serves 2

1 tsp olive oil
1 clove garlic, thinly sliced
1 head of broccoli, cut into florets
½ lemon

1. Heat the oil in a small pan and fry the garlic over a low heat until softened and just starting to colour.
2. Zest and juice the lemon into a small bowl then add the cooked garlic.
3. Prepare your steamer and bring the water to the boil. Pop the squeezed lemon half into the water.
4. Tip the broccoli into the steamer, cover and steam for 5 minutes or until just tender.
5. Transfer to a serving dish, toss in the lemon and garlic and season to taste.

Vegetable Boulangère

Sometimes my clients say they are bored with plain veg, but this recipe is far from boring. It's my alternative to dairy-laden potato Dauphinoise but made with mixed root vegetables for varied sources of fibre and added nutrients. If I have leftovers the next day, I'll add more hot stock and blend into a soup.

Serves 4

1 tsp olive oil
2 carrots
1 large parsnip

1 bulb of fennel
1 medium leek
500ml vegetable stock

1. Preheat the oven to 180°C.
2. Use the olive oil to grease a deep baking dish, approximately 20cm x 30cm.
3. Slice the vegetables as thinly as possible; you may find this easiest to do using a mandolin.
4. Arrange the parsnips in a thin layer to cover the bottom of the dish. Season lightly with salt and pepper then layer the rest of the vegetables in the same way, seasoning each layer as you go.
5. Pour over the stock then cover with foil. Cook in the oven for 40 minutes then remove the foil and cook for a further 20 minutes, or until the vegetables are tender and most of the stock has been absorbed.

SAUCES AND DRESSINGS

I've included the recipes for the four sauces and dressings that people tell me they make on repeat. They will make at least two servings and where they make more, these are good in the fridge for up to five days.

Lemon Gremolata

20g fresh parsley, leaves only, finely chopped
1 tsp lemon zest
1 tsp freshly squeezed lemon juice
1 clove garlic, minced
2 tbsp extra virgin olive oil
Salt

Stir everything together and season with salt to taste.

Everyday Dressing

Juice of ½ lemon
1 tbsp organic apple cider vinegar
1 tsp Dijon mustard
Zest of an unwaxed lemon
5 tbsp extra virgin olive oil
Pinch of sea salt and fresh black pepper
1 tbsp freshly chopped parsley or basil

Put all ingredients into a jam jar and shake to mix well.

Pumpkin Seed Pesto

You can adapt this recipe by using other nuts and seeds – pine nuts are the classic and walnuts are very good – and with different herbs as well as spinach and rocket.

30g pumpkin seeds
1 clove garlic
25g basil, leaves only
15g parsley, leaves and tender stems only

Juice of 1 lemon
½ tsp flaked sea salt
60ml extra virgin olive oil

Add the garlic, basil, parsley, lemon juice and salt to the food processor and blend until finely chopped. With the processor still going, slowly add the olive oil. Check for seasoning and adjust as needed.

Miso Tahini Dressing

2 tbsp tahini
2 tbsp sweet white miso paste
3 tsp lemon juice
3 tbsp extra virgin olive oil

1 crushed garlic clove
2 tsp hot water
¼ tsp tamari

Whisk together the tahini, miso, lemon juice, tamari, olive oil, garlic and a pinch of salt and pepper. Add the water a spoonful at a time to achieve your desired consistency. Taste for seasoning and adjust as needed.

CAKES AND PUDDINGS

You might not expect to see these in this book. But the PCM approach isn't about denial, it's about living 80:20. That means that if you want to, you can have delicious, sweet foods – just not every day. And if you do enjoy something sweet, why not go for the options that are not only tasty but have nutritional value?

Apricot Seeded Flapjacks

There are flapjacks, then there are PCM flapjacks, with the goodness and fibre of four different nuts and seeds. Pumpkin seeds alone give you healthy fats, protein, magnesium (for bone health, sleep regulation and mood), zinc (for immune function and skin health) and phytoestrogens that may help balance hormones.

Makes 12

- 175g Medjool dates, destoned
- 240ml warm water
- 2 tbsp coconut oil, melted
- ½ tsp vanilla extract
- 200g gluten-free oats
- 40g pistachios, roughly chopped
- 35g desiccated coconut
- 25g pumpkin seeds
- 25g sunflower seeds
- ½ tsp cinnamon
- 1½ tsp baking powder

1. Preheat the oven to 180°C and line a 20cm square baking tin with baking paper.
2. Tip the dates and water into a food processor and blend into a smooth paste. Mix in the coconut oil and vanilla then tip into a large mixing bowl.
3. Add the dry ingredients and mix well. Tip the mixture into the prepared tin and use the back of a spoon to press the mixture firmly into the tin.
4. Bake for 20 minutes or until golden and cooked through. Allow to cool in the tin then use a sharp knife to cut it into 12 squares.

Avocado Lime Cheesecake

This cheesecake came about many years ago, when I spent a year in the US and fell in love with key lime pie. At the time, I had intolerances to gluten and dairy, but I thought, Why should I miss out on eating something I love? *So I created this recipe and I've been tweaking it ever since.*

Serves 12

For the base:
100g Medjool dates, destoned
250g almonds
2 tbsp cacao powder
2 tbsp coconut oil

For the filling:
240g cashews
50g coconut oil
90g coconut cream
2 ripe avocados
Juice of 8 limes
Zest of 2 limes
6 tbsp maple syrup
3 tbsp pistachios, roughly chopped, to serve

1. Tip the cashews into a jug and pour in enough water to cover. Leave to soak for at least 4 hours.
2. Meanwhile, prepare the base by blending the four ingredients in a food processor into a biscuit crumb consistency. Tip the crumb into a 20cm loose bottomed tart or cake tin and press down firmly into an even layer. Refrigerate for at least 2 hours.
3. Once the cashews have finished soaking, drain them thoroughly and tip into the bowl of a food processor along with the rest of the filling ingredients. Blend on high until smooth then pour over the prepared base. Smooth out the top then refrigerate for 12 hours or overnight.
4. When ready to serve, carefully remove from the tin and scatter with the chopped pistachios.

Carrot Cake Muffins

This is the most joyful thing you can do with a carrot! They're like little mini carrot cakes that you can put in your lunch box. You don't have to add the frosting but it's the icing on the cake (literally).

Makes 12

125g almond flour
25g arrowroot powder
½ tsp baking powder
½ tsp bicarbonate of soda
½ tsp cinnamon
25g desiccated coconut
2 medium free-range eggs
50ml maple syrup
85ml coconut oil, melted
2 tbsp almond milk (or other plant-based milk)
Zest and juice of 1 orange
Zest of 1 lemon

100g carrot, coarsely grated
1 medium eating apple, coarsely grated
35g pecans, chopped

For the cashew butter frosting:
100g cashew butter
1½ tbsp maple syrup
4 tbsp almond milk (or other plant-based milk)
Shredded coconut to decorate (optional)

1. Preheat the oven to 180°C and line a 12-hole muffin tin with paper cases.
2. Sift the almond flour, arrowroot, baking powder, bicarbonate of soda and cinnamon into a large mixing bowl, then stir in the desiccated coconut.
3. In a separate bowl, whisk the eggs with the maple syrup, coconut oil, almond milk, orange and lemon zest, and orange juice.
4. Stir in the carrot, apple and pecans, then mix into the dry ingredients. Divide the batter between the muffin cases and

bake for 20–25 minutes or until golden and a skewer inserted into the centre comes out clean. Transfer to a wire rack to cool completely.
5. Meanwhile, prepare the frosting by beating the cashew butter and maple syrup together with an electric whisk. Add the almond milk a little at a time until you reach a creamy, spreadable consistency. You may not need all of the milk.
6. Once your muffins are cool, spread over the frosting and add a sprinkle of shredded coconut if using.

Chocolate and Hazelnut Cookies

People can't tell these are flour- and refined sugar-free – they often assume they are some kind of sophisticated Italian recipe because of the hazelnuts. Hazelnuts are packed with healthy monounsaturated fats (for heart health), vitamin E (for skin), magnesium (for sleep) and calcium (for bones).

Makes 8

125g hazelnut butter
75g coconut oil, melted
6 tbsp maple syrup
2 tsp vanilla extract
1 medium free-range egg, beaten

45g ground almonds
½ tsp baking powder
½ tsp fine sea salt
60g dark chocolate, chopped
Flaked sea salt

1. Beat the hazelnut butter, coconut oil, maple syrup and vanilla extract together with an electric whisk until completely smooth, then beat in the egg.
2. Add the ground almonds, baking powder and salt, and beat again until fully combined.
3. Stir in the chocolate by hand then chill the dough in the fridge for at least 2 hours (ideally overnight) or until firm.
4. Preheat the oven to 180°C and line a large baking tray with baking paper.
5. Spoon heaped tablespoons of dough onto the baking tray, spacing well apart. Sprinkle with a little flaked salt then bake for 10–12 minutes or until golden. Cool on the tray for 5 minutes then transfer to a wire rack to cool completely.

Chocolate and Walnut Brownies

The walnut and chocolate combination in these rich brownies is a tried-and-tested crowd pleaser. You can't buy coconut butter in the supermarket, but it's available online and often in health food shops.

Makes 12

80g coconut butter
250g dark chocolate, roughly chopped
3 medium free-range eggs
2 tbsp almond milk (or plant-based milk of choice)

1 tsp vanilla extract
30g cacao powder
40g arrowroot powder
¼ tsp fine sea salt
150g coconut sugar
50g walnuts, roughly chopped

1. Preheat the oven to 180°C and grease and line a 20cm square tin with baking paper.
2. Melt the coconut butter with 200g of the dark chocolate in a bain-marie then leave to cool while you prepare the other ingredients.
3. Whisk the eggs with the almond milk and vanilla extract.
4. In a separate bowl, sieve the cacao, arrowroot and salt together.
5. Stir the coconut sugar into the melted chocolate then add the beaten egg mixture and stir well to combine.
6. Add the sieved cacao and arrowroot and fold in along with the walnuts and remaining 50g chocolate chunks. Pour into the prepared tin and spread into an even layer.
7. Bake for 20 minutes for a gooey brownie or 25 minutes if you prefer it a little firmer.

Chocolate Cheesecake

This version of a plant-based cheesecake is probably the most indulgent pudding I make. Cacao is a great source of flavonoids, which are good for bone health, liver health and for mood too, as well as anti-inflammatory compounds. It even contains some fibre!

Serves 12

For the crust:
195g almonds
9 Medjool dates
3 tbsp cacao powder
3 tbsp coconut oil, melted
¼ tsp fine sea salt

For the filling:
300g cashew nuts
5 tbsp maple syrup
100g coconut oil, melted
75g dark chocolate, chopped
130g cashew butter
260g coconut cream
1 tsp vanilla extract
2 tbsp cacao powder
¼ tsp fine sea salt

Cacao nibs, to serve (optional)

1. Begin by soaking the cashews for at least 1 hour in enough boiling water to cover them.
2. Meanwhile, prepare the crust by placing all the ingredients into a food processor and process into a coarse, uniform crumb. Tip into a 20cm loose-bottomed tin and press firmly into an even layer. Chill in the fridge while you make the filling.
3. In a small pan, melt together the maple syrup, coconut oil, dark chocolate and cashew butter over a medium/low heat and whisk until smooth.
4. Once the cashews have finished soaking, rinse and drain them. In a high-power blender, blend the cashews with the coconut cream and vanilla until smooth.

5. Add the melted chocolate mix, cacao powder and salt to the blender and blend on high until silky smooth, scraping down the sides of the blender as necessary.
6. Pour the filling over the prepared base and return to the fridge for 4–6 hours, or until firm. Scatter with cacao nibs before serving, if you'd like to.

Lemon Drizzle Cake

This is slightly heavier than the usual lemon drizzle cake, due to the flour being replaced by ground almonds, but it's just as more-ish. Lemons are packed with vitamin C, which supports immune function and collagen synthesis, and including the zest makes it good for liver function too.

Serves 8

330g ground almonds
1 tsp baking powder
½ tsp bicarbonate of soda
Juice and zest of 4 lemons
80g coconut oil, melted
80g maple syrup

2 tsp vanilla extract
4 medium free-range eggs

For the drizzle:
Zest and juice of 2 lemons
3 tbsp maple syrup
2 tbsp water

1. Preheat the oven to 160°C and line a 2lb loaf tin with parchment paper.
2. Whisk together the ground almonds, baking powder, bicarbonate of soda and lemon zest.
3. In a separate bowl or jug, whisk together the lemon juice, coconut oil, maple syrup, vanilla and eggs.
4. Stir the wet ingredients into the dry then spoon into the prepared tin. Bake for 50–55 mins or until a skewer inserted into the centre comes out clean.
5. Meanwhile, prepare the drizzle. Bring all the ingredients to the boil in a small saucepan, then simmer until reduced to the consistency of maple syrup. Set aside until the cake is cooked.
6. As soon as the cake is out of the oven, prick holes all over the top using a skewer or cocktail stick, going deep into the cake. Pour over the drizzle and leave to cool in the tin for 10 minutes before transferring to a wire rack to cool completely.

Millionaire Shortcake

The pecan base is smoky and nutty, a lovely contrast to the caramel and chocolate. And pecans are full of good fats, fibre and vitamin E. Plus, the combination of salt and sweet is so delicious.

Makes 12

For the shortcake:
300g pecans
1 tbsp coconut oil, melted
5 Medjool dates, destoned

For the caramel:
70ml maple syrup
150g coconut oil
180g cashew butter

1 tsp vanilla extract
Pinch fine sea salt

For the chocolate:
100g coconut oil
60g cacao powder
2 tbsp maple syrup
1 tsp vanilla extract
Pinch fine sea salt

1. Line a 20cm square tin with baking paper.
2. Prepare the shortcake by blending the pecans, coconut oil and dates in a food processor into a fine crumb. Tip into the lined tin and press down firmly into an even layer. Place in the fridge whist you make the caramel.
3. Put the maple syrup, coconut oil, cashew butter, vanilla and salt into a small saucepan and heat over a medium/low heat, whisking until smooth. Pour over the shortcake base and return to the fridge for 1–2 hours or until completely firm.
4. Melt the chocolate ingredients together in a small saucepan over a medium/low heat until smooth. Set aside to cool.
5. Once the chocolate has cooled, pour over the caramel layer and chill for 30–60 minutes or until firm. To serve, remove from the tin and slice into 12 pieces.

Raspberry and Blueberry Almond Cake

Berries are very high in flavonoids, blue-red antioxidant compounds that support liver health, are anti-inflammatory and are great for skin. This cake is so easy to make that I used to throw it together in the morning to put in my daughter Poppy's school lunch box. As the recipe is based on ground almonds and contains very little sugar, it's filling and doesn't spike blood sugar. And if she didn't finish it, her friends would always call first dibs on what was left!

Serves 8

200g ground almonds
1 tbsp arrowroot powder
3 tbsp coconut sugar
½ tsp bicarbonate of soda
3 medium free-range eggs

3 tbsp coconut butter, melted
1 tsp vanilla extract
75g raspberries
75g blueberries
2 tbsp flaked almonds

1. Preheat oven to 180°C and grease and line a 20cm round cake tin with baking paper.
2. Whisk together the ground almonds, arrowroot, coconut sugar and bicarbonate of soda.
3. In a separate bowl, beat the eggs together with the coconut butter and vanilla.
4. Gently mix the wet ingredients into the dry then pour into the tin. Use a spatula to spread into an even layer then press the berries into the batter. Scatter over the flaked almonds then bake for 25–30 minutes or until golden and a skewer inserted into the centre comes out clean.

Seed Crusted Banana Bread

You probably already have a banana bread recipe but please don't discount this one! With almonds, flaxseeds, walnuts and a variety of mixed seeds to top it off, it's a great source of good fats. Bananas and walnuts are two of the plant foods that contain tryptophan, an amino acid that the body converts into serotonin, enhancing mood and promoting better sleep.

Serves 12

- 3 medium very ripe bananas
- 50g coconut butter or oil, melted
- 3 tbsp maple syrup
- 2 tsp vanilla extract
- 3 medium free-range eggs, beaten
- 200g ground almonds
- 40g ground flaxseed
- 1 tsp baking powder
- ½ tsp bicarbonate of soda
- 1 tsp ground cinnamon
- 40g walnuts, chopped
- 25g mixed seeds, such as pumpkin, sunflower or flax

1. Preheat the oven to 180°C and grease and line a 2lb loaf tin.
2. Mash the bananas with a fork in a mixing bowl, then stir in the coconut butter or oil, maple syrup, vanilla and beaten eggs.
3. In a separate bowl whisk together the ground almonds, ground flaxseed, baking powder, bicarbonate of soda, cinnamon and walnuts.
4. Add the wet ingredients to the dry and mix until just combined. Pour into the prepared tin then scatter the mixed seeds over the top. Bake for 30–35 minutes or until golden and a skewer inserted into the centre comes out clean.

TEAS

Pippa's Sleepy Witches' Brew

This powerful combination of herbs works on the nervous system to relax the mind and body before sleep. Just the act of making this tea is therapeutic, an important part of my evening wind-down routine. My husband named it my 'witches' brew' because he finds it amusing to watch me pick and measure out the herbs for the concoction – and because he finds it so effective that if I'm not around, he'll now make it for himself.

Serves 2

1 tsp each chamomile, valerian, passionflower, lemon balm
dried herbs

Add freshly boiled hot water, infuse for 10 minutes and drink.

Stress and Anxiety Support Tea

Oat straw and skullcap leaf both support the nervous system and can increase resilience to stress. This is my go-to tea for when I'm feeling a little anxious. Like many nerve restorative herbs, these have an almost sweet taste, so you can easily drink this tea all day.

Serves 1

1 tsp each oat straw and skullcap

½ tsp lemon balm (optional, to lift mood)

Add freshly boiled hot water, infuse for 10 minutes and drink.

Liver Support Tea

This is the recipe I give clients who do my yearly January Detox Plan. Dandelion root increases both the production of bile in the liver and stored bile in the gall bladder. Milk thistle supports and regenerates the liver by increasing levels of the antioxidant glutathione. Burdock root is a diuretic which helps to eliminate excess water. For this reason, don't drink this tea close to bedtime!

2 parts dandelion root
1 part burdock root

1 part artichoke leaf
1 part crushed milk thistle seeds

Place herbs in a pan and add 2 cups water. Simmer for 15 minutes, strain and drink throughout the morning.

Acid Reflux Tea

Marshmallow root is so helpful during perimenopause because it's soothing and anti-inflammatory. It's helpful for managing dryness of mucous membranes including the skin, digestive tract and vaginal area. And it's soothing for indigestion or acid reflux, which some women experience more at this time.

Serves 1

1 tsp marshmallow root

Add freshly boiled hot water, infuse for 10 minutes and drink.

Cold Remedy Tea

This tea is slightly more hardcore due to the addition of sliced garlic. That said, when you have a cold, you won't taste it while it's working its magic! Both rosemary and garlic have anti-inflammatory and antimicrobial properties, plus the lemon gives a dose of vitamin C.

2 sprigs fresh rosemary
1 fresh garlic clove, sliced
Juice of 1 lemon
A little raw honey to sweeten (optional)

Add freshly boiled hot water. Infuse for 10 minutes and drink.

Endnotes

CHAPTER 1

Page 22: For example, one study showed that midlife women going though stressful life events have 21 per cent more hot flushes.

Arnot ,M., Emmott, E.H., Mace, R. The relationship between social support, stressful events, and menopause symptoms. PLoS One. 2021 Jan 27;16(1):e0245444. doi: 10.1371/journal.pone.0245444. PMID: 33503073; PMCID: PMC7840006.

CHAPTER 2

Page 42: People aged under 40 can have 17 to 41 per cent less muscle strength than people over 40.

Keller, K., Engelhardt, M. Strength and muscle mass loss with aging process. Age and strength loss. Muscles Ligaments Tendons J. 2014 Feb 24;3(4):346–50. PMID: 24596700; PMCID: PMC3940510.

Page 42: One study showed that people who eat more brightly coloured yellow/orange/red vegetables, beans and pulses, and cruciferous vegetables tend to feel less stressed.

Radavelli-Bagatini, S., Sim, M., Blekkenhorst, L.C. et al. Associations of specific types of fruit and vegetables with perceived stress in adults: the AusDiab study. Eur J Nutr 61, 2929–2938 (2022).

CHAPTER 3

Page 56: Studies also suggest they could also help reduce appetite, improve skin and support bone health.

Desmawati, D., Sulastri, D. Phytoestrogens and Their Health Effect. Open Access Maced J Med Sci. 2019 Feb 14;7(3):495–499. doi: 10.3889/oamjms.2019.044. PMID: 30834024; PMCID: PMC6390141.

Page 58: In a study of women who had been diagnosed with PCOS, the group that did seed cycling as well as portion control had better hormone balance at the end of three months.

Rasheed, N., Ahmed, A., Nosheen, F., Imran, A., Islam, F., Noreen, R., Chauhan, A., Shah, M.A., Amer, Ali, Y. Effectiveness of combined seeds (pumpkin, sunflower, sesame, flaxseed): As adjacent therapy to treat polycystic ovary syndrome in females. Food Sci Nutr. 2023 Mar 25;11(6):3385–3393. doi: 10.1002/fsn3.3328. PMID: 37324929; PMCID: PMC10261760.

Page 59: If your cycle has stopped, start day one of seed cycling on the first day of the new moon; it may be that seed cycling helps reboot your cycle.

Brooks, J.D., Ward, W.E., Lewis, J.E., Hilditch, J., Nickell, L., Wong, E., Thompson, L.U. Supplementation with flaxseed alters oestrogen metabolism in postmenopausal women to a greater extent than does supplementation with an equal amount of soy. Am, J. Clin Nutr. 2004 Feb;79(2):318--25. doi: 10.1093/ajcn/79.2.318. PMID: 14749240.

CHAPTER 4

Pages 66-67: It's been shown to work for anxiety, depression, sleep and even to reduce hot flushes. It's clear that the more you practise, the better the results.

Xiao, C., Mou, C., Zhou, X., Effect of mindfulness meditation training on anxiety, depression and sleep quality in perimenopausal women]. Nan Fang Yi Ke Da Xue Xue Bao. 2019 Aug 30;39(8):998–1002. Chinese. doi: 10.12122/j.issn.1673-4254.2019.08.19. PMID: 31511223; PMCID: PMC6765589.

ENDNOTES | 321

Page 67: Mindfulness-based cognitive therapy (MBCT) is a structured course that's been shown to help with menopausal symptoms. You can find more information at oxfordmindfulness.org.

John, J.B., Chellaiyan, D.V.G., Gupta, S., Nithyanandham, R. How Effective the Mindfulness-Based Cognitive Behavioral Therapy on Quality of Life in Women With Menopause. J Midlife Health. 2022 Apr–Jun;13(2):169–174. doi: 10.4103/jmh.jmh_178_21. Epub 2022 Sep 16. PMID: 36276630; PMCID: PMC9583372.

Page 67: In a 12-week trial of people who'd been put into menopause due to breast cancer treatment, the group that did yoga and meditation had fewer psychological symptoms, less fatigue and an improved quality of life, but also fewer urogenital symptoms.

Cramer, H., Rabsilber, S., Lauche, R., Kümmel, S., Dobos, G. Yoga and meditation for menopausal symptoms in breast cancer survivors – A randomized controlled trial. Cancer. 2015 Jul 1;121(13):2175–84. doi: 10.1002/cncr.29330. Epub 2015 Mar 4. PMID: 25739642.

Page 68: In a recent study, this came out as the most effective way to reduce anxiety and improve mood, over other types of breathwork and meditation. Inhale slowly through your nose until your lungs feel full, then inhale again until they feel very full. The second inhale will be short. Let your breath out slowly through your mouth.

Balban, M.Y., Neri, E., Kogon, M.M., Weed, L., Nouriani, B., Jo, B., Holl, G., Zeitzer, J.M., Spiegel, D., Huberman, A.D. Brief structured respiration practices enhance mood and reduce physiological arousal. Cell Rep Med. 2023 Jan 17;4(1):100895. doi: 10.1016/j.xcrm.2022.100895. Epub 2023 Jan 10. PMID: 36630953; PMCID: PMC9873947.

Page 69: Going barefoot, a.k.a. grounding. Not only is this good for the many little muscles in our feet and ankles, but there is a small amount of research to show that being barefoot outside or on natural surfaces helps lower cortisol levels

Sinatra, S.T., Sinatra, D.S., Sinatra, S.W., Chevalier, G. Grounding The universal anti-inflammatory remedy. Biomed J. 2023 Feb;46(1):11–16. doi: 10.1016/j.bj.2022.12.002. Epub 2022 Dec 15. PMID: 36528336; PMCID: PMC10105021.

Page 69: Research shows that spending 120 minutes a week in nature leads to better wellbeing and health overall.

White, M.P., Alcock, I., Grellier, J., et al. Spending at least 120 minutes a week in nature is associated with good health and wellbeing. Sci Rep 9, 7730 (2019). https://doi.org/10.1038/s41598-019-44097-3

Page 71: I'm also seeing a lot of clients who put their body under stress by fasting for too long, or over too many days, or who are doing cold plunges or cold-water swimming despite feeling worse afterwards.

Li, X., Yang, T., Sun, Z., Hormesis in Health and Chronic Diseases. Trends Endocrinol Metab. 2019 Dec;30(12):944–958. doi: 10.1016/j.tem.2019.08.007. Epub 2019 Sep 11. PMID: 31521464; PMCID: PMC6875627.

Page 72: A lot of women are nervous of building muscle but it's such a positive thing to do, not just to look good but because it counters the natural loss of muscle that comes with age, improves the lean muscle to fat ratio, plus muscle is metabolically active, which means building muscle helps with blood sugar control.

Chapman-Lopez, T., Wilburn, D., Fletcher, E., Adair, K., Ismaeel, A., Heileson, J., Gallucci, A., Funderburk, L., Koutakis, P., Forsse, J.S. The influence of resistance training on adipokines in post-menopausal women: A brief review. Sports Med Health Sci. 2022 Sep 20;4(4):219–224. doi: 10.1016/j.smhs.2022.09.001. PMID: 36600971; PMCID: PMC9806702.

Page 74: As you up the intensity of your exercise, research suggests consistency and rest are key.

Athanasiou, N., Bogdanis, G.C., Mastorakos, G., Endocrine responses of the stress system to different types of exercise. Rev Endocr Metab Disord. 2023 Apr;24(2):251–266. doi: 10.1007/s11154-022-09758-1. Epub 2022 Oct 15. PMID: 36242699; PMCID: PMC10023776.

Page 73: You can get the cardiovascular benefits of exercise with HIIT and even with strength training and walking. And you can get the muscle maintaining benefits of exercise with HIIT too.

Qian, J., Sun, S., Wang, M., Sun, Y., Sun, X., Jevitt, C., Yu, X. The effect of exercise intervention on improving sleep in menopausal women: a systematic review and meta-analysis. Front Med (Lausanne). 2023 Apr 25;10:1092294. doi: 10.3389/fmed.2023.1092294. PMID: 37181372; PMCID: PMC10167708.

ENDNOTES | 323

Page 74: There's some powerful research showing that yoga not only makes you bendy and helps with joint pain but can also improve perimenopausal mood changes and reduce hot flushes.

Shepherd-Banigan, M., Goldstein, K.M., Coeytaux, R.R., McDuffie, J.R., Goode, A.P., Kosinski, A.S., Van Noord, M.G., Befus, D., Adam, S., Masilamani, V., Nagi, A., Williams, J.W. Jr. Improving vasomotor symptoms; psychological symptoms; and health-related quality of life in peri- or post-menopausal women through yoga: An umbrella systematic review and meta-analysis.

Page 75: This mix-and-match approach has been shown to be a really positive way to build and maintain muscle and bone.

Martyn-St James, M., Carroll, S., A meta-analysis of impact exercise on postmenopausal bone loss: the case for mixed loading exercise programmes. Br J Sports Med. 2009 Dec;43(12):898–908. doi: 10.1136/bjsm.2008.052704. Epub 2008 Nov 3. PMID: 18981037.

Page 75: A 2017 study by the American Menopause Society showed that 32 to 42 per cent of perimenopausal women have insomnia symptoms, compared to 16 per cent across all women.

Ciano, C., King, T.S., Wright, R.R., Perlis, M., Sawyer, A.M.Longitudinal Study of Insomnia Symptoms Among Women During Perimenopause. J. Obstet Gynecol Neonatal Nurs. 2017 Nov–Dec;46(6):804–813. doi: 10.1016/j.jogn.2017.07.011. Epub 2017 Sep 5. PMID: 28886339; PMCID: PMC5776689.

Page 77: Even better, as movement is also a waking signal, do some of your workout outside. If it's winter, you can use a light box.

Bedrosian, T.A., Nelson, R.J. Timing of light exposure affects mood and brain circuits. Transl Psychiatry. 2017 Jan 31;7(1):e1017. doi: 10.1038/tp.2016.262. PMID: 28140399; PMCID: PMC5299389.

Page 78: Stick to cool cotton pyjamas or a nightie and consider changing to a cooler summer-weight duvet.

Okamoto-Mizuno, K., Mizuno, K. Effects of thermal environment on sleep and circadian rhythm. J. Physiol Anthropol. 2012 May 31;31(1):14. doi: 10.1186/1880-6805-31-14. PMID: 22738673; PMCID: PMC3427038.

CHAPTER 5

Page 105: After this, keep lights low and screens to a minimum.

Irish, L.A., Kline, C.E., Gunn, H.E., Buysse, D.J., Hall, M.H. The role of sleep hygiene in promoting public health: A review of empirical evidence. Sleep Med Rev. 2015 Aug;22:23-36. doi: 10.1016/j.smrv.2014.10.001. Epub 2014 Oct 16. PMID: 25454674; PMCID: PMC4400203.

Page 105: Nurture your relationships and make new ones by joining groups where you have a shared interest – whether it's hiking, pottery or roller skating – as that will bring you extra joy.

Campagne DM. Stress and perceived social isolation (loneliness). Arch Gerontol Geriatr. 2019 May–Jun;82:192-199. doi: 10.1016/j.archger.2019.02.007. Epub 2019 Feb 22. PMID: 30825769.

CHAPTER 6

Page 124: When your lungs feel full, take a second sip of air to expand your lungs as much as you can. Exhale through your mouth, very slowly and completely. Repeat.

Balban, M.Y., Neri, E., Kogon, M.M., Weed, L., Nouriani, B., Jo, B., Holl, G., Zeitzer, J.M., Spiegel, D., Huberman, A.D. Brief structured respiration practices enhance mood and reduce physiological arousal. Cell Rep Med. 2023 Jan 17;4(1):100895. doi: 10.1016/j.xcrm.2022.100895. Epub 2023 Jan 10. PMID: 36630953; PMCID: PMC9873947.

Page 124: Research shows that meditation reduces cortisol levels and it works best for people with high levels of stress.

Adam Koncz, Zsolt Demetrovics & Zsofia, K. Takacs (2021) Meditation interventions efficiently reduce cortisol levels of at-risk samples: a meta-analysis, Health Psychology Review, 15:1, 56–84, DOI: 10.1080/17437199.2020.1760727

Page 124: Brief structured respiration practices enhance mood and reduce physiological arousal

Melis Yilmaz Balban, Eric Neri, Manuela, M., Kogon, Jamie, M. Zeitzer, David Spiegel, Andrew, D. Huberman. Open Access Published:January 10, 2023DOI. :https://doi.org/10.1016/j.xcrm.2022.100895. Cell 4:1 Published: 17 January, 2023

Page 125: Research shows high-intensity exercise ups your cortisol level, while low-intensity exercise can lower it.

Hill, E.E., Zack, E., Battaglini, C., Viru, M., Viru, A., Hackney, A.C., Exercise and circulating cortisol levels: the intensity threshold effect. J. Endocrinol Invest. 2008 Jul;31(7):587–91. doi: 10.1007/BF03345606. PMID: 18787373.

Page 125: A handful of studies have shown that yoga helps reduce stress and cortisol. The meditative part helps but so does the stretching, which can activate the relaxation response.

Cahn, B.R., Goodman, M.S., Peterson, C.T., Maturi, R., Mills, P.J. Yoga, Meditation and Mind-Body Health: Increased BDNF, Cortisol Awakening Response, and Altered Inflammatory Marker Expression after a 3-Month Yoga and Meditation Retreat. Front Hum Neurosci. 2017 Jun 26;11:315. doi: 10.3389/fnhum.2017.00315.

Page 125: One way to do this is not to drink alcohol (see chapter three) – even moderate drinkers tend to have less restful sleep.

Helaakoski, V., Kaprio, J., Hublin, C., Ollila, H.M., Latvala, A., Alcohol use and poor sleep quality: a longitudinal twin study across 36 years. Sleep Adv. 2022 Jul 6;3(1):zpac023. doi: 10.1093/sleepadvances/zpac023. PMID: 37193395; PMCID: PMC10104364.

Page 125: You could also try a white noise app: research suggests this helps people who have noisy bedrooms (from outside noise) get to sleep faster and/or wake less at night.

Ebben, M.R., Yan, P, Krieger, A.C., The effects of white noise on sleep and duration in individuals living in a high noise environment in New York City. Sleep Med. 2021 Jul;83:256–259. doi: 10.1016/j.sleep.2021.03.031. Epub 2021 Apr 6. PMID: 34049045.

Page 127: A recent study showed that taking saffron twice a day improved both anxiety and depression scores by a third in perimenopausal women (also in PCH Mood & Sleep).

Lopresti, A.L., Smith, S.J.,The Effects of a Saffron Extract (affron®) on Menopausal Symptoms in Women during Perimenopause: A Randomised, Double-Blind, Placebo-Controlled Study. J Menopausal Med. 2021 Aug;27(2):66-78. doi: 10.6118/jmm.21002. PMID: 34463070; PMCID: PMC8408316.

Page 129: When progesterone is low, you can become over-sensitive to even minor changes in body temperature, leading to overheating and night sweats.

Charkoudian, N., Stachenfeld, N. Sex hormone effects on autonomic mechanisms of thermoregulation in humans. Auton Neurosci. 2016 Apr;196:75-80. doi: 10.1016/j.autneu.2015.11.004. Epub 2015 Nov 30. PMID: 26674572.

Page 130: Having low progesterone can also interfere with the rhythmic contractions of the gut muscles that move food along the gut.

Relationship between Aldosterone and Progesterone in the Human Menstrual Cycle. Emily, D. Szmuilowicz, Gail, K. Adler, Jonathan, S. Williams, Dina E. Green, Tham M. Yao, Paul, N. Hopkins, Ellen, W. Seely. The Journal of Clinical Endocrinology & Metabolism, Volume 91, Issue 10, 1 October 2006, Pages 3981-3987, https://doi.org/10.1210/jc.2006-1154 Published: 01 October 2006 Article history

CHAPTER 8

Page 155: Once your periods have stopped for a year –menopause itself – you will have an oestrogen level that's much lower than in your fertile years (unless you're taking HRT).

Peacock, K., Ketvertis, K.M. Menopause. [Updated 2022 Aug 11]. In: StatPearls [Internet]. Treasure Island (FL): StatPearls Publishing; 2023 Jan- Available from: https://www.ncbi.nlm.nih.gov/books/NBK507826/

Page 156: When phytoestrogens also bind to oestrogen receptors, they leave less space for xenoestrogens to attach.

Varun Reddy, Micheline McCarthy, Ami, P., Raval, Xenoestrogens impact brain estrogen receptor signaling during the female lifespan: A precursor to neurological disease?, Neurobiology of Disease, Volume 163, 2022, 105596, ISSN 0969-9961, https://doi.org/10.1016/j.nbd.2021.105596.

Page 156: This makes sense: why would your body prioritise fertility when it's constantly getting a message that you're in a life-threatening situation?

Slavich, G.M., Sacher, J., Stress, sex hormones, inflammation, and major depressive disorder: Extending Social Signal Transduction Theory of Depression to account for sex differences in mood disorders. Psychopharmacology (Berl). 2019 Oct;236(10):3063–3079. doi: 10.1007/s00213-019-05326-9. Epub 2019 Jul 29. PMID: 31359117; PMCID: PMC6821593.

Page 158: There's lots you can do. For example, you can make your exercise routine more restorative by doing yoga. You can do meditation or deep breathing exercises while walking or making tea.

Namazi, M., Sadeghi, R., Behboodi Moghadam, Z., Social Determinants of Health in Menopause: An Integrative Review. Int J Womens Health. 2019 Dec 9;11:637–647. doi: 10.2147/IJWH.S228594. PMID: 31849539; PMCID: PMC6910086.

Page 161: Vitamin E – some women find it helpful to apply it directly to the vaginal area.

Porterfield, L., Wur, N., Delgado, Z.S., Syed, F., Song, A., Weller, S.C., Vaginal Vitamin E for Treatment of Genitourinary Syndrome of Menopause: A Systematic Review of Randomized Controlled Trials. J Menopausal Med. 2022 Apr;28(1):9–16. doi: 10.6118/jmm.21028. PMID: 35534426; PMCID: PMC9086347.

Page 161: At the same time, muscle mass and metabolic rate both decline with age.

Chopra, S., Sharma, K,A., Ranjan, P., Malhotra, A., Vikram, N.K., Kumari, A., Weight Management Module for Perimenopausal Women: A Practical Guide for Gynecologists. J Midlife Health. 2019 Oct–Dec;10(4):165–172. doi: 10.4103/jmh.JMH_155_19. PMID: 31942151; PMCID: PMC6947726.

Page 161: Research suggests that blood sugar control is best when exercise is regular and includes resistance exercise, that you move after eating (or before if that suits you better), and that you break up your day with regular three-minute 'exercise snacks'.

U.S. Afsheen Syeda, Daniel Battillo, Aayush Visaria, Steven, K., Malin, The importance of exercise for glycemic control in type 2 diabetes, American Journal of Medicine Open, Volume 9, 2023, 100031, ISSN 2667-0364, https://doi.org/10.1016/j.ajmo.2023.100031.

Pages 161-162: Oestrogen is needed to make serotonin, which supports the production of the sleepy hormone melatonin. It helps regulate your sleep-wake cycle and lulls you into a deeper sleep. So when it drops, so does your sleep quality and often the hours you sleep too.

Tandon, VR., Sharma, S., Mahajan, A., Mahajan, A., Tandon, A. Menopause and Sleep Disorders. J Midlife Health. 2022 Jan–Mar;13(1):26–33. doi: 10.4103/jmh.jmh_18_22. Epub 2022 May 2. PMID: 35707298; PMCID: PMC9190958.

Page 162: If you have fatigue, you are not alone: nearly half of women in perimenopause report symptoms of physical and mental exhaustion.

Chedraui, P., Aguirre, W., Hidalgo, L., Fayad, L. Assessing menopausal symptoms among healthy middle aged women with the Menopause Rating Scale. Maturitas. 2007;57(3):271–278.

Page 162: And research shows that in late menopause in particular, as oestrogen falls lower, fatigue can add to stress, which makes you more tired.

Taylor-Swanson, L., Wong, A.E., Pincus, D., Butner J.E., Hahn-Holbrook J., Koithan, M., Wann, K., Woods, N.F., The dynamics of stress and fatigue across menopause: attractors, coupling, and resilience. Menopause. 2018 Apr;25(4):380–390. doi: 10.1097/GME.0000000000001025. PMID: 29189603; PMCID: PMC5866170.

Page 165: Before you supplement vitamin D, you may want to test to see if you're deficient. A recent UK survey showed that half of Asian people aged 40 to 69 are deficient, around a third of Black people and 12 per cent of white people.

Lin, L., Smeeth L, Langan, S. et al. Distribution of vitamin D status in the UK: a cross-sectional analysis of UK Biobank. BMJ Open 2021;11:e038503. doi: 10.1136/bmjopen-2020-038503

CHAPTER 9

Page 174: There are specific foods you can eat to support your body to make SHBG

Maggio, M., Lauretani, F., Basaria, S., et al. Sex hormone binding globulin levels across the adult lifespan in women – the role of body mass index and fasting insulin. J Endocrinol Invest. 2008. 31. 597–601.

Page 175: Spearmint tea has been shown to reduce free (active) testosterone levels.

Grant P. Spearmint herbal tea has significant anti-androgen effects in polycystic ovarian syndrome. A randomized controlled trial. Phytother Res. 2010;24(2):186–8. Dixon RA. Phytoestrogens. Annu Rev Plant Biol. 2004;55:225–61.

Page 176: Oxidative stress has been shown to reduce levels of SHBG.

Longcope, C., Feldman. H.A., McKinlay, J.B., Araujo, A.B., Diet and sex hormone-binding globulin. J Clin Endocrinol Metab. 2000. 85. 293–296.

Page 176: One study showed that supplementing with CoQ10 and vitamin E led to a rise in SHBG levels and a drop in total testosterone. Eat: sunflower seeds, peanuts, almonds, avocados, spinach, organ meats (e.g. liver), oily fish, olive oil.

Izadi, A., Ebrahimi, S., Shirazi, S., Taghizadeh, S., Parizad, M., Farzadi, L., Gargari, BP., Hormonal and Metabolic Effects of Coenzyme Q10 and/or Vitamin E in Patients With Polycystic Ovary Syndrome. J Clin Endocrinol Metab. 2019 Feb 1;104(2):319–327. doi: 10.1210/jc.2018-01221. PMID: 30202998.

Page 176: Phytoestrogen foods, such as soy foods, flaxseeds, sesame seeds and lentils.Phytoestrogen foods. Eat: soy foods, flaxseeds, sesame seeds and lentils

Pino, A.M., Valladares, L.E., Palma, M.A., Mancilla, A.M., Yáñez, M., Albala, C. Dietary isoflavones affect sex hormone-binding globulin levels in postmenopausal women. J Clin Endocrinol Metab. 2000 Aug;85(8):2797–800. doi: 10.1210/jcem.85.8.6750. PMID: 10946884.

Page 177: High-intensity interval training (HIIT) – short bursts of intense activity – has been shown to reduce levels of the androgen DHEA-S. N.B. whatever you do, consistency is key.

Shele, G., Genkil, J., Speelman, D. A., Systematic Review of the Effects of Exercise on Hormones in Women with Polycystic Ovary Syndrome. J Funct Morphol Kinesiol. 2020 May 31;5(2):35. doi: 10.3390/jfmk5020035. PMID: 33467251; PMCID: PMC7739243.

Page 177: Women with androgen dominance had lower testosterone levels after doing regular strength training for 16 weeks

Ramos, F.K., Lara, L.A., Kogure, G.S., Silva, R.C., Ferriani, R.A., Silva de Sá, M.F., Reis, R.M. Quality of Life in Women with Polycystic Ovary Syndrome after a Program of Resistance Exercise Training. Rev Bras Ginecol Obstet. 2016 Jul;38(7):340–7. doi: 10.1055/s-0036-1585457. Epub 2016 Jul 29. PMID: 27472811; PMCID: PMC10374239.

Page 177: After three months of doing yoga, women with androgen dominance had lower levels of free testosterone, and reported better mood as well as reductions in anxiety and depression.

Patel, V., Menezes, H., Menezes, C., Bouwer, S., Bostick-Smith, C.A., Speelman, D.L. Regular Mindful Yoga Practice as a Method to Improve Androgen Levels in Women With Polycystic Ovary Syndrome: A Randomized, Controlled Trial. J Am Osteopath Assoc. 2020 Apr 14. doi: 10.7556/jaoa.2020.050. PMID: 32285088.

Page 179: Stinging nettle and Saw palmetto both target 5AR, reducing DHT.

Chrubasik, J.E., Roufogalis, B.D., Wagner, H., Chrubasik, S. A comprehensive review on the stinging nettle effect and efficacy profiles. Part II: urticae radix. Phytomedicine. 2007 Aug;14(7-8):568-79. doi: 10.1016/j.phymed.2007.03.014. Epub 2007 May 16. PMID: 17509841.

Page 179: one study showed that out of all the medicinal mushrooms, reishi are the most powerful anti-androgen.

Fujita, R., Liu, J., Shimizu, K., Konishi, F., Noda, K., Kumamoto, S., Ueda, C., Tajiri, H., Kaneko, S., Suimi, Y., Kondo, R. j Anti-androgenic activities of Ganoderma lucidum. J Ethnopharmacol. 2005 Oct 31;102(1):107–12. doi: 10.1016/j.jep.2005.05.041. PMID: 16029938.

CHAPTER 10

Page 185: The drop in testosterone during this time is not as big as the drop in oestrogen, but because androgens are so potent, it can have big effects.

John, E., Morley, H., Mitchell Perry, Androgens and Women at the Menopause and Beyond, The Journals of Gerontology: Series A, Volume 58, Issue 5, May 2003, Pages M409–M416 https://doi.org/10.1093/gerona/58.5.M409

Page 186: If you put on weight around your middle (which most people do in midlife), or you have an inflammatory diet, or you have high insulin levels, you produce more aromatase, and so convert more testosterone to oestrogen.

Insulin and aromatase: Randolph, J.F., et al., The effect of insulin on aromatase activity in isolated human endometrial glands and stroma. Am J Obstet Gynecol, 1987. 157(6): p. 1534–9.

Page 191: To reduce the production of aromatase, the enzyme that converts testosterone to oestrogen, it's a good idea to eat high-fibre foods, flaxseeds, soy, green tea and white button mushrooms.

Novaes, M.R., et al., The effects of dietary supplementation with Agaricales mushrooms and other medicinal fungi on breast cancer: evidence-based medicine. Clinics (Sao Paulo), 2011. 66(12): p. 2133-

Page 191: Research also suggests that lifting weights and large compound movements such as squats and deadlifts are good for testosterone levels, at least in the short term.

Nindl, B.C,. Kraemer, W.J., Gotshalk, L.A., Marx, J.O., Volek, J.S., Bush, F.A., Häkkinen, K., Newton, R.U., Fleck, S.J., Testosterone responses after resistance exercise in women: influence of regional fat distribution. Int J Sport Nutr Exerc Metab. 2001 Dec;11(4):451–65. doi: 10.1123/ijsnem.11.4.451. PMID: 11915780.

Page 191: Research suggests that interval training is good for mitochondrial function.

Chrøis, K.M., Dohlmann, T.L., Søgaard, D., Hansen C.V., Dela, F., Helge J.W., Larsen S., Mitochondrial adaptations to high intensity interval training in older females and males. Eur J Sport Sci. 2020 Feb;20(1):135–145. doi: 10.1080/17461391.2019.1615556. Epub 2019 May 30. PMID: 31145037.

Page 192: you are probably not a great candidate for longer fasting, as research suggests it lowers testosterone levels.

Cienfuegos, S., Corapi, S., Gabel, K., Ezpeleta, M., Kalam, F., Lin, S., Pavlou V., Varady, K.A., Effect of Intermittent Fasting on Reproductive Hormone Levels in Females and Males: A Review of Human Trials. Nutrients. 2022 Jun 3;14(11):2343. doi: 10.3390/nu14112343. PMID: 35684143; PMCID: PMC9182756.

Page 192: A study showed that when midlife women had less than six hours sleep or more than nine hours sleep, they had lower testosterone levels than adults who slept seven to eight hours.

Hernández-Pérez, J.G., Taha, S., Torres-Sánchez, L.E., Villasante-Tezanos A., Milani, S.A., Baillargeon J., Canfield S., Lopez, D.S., Association of sleep duration and quality with serum testosterone concentrations among men and women: NHANES 2011-2016. Andrology. 2023 Jul 15:10.1111/andr.13496. doi: 10.1111/andr.13496. Epub ahead of print. PMID: 37452666; PMCID: PMC10788378.

Page 193: Research shows that having more zinc in the diet helps raise testosterone – and sex drive – in midlife women with low sex drive.

Mazaheri Nia, L., Iravani M., Abedi, P., Cheraghian. B. Effect of Zinc on Testosterone Levels and Sexual Function of Postmenopausal Women: A Randomized Controlled Trial. J Sex Marital Ther. 2021;47(8):804-813. doi: 10.1080/0092623X.2021.1957732. Epub 2021 Jul 27. PMID: 34311679.

Page 194: Chrysin, found in honey, propolis and some passionflowers, has been studied for its potential to inhibit aromatase....chrysin has been studied for its potential to inhibit aromatase.

Balam, F.H., Ahmadi, Z.S., Ghorbani, A. Inhibitory effect of chrysin on estrogen biosynthesis by suppression of enzyme aromatase (CYP19): A systematic review. Heliyon. 2020 Mar 7;6(3):e03557. doi: 10.1016/j.heliyon.2020.e03557. PMID: 32181408; PMCID: PMC7063143.

Page 194: Creatine monohydrate and amino acids have been researched for their benefits in muscle growth and maintenance.

Wu, S.H., Chen, K.L., Hsu C., Chen, H.C., Chen JY, Yu S.Y., Shiu Y.J. Creatine Supplementation for Muscle Growth: A Scoping Review of Randomized Clinical Trials from 2012 to 2021. Nutrients. 2022 Mar 16;14(6):1255. doi: 10.3390/nu14061255. PMID: 35334912; PMCID: PMC8949037.

CHAPTER 11

Page 200: If used-up thyroid hormones are still circulating in your body, the hypothalamus might sense there is enough and scale back production.

Knezevic, J., Starchl, C., Tmava Berisha A., Amrein K. Thyroid-Gut-Axis: How Does the Microbiota Influence Thyroid Function? Nutrients. 2020 Jun 12;12(6):1769. doi: 10.3390/nu12061769. PMID: 32545596; PMCID: PMC7353203

Page 202: But there's even more reason to avoid gluten if your thyroid is low as, for some people, gluten can make symptoms worse.

Ihnatowicz, P., Wątor, P., Drywień, M.E. The importance of gluten exclusion in the management of Hashimoto's thyroiditis. Ann Agric Environ Med. 2021 Dec 29;28(4):558–568. doi: 10.26444/aaem/136523. Epub 2021 May 28. PMID: 34969211.

Page 203: Cooking and fermenting deactivate compounds that interfere with thyroid function.

Bajaj, J.K., Salwan, P., Salwan, S. Various Possible Toxicants Involved in Thyroid Dysfunction: A Review. J Clin Diagn Res. 2016 Jan;10(1):FE01-3. doi: 10.7860/JCDR/2016/15195.7092. Epub 2016 Jan 1. PMID: 26894086; PMCID: PMC4740614.

Page 203: the best way to get vitamin D is exposure to 20 minutes of sunshine a day on your limbs with no sunscreen. (N.B. In summer months, avoid 12pm to 3pm.)

Xu, J., Zhu, X.Y., Sun, H., Xu X.Q., Xu, S.A., Suo, Y., Cao, L.J,, Zhou, Q., Yu, H.J., Cao, W.Z. Low vitamin D levels are associated with cognitive impairment in patients with Hashimoto thyroiditis. BMC Endocr Disord. 2018 Nov 26;18(1):87. doi: 10.1186/s12902-018-0314-7. PMID: 30477467; PMCID: PMC6260768.

Page 204: Half of people with thyroid issues have low levels of B12

Vitamin B12: Jabbar, A., Yawar, A., Waseem, S., Islam, N., Ul Haque. N., Zuberi, L., Khan, A., Akhter J. Vitamin B12 deficiency common in primary hypothyroidism. J Pak Med Assoc. 2008 May;58(5):258–61. Erratum in: J Pak Med Assoc. 2009 Feb;59(2):126. Wasim, Sabeha [corrected to Waseem, Sabiha]. PMID: 18655403.

Page 204: Iron: Vital for converting T4 to active T3

Zimmermann, M.B, Köhrle J. The impact of iron and selenium deficiencies on iodine and thyroid metabolism: biochemistry and relevance to public health. Thyroid. 2002 Oct;12(10):867–78. doi: 10.1089/105072502761016494. PMID: 12487769.

Page 204: A DUTCH study showed only a sixth of women diagnosed with hypothyroidism do even the minimum of exercise.

Lankhaar, J.A.C., Kemler, E., Stubbe, J.H., Backx, F.J.G. Physical Activity in Women With Hypothyroidism on Thyroid Hormone Therapy: Associated Factors and Perceived Barriers and Benefits. J Phys Act Health. 2021 Oct 9;18(11):1383–1392. doi: 10.1123/jpah.2021-0230. PMID: 34627125.

Page 205: In the study authors said that after four months, they showed 'remarkable improvements' in their general fitness and physical and emotional health too.

Werneck, F.Z., Coelho, E.F, Almas. S.P., Garcia, M.M.D.N., Bonfante, H.L.M., Lima, J.R.P., Vigário, P.D.S., Mainenti, M.R.M, Teixeira, P.F.D.S., Vaisman, M. Exercise training improves quality of life in women with subclinical hypothyroidism: a randomized clinical trial. Arch Endocrinol Metab. 2018 Oct;62(5):530–536. doi: 10.20945/2359-3997000000073. PMID: 30462806; PMCID: PMC10118651.

Page 205: There's a lot of evidence to indicate that aerobic exercise, strength training and a combination of the two have positive effects on thyroid hormones – although including some resistance exercise seems to give the edge.

Impact of Aerobic and Resistance Training on Thyroid-Stimulating Hormone in Hypothyroidism. (2022). Journal of Pharmaceutical Negative Results, 1751–1762.

Page 205: A study of women who were overweight due to being hypothyroid showed combining aerobic and resistance exercise was effective for weight loss too.

Patel, B. R., G. Varadharajulu, & Jagtap, V. (2021). Effect of Structured Physical Therapy Exercise Protocol on Obesity Secondary to Hypothyroidism. Indian Journal of Public Health Research & Development, 12(3), 624–627. https://doi.org/10.37506/ijphrd.v12i3.16445

Page 205: There's an ongoing study looking at whether specific yoga poses that work on the throat can help support the thyroid too.

Nilkantham, S., Majumdar, V., Singh, A. Scientific yoga module for hypothyroidism: A study protocol for tele-yoga RCT. Contemp Clin Trials Commun. 2023 Jun 10;33:101157. doi: 10.1016/j.conctc.2023.101157. PMID: 37342177; PMCID: PMC10277449.

CHAPTER 12

Page 218: In one study, healthy men were given 6,000 calories a day of the standard American diet, which is admittedly a lot. They put on 3.5kg each, which wasn't that surprising. What was eye opening is that after two to three days, they developed insulin resistance.

Boden, G., Homko, C., Barrero, C.A., Stein, T.P., Chen, X., Cheung, P., Fecchio. C., Koller S., Merali, S. Excessive caloric intake acutely causes oxidative stress, GLUT4 carbonylation, and insulin resistance in healthy men. Sci Transl Med. 2015 Sep 9;7(304):304re7. doi: L

Pages 218-219: You can be thin but still develop insulin resistance. This is due to a specific type of fat called visceral fat, that is around your organs. This is why you might have noticed your waist thickening or your stomach sticking out more, even while the rest of you is slim.

Klein, S., Gastaldelli, A., Yki-Järvinen, H., Scherer, P.E. Why does obesity cause diabetes? Cell Metab. 2022 Jan 4;34(1):11-20. doi: 10.1016/j.cmet.2021.12.012. PMID: 34986330; PMCID: PMC8740746.

Page 219: In addition, exercise increases insulin sensitivity – that is, how effectively your body stores and uses glucose.

Gratas-Delamarche, A., Derbré, F., Vincent, S., Cillard, J. Physical inactivity, insulin resistance, and the oxidative-inflammatory loop. Free Radic Res. 2014 Jan;48(1):93-108. doi: 10.3109/10715762.2013.847528. Epub 2013 Oct 17. PMID: 24060092.][Dempsey P.C., Larsen, R.N., Winkler, E.A.H., Owen, N., Kingwell, B.A., Dunstan, D.W.

Page 219: One study showed that just three days of bed rest – i.e. not moving much – brought was enough to bring on insulin resistance.

Hamburg, N.M., McMackin, C.J., Huang, A.L., Shenouda, S.M., Widlansky, M.E., Schulz, E., Gokce, N., Ruderman, N.B., Keaney, J.F. Jr, Vita, J.A. Physical inactivity rapidly induces insulin resistance and microvascular dysfunction in healthy volunteers. Arterioscler Thromb Vasc Biol. 2007 Dec;27(12):2650-6. doi: 10.1161/ATVBAHA.107.153288. Epub 2007 Oct 11. PMID: 17932315; PMCID: PMC2596308.

Page 219: For example, research has established a connection between people who report that their jobs are stressful and the development of insulin resistance.

Yan, Y.X., Xiao, H.B., Wang, S.S., Zhao, J., He, Y., Wang, W., Dong, J. Investigation of the Relationship Between Chronic Stress and Insulin Resistance in a Chinese Population. J Epidemiol. 2016 Jul 5;26(7):355-60. doi: 10.2188/jea.JE20150183. Epub 2016 Jan 30. PMID: 26830350; PMCID: PMC4919480. Yang, S., Yang, C., Pei, R., Li.

Page 220: And the more of those you eat, the more likely you are, over time, to become insulin resistant.

Koren, D., Taveras, E.M. Association of sleep disturbances with obesity, insulin resistance and the metabolic syndrome. Metabolism. 2018 Jul;84:67-75. doi: 10.1016/j.metabol.2018.04.001. Epub 2018 Apr 6. PMID: 29630921.

Page 222: Green tea is high in the antioxidant epigallocatechin gallate (EGCG), which improves insulin sensitivity.

Wen, L., Wu, D., Tan, X., Zhong, M., Xing, J., Li, W, Li, D., Cao, F. The Role of Catechins in Regulating Diabetes: An Update Review. Nutrients. 2022 Nov 4;14(21):4681. doi: 10.3390/nu14214681. PMID: 36364943; PMCID: PMC9654920.

Page 222: Research shows that replacing vegetable oils with extra virgin olive oil can minimize blood sugar spikes and improve insulin resistance.

Álvarez-Amor, L., Sierra, A.L., Cárdenas, A. et al. Extra virgin olive oil improved body weight and insulin sensitivity in high fat diet-induced obese LDLr−/−.Leiden mice without attenuation of steatohepatitis. Sci Rep 11, 8250 (2021). https://doi.org/10.1038/s41598-021-87761-3

Page 223: It also increases appetite and the likelihood of being overweight, and so increases insulin resistance via these mechanisms too.

Singh, T., Ahmed, TH., Mohamed, N., Elhaj, M.S., Mohammed, Z., Paulsingh C.N., Mohamed, M.B., Khan, S. Does Insufficient Sleep Increase the Risk of Developing Insulin Resistance: A Systematic Review. Cureus. 2022 Mar 26;14(3):e23501. doi: 10.7759/cureus.23501. PMID: 35494895; PMCID: PMC9036496.

Page 223: Studies suggest that having least seven hours of uninterrupted sleep each night is best for insulin function.

Cedernaes, J., Lampola, L., Axelsson, E.K., Liethof, L., Hassanzadeh, S., Yeganeh, A., Broman, J.E., Schiöth, H.B., Benedict, C. A single night of partial sleep loss impairs fasting insulin sensitivity but does not affect cephalic phase insulin release in young men. J Sleep Res. 2016 Feb;25(1):5–10. doi: 10.1111/jsr.12340. PMID: 26361380.

Page 224: Get up often (and sit down less). Sitting down for long periods leads to higher blood sugar levels after meals.

Dempsey, P.C., Larsen, R.N., Winkler, E.A.H., Owen, N., Kingwell, B., Dunstan, D,W. Prolonged uninterrupted sitting elevates postprandial hyperglycaemia proportional to degree of insulin resistance. Diabetes Obes Metab. 2018 Jun;20(6):1526–1530. doi: 10.1111/dom.13254. Epub 2018 Mar 6. PMID: 29431272.

Page 224: One study showed that doing three-minute exercise 'snacks' – for example jumping jacks, stairs, squats – every 30 minutes was enough.

Smith, J.A.B., Savikj, M., Sethi, P., Platt, S., Gabriel, B.M., Hawley, J.A., Dunstan, D., Krook, A,. Zierath, J.R., Näslund, E. Three weeks of interrupting sitting lowers fasting glucose and glycemic variability, but not glucose tolerance, in free-living women and men with obesity. Am J Physiol Endocrinol Metab. 2021 Aug 1;321(2):E203–E216.

Page 224: Another study showed that 170 minutes of exercise a week – 20 minutes more than NHS guidelines – increases insulin sensitivity more than doing 115 minutes a week. Don't forget, you can break it up into short chunks that suit your schedule.

Iaccarino, G., Franco, D., Sorriento, D., Strisciuglio, T., Barbato, E., Morisco, C. Modulation of insulin sensitivity by exercise training: implications for cardiovascular prevention. J Cardiovasc Transl Res. 2021;14(2):256–270. doi:10.1007/s12265-020-10057-w

Page 224: Aerobic exercise improves insulin sensitivity and resistance training increases muscle mass, which means a greater uptake of which improves uptake of glucose from the blood. This is especially important in midlife because as we age, we lose muscle

Fealy, C.E., Nieuwoudt, S., Foucher, J.A., et al. Functional high-intensity exercise training ameliorates insulin resistance and cardiometabolic risk factors in type 2 diabetes. Exp Physiol. 2018;103(7):985–994. doi:10.1113/EP086844

Page 224: Research suggests that HIIT is effective at lowering blood glucose and even more so when you do it in the afternoon rather than the morning.

Savikj, M., Gabriel, B.M., Alm, P.S., et al. Afternoon exercise is more efficacious than morning exercise at improving blood glucose levels in individuals with type 2 diabetes: a randomised crossover trial. Diabetologia. 2019;62(2):233–237. doi:10.1007/s00125-018-4767-z

Page 225: Studies show that people exposed to some pollutants including certain pesticides and plastics are more likely to develop insulin resistance and diabetes.

Kim, Y.A., Park, J.B., Woo, M.S., Lee, S.Y., Kim, H.Y., Yoo, Y.H. Persistent Organic Pollutant-Mediated Insulin Resistance. Int J Environ Res Public Health. 2019 Feb 3;16(3):448. doi: 10.3390/ijerph16030448. PMID: 30717446; PMCID: PMC6388367.

Page 227: The brain can also become insulin resistant, which has been linked to dementia and cognitive decline, as well as your ability to keep your weight stable.

Milstein, J.L., Ferris, H.A. The brain as an insulin-sensitive metabolic organ. Mol Metab. 2021 Oct;52:101234. doi: 10.1016/j.molmet.2021.101234. Epub 2021 Apr 15. PMID: 33845179; PMCID: PMC8513144.

Page 228: In an eight-week study of overweight non-exercisers who started to work out regularly, their brain insulin sensitivity improved until it was the level of someone at a healthy weight.

Kullmann, S., Goj, T., Veit, R., Fritsche, L., Wagner, L., Schneeweiss, P., Hoene, M., Hoffmann, C., Machann, J., Niess, A., Preissl, H., Birkenfeld, AL., Peter, A., Häring, H.U., Fritsche, A., Moller, A., Weigert, C., Heni, M. Exercise restores brain insulin sensitivity in sedentary adults who are overweight and obese. JCI Insight. 2022 Sep 22;7(18):e161498. doi: 10.1172/jci.insight.161498. PMID: 36134657; PMCID: PMC9675563.

Index

5-HTP 128, 162, 227
5AR (5-alpha reductase) 172, 175, 178, 179

A
acetylcholine 228
acne and oily skin 93, 122, 172, 178
acupuncture and acupressure 146
adaptogenic herbs 62, 103, 106, 110, 145, 193, 194
adrenal dysfunction
    causes 101-2
    diet/what to eat 101, 102-4, 106-11
    lifestyle guidelines 104-5, 106-11
    sex hormones under stress 99-101, 102
    stress hormone connection 98-9, 100-2, 106-11
    symptoms and treatment 89-90, 97-8, 98-9, 106-11
adrenal glands 22-3, 24, 41, 98-101, 119, 145, 154, 155, 156, 172, 173, 184, 185, 186, 187, 198
adrenaline 82, 98, 101, 226
air filters 81

alcohol consumption 26, 38, 47, 61, 104, 136, 165
aldosterone 110
aloe vera juice 208-9
alpha lipoic acid (ALA) 191
amino acids 38, 43, 50, 51, 77, 108, 123, 127, 128, 146, 180, 196, 221
anaemia 126, 208
anandamide 55
androgens 172-4, 184-5
    deficiency
    causes 185-7
    diet/what to eat 190-1, 193-6
    lifestyle guidelines 191-6
    symptoms and treatment 93-4, 183-4, 191-6
    dominance 93
    causes 173-4
    diet/what to eat 175-81
    lifestyle guide 177-81
    symptoms and treatment 93, 171-3, 175-81
anger/rage 2, 16, 31, 91, 93, 138, 143, 180-1
anti-androgens 192

anti-inflammatories 37, 52, 103, 109, 123, 127, 146–7, 157, 163–4, 178
anti-stress toolkit 66–71, 104, 107, 124, 141, 143, 158, 177, 179, 192, 206, 224
antidepressants 162, 227
antihistamines 136
antioxidants 50, 53, 107, 123, 140, 146, 147, 163, 164, 176, 194, 203
anxiety ix, 4, 40, 66, 82, 90–1, 92, 118, 122, 127–8, 177
appetite and satiety 56, 161, 180, 207, 223
apple cider vinegar 225
apps 67, 80
aromatase 154, 181, 186, 191
ashwagandha 63, 103, 128, 195
avocados 43, 53, 123, 143, 157, 176, 221, 228
Ayurvedic medicine 62, 128, 195

B

Bacopa monnieri 195
bacteria, gut 36, 39, 53, 55, 141
balance exercises *see* flexibility, balance and mobility exercise
beans and pulses 37, 42, 51, 55, 123, 129, 143, 158, 162, 176, 178, 204, 207, 209, 221, 228
beauty products 80, 83
bedtime routines 41, 227
berberine 144
berries 53, 103, 109, 110, 123, 140, 146, 163, 164, 176, 178, 194, 203, 222, 229
see also fruit
beta carotene 223
beta glucuronidase 39, 141
bile 55, 141, 200, 209
bile salts 38–9
bitter foods 39, 40, 209

bloating 49–50, 60, 91, 122, 130, 207
blood circulation 179
blood glucose monitors 229–30
blood pressure 63, 106, 108, 181
blood sugar levels 23, 40, 45, 49, 51, 61, 72, 101, 102, 104, 107, 108, 109, 110, 129, 143, 144, 157, 161, 174, 175–6, 178, 180, 194, 202
  dysregulation 216–19
  causes 219–20
  diet/what to eat 220–3, 226–30
  lifestyle guidelines 223–30
  symptoms and treatments 95, 215, 226–30
blood tests 28, 30, 95, 198, 201, 230
body image 193
body temperature *see* hot flushes; temperature, body
bone health 8, 21, 29, 42, 55, 56, 62, 92–3, 125, 165–6, 172
bowel movements 32, 37, 39, 94, 208–9
box breathing 68
BPA (bisphenol-A) 37, 80–1, 139, 192, 205
brain fog 90, 95, 163, 227–8
brain function 23, 41, 42–3, 98, 100, 127, 136, 143, 145, 146, 159, 162, 163, 180, 189, 227–8
Brazil nuts 210
bread 32–3
breast cancer 25–6, 67, 155
breast tenderness and swelling 4, 19, 31, 32, 33, 91–2, 122, 147
breath exercises/breathwork 41, 66, 67–8, 83, 111, 124, 158, 178, 207, 226
broccoli/broccoli sprouts 142, 158, 176, 190, 222

C

caffeine 61, 80, 89, 101, 106
calcium 55, 165, 166
calcium-D-glucarate 145
carbohydrates 40, 51-2, 95, 102, 122, 143, 144, 175-6, 178, 202, 216-17, 219, 220, 225
    white and refined 60-1, 101, 102, 144, 202
carcinogens 60
cardio or aerobic exercise 73-4, 160, 161, 177, 224, 229
cardiovascular disease 8, 87, 219, 228
cardiovascular health 42, 53, 73
cartilage 163
catechins 179
cayenne pepper 107, 161, 207, 229
CBTi 80
chewing your food 49-50, 104
Chinese medicine 62, 146, 181
chlorine 205
chocolate and cocoa 32
    dark 55, 123, 127, 163, 176, 194, 222
cholesterol 21, 95, 99-100, 123, 186, 209-10
choline 140, 204
chromium 107, 110, 130, 161, 207, 220
    picolinate 180, 226, 228, 229
circadian rhythms 102, 128
cleaning products 81
coffee 61, 101, 106
cognitive behavioural therapy (CBT) 82, 143, 180, 196
cognitive issues 92, 93-4, 107, 143, 163, 194-5, 227-8
cold, feeling 94, 207
cold therapy 71-2, 86, 184, 186
collagen 163, 165
community 82
compassion meditation 67
concentration difficulties 16, 93-4, 194-5, 227
confidence, low 118
constipation 49-50, 207-8
contraceptive pills 121
CoQ10 (coenzyme Q10) 176, 191
corpus luteum 119, 120
cortisol 22, 37, 61, 65, 67-8, 76, 78, 98-9, 100, 101-2, 103, 105, 106-11, 119, 125, 128, 156, 178, 186, 216, 219, 223, 226, 227
COVID-19 global pandemic ix
cravings 90, 95, 110, 129, 130, 144, 207, 229
creatine monohydrate 194
curcumin 103, 109, 147, 164, 177
cyclic sighing 68, 77, 124
cysts 91, 146-7, 174

D

dairy foods 31-2, 60, 202
dandelion root tea 209
dehydration *see* hydration
depression 90, 127-8, 177
detoxification 37-8, 53, 55, 81-2, 138-9, 156
    support for liver detox 140-1, 145, 157-8, 176-7
DHEA/'mother hormone' 21, 100, 172-3, 184, 185, 186-7, 194, 195
DHEA (androgen) pessary 160, 195
DHT (Dihydrotestosterone) 172, 173, 174, 175, 178-9
diabetes 40, 218, 219, 224-5, 228, 229
diagnosis of perimenopause 4-5
digestive system 49, 94, 140, 207-8, 209
diuretics 130, 147
diversity, microbiome 36-7

dizziness 89, 108
DNA tests 30
dopamine 42, 50, 127, 143, 180, 193, 195, 196
dryness, vaginal 26
DUTCH tests 6–7, 20, 28, 29, 138

E

E1 (estriol/estrone) 23, 154–5
E2 (estradiol) 23
eating speed 49–50, 104, 180, 209, 225, 229
egg stores/production 17, 18, 20, 120
eggs 51, 123, 140, 158, 165, 175, 179, 190, 203, 204
electrolytes 109
emotional eating 110
endocrine disruptors 37, 80, 139, 156, 205
endometrial cancer 122
endometriosis 91, 137, 140, 146–7
endorphins 144
energy levels 21, 33, 43, 55, 72, 90, 98, 104, 109, 145, 162, 189, 193–4, 196, 216
environmental toxins/chemicals 37, 80–2, 83, 138–9, 142, 225
epigenetics 30
Epsom salts 81, 109, 146
estrobolome 36–7, 39, 50
evening primrose oil 147
exercise 40, 42, 66, 83, 105
    adrenal dysfunction 105, 107, 108, 109, 110, 111
    androgen deficiency 185, 191–2, 194
    androgen dominance 177, 180
    blood sugar dysregulation 219, 224, 226, 228, 229
    cardio or aerobic exercise 73–4, 160, 161, 177, 224, 229
    flexibility, balance and mobility 74–5, 142, 159, 164
    low progesterone 125, 127, 130
    low thyroid function 204–5, 208, 209–10
    low to moderate intensity 42, 105, 125, 162, 164
    oestrogen deficiency 159, 160, 161, 164, 165
    oestrogen dominance 142, 145
    overdoing it 71–2, 145, 184, 200
    pelvic floor 193
    putting a routine together 75
    strength-training/resistance exercise 72–3, 125, 130, 144, 164, 165, 177, 205, 224, 229
eyebrow loss 94, 208

F

family and friends 105, 158
fasting 72, 184, 200, 202
fat digestion 38, 39, 200
fat storage, body 23, 49, 61, 107, 129, 137, 143–4, 154, 216, 218, 228
fatigue 27, 33, 49, 51, 60, 82, 89, 91, 93, 95, 106, 145, 162–3, 194, 198, 206, 226
    see also tiredness
fats, healthy 40, 43, 52–3, 102, 103, 123, 145, 157, 190, 202, 220, 221, 227
fatty foods 94, 197, 209
Female Food Club 48
fermented foods 37, 55, 63, 123, 165, 203
fibre 32, 37, 40, 52, 53, 102, 129, 141, 157, 179–80, 191, 202, 207, 209, 220, 221, 227, 228
fibroids 19, 91, 137, 140, 146–7

fight or flight response 78, 104, 219
fish and seafood 43, 50-1, 53, 55, 103, 109, 123, 127, 140, 143, 157, 163, 164, 165, 176, 178, 190, 193, 194, 196, 203, 204, 208, 221, 227, 228
flavonoids 38, 40, 163, 177
flaxseeds 37, 56, 58-9, 63, 129, 141, 157, 159, 163, 164, 176, 178, 191, 203, 222-3, 228
flexibility, balance and mobility exercise 74-5, 142, 159, 164
fluoride 205
Food Framework, PCM 37, 39-40, 42-3, 47-8, 106, 162
    dietary supplements 61-2, 106
    Five Rules
    1. starting meals with protein 49, 63
    2. time between meals 49, 63
    3. daily water consumption 49, 63
    4. chewing your food 49-50, 63
    5. vegetable variety 50, 63
    foods to leave out/cut back 59-61
    what to eat
    carbohydrates 51-2
    fats 52-3
    gut supporting foods 55
    herbs and spices 56-8
    iron-rich foods 55
    phytoestrogen foods 56, 63
    polyphenol foods 55
    protein 50-1
    vegetables 53-5, 63
    see also Recipes, PCM Hormone Balance
friends *see* family and friends; support network, social
fruit 52, 81, 103, 108, 109, 110, 123, 129, 140, 146, 163, 164, 176, 178, 207, 209, 229

fullness and satiety 50, 52, 55, 143, 161, 180, 220, 225, 229
functional medicine 16, 35

G

gall bladder 38, 39, 141, 200, 209
gamma-aminobutyric acid (GABA) 118, 127, 128, 180
genetics 30, 178, 179
ghrelin 143
ginger 56, 57, 140, 146, 164, 176, 206, 222
ginseng 108, 194
glucose 40, 52, 61, 130, 216-17, 219, 220, 225, 226, 227, 229-30
glucosinolates 140
glutathione 203
gluten 60, 202
glycaemic index foods, low (GI) 40, 52, 109, 122, 102, 122, 202, 220, 227, 228, 229
glycogen 219
GPs and gynaecologists 4, 6, 24-7, 28, 35, 79, 80, 126, 160, 193, 198, 206
green tea/green tea extract 106, 140, 143, 144, 147, 164, 175, 176, 179, 191, 222, 228
gut bacteria 36, 39, 53, 55, 141
gut function/health 24, 36-7, 43, 53, 55, 56, 62, 111, 123, 130, 139, 140, 200

H

haem iron 126
hair, facial and body 93, 172, 178, 208-9
hair, thinning 93, 94, 122, 172, 178-9, 208
hay fever 136
HDL cholesterol 95, 198, 209
headaches/migraines 19, 32, 91, 122, 145-6
heart health 25, 73

herbal teas 41, 56, 106, 130, 143, 175, 209
  see also under Recipes, PCM
    Hormone Balance
herbs and herbal remedies 27, 56-8, 62,
  123, 127, 162, 179, 194, 196
  see also adaptogenic herbs
HIIT (high intensity interval training)
  73-4, 177, 180, 191, 224
hobbies 82
hormone tracking journal see journal,
  hormone tracking
hormones 15-16, 28-9
  balance 13, 19, 20-1, 36-7, 56,
    122, 123, 137, 139, 145, 146, 147,
    157, 159, 174 (see also Food
    Framework, PCM)
  production 22-3, 41, 42-3, 50, 52,
    62, 99-100, 101, 154-5, 159,
    172-3, 184, 185-6, 216
  used-up/old 37, 38, 63, 139, 140, 200
  see also androgens; gut health;
    liver function; oestrogen;
    progesterone; testosterone
hot flushes 5, 20, 22, 25, 82, 154, 159-60
HPA (hypothalamic-pituitary-adrenal)
  axis 23, 98-9, 101, 106, 143, 198, 200
HPO (hypothalamicpituitary-ovarian)
  axis 23, 100, 198
HPT (HP-thyroid) axis 198-9, 200
HRT xi, 5, 15-16, 24-7, 28-9, 38, 39, 48,
  121-2, 137, 147, 187-90, 199
Huberman, Professor Andrew 79
hunger and 'hanger' 40, 43, 49, 51, 52, 95,
  104, 111, 143, 161, 216, 217, 220, 226,
  229-30
hydration 49, 103, 110, 128, 160, 164, 195,
  208, 222
hypoglycaemia 226
hypothalamus 23, 159, 198, 200

I
immune system 36, 62, 110-11, 145
incontinence, urinary 26, 27
indigestion 94, 209
inflammation 36, 37, 53, 60, 62, 99, 103,
  127, 128, 139, 163, 164, 178, 186, 195,
  223, 228
insomnia see sleep
insulin 23, 49, 60, 109, 178, 186, 216-17,
  219, 230
  resistance and sensitivity 40, 61, 107,
    125, 129, 130, 144, 173-4, 177, 179,
    180, 202, 217-19, 220, 222-3,
    224-5, 226, 227, 228, 229
iodine 203, 206
iron 55, 126, 162, 179, 190, 204, 208
irritability ix, 2, 91, 93, 138, 143, 144
isoflavones 157, 160, 161
itchy skin/hives 136

J
joint pain 16, 42, 60, 90, 92, 109, 163-4
journal, hormone tracking 9-10

K
keto diets 122, 200, 202

L
L-theanine 85, 106, 127, 143
L-tyrosine 196
LDL cholesterol 95, 198, 209
'leaky gut' 36
legumes see beans and pulses
leptin 143, 180
levonorgestrel 122
libido 21, 27, 93, 172, 184-5, 188-9,
  193
lignans 141, 157, 178
lipids 209

liquorice supplements 63, 107, 108, 181, 194
liver function 21, 24, 37-8, 43, 53, 55, 82, 138, 139, 140-1, 142, 156, 157-8, 176-7, 200-1, 203, 209, 219
low mood 31, 90, 94, 108, 119, 127-8, 195-6
lumpy breasts 147
lymph system 82

M

maca 62, 193, 196
magnesium 62, 78, 101, 109, 110, 123, 128, 143, 144, 145, 146, 162, 165, 190, 208, 226-7, 228, 229
massages 83, 179
meal portion sizes 221-2
meat and poultry 50-1, 55, 60, 123, 127, 140, 176, 178, 180, 190, 191, 193, 194, 196, 203, 204, 209, 221, 227
meditation 65-7, 124, 128, 144, 158, 178, 196
melatonin 76, 128, 161, 227
memory issues 92, 107, 163, 194, 227
menopause 2, 3, 6, 28, 67, 82, 120, 154, 155, 157, 162, 163, 173, 187
menstrual cycle x, 16-20, 21, 58-9, 126, 137, 140, 146
    see also periods; PMS
mental clarity 145, 189, 216
    see also brain fog; cognitive issues
metabolism 23, 45, 107, 136, 144, 145, 161, 184, 198, 206, 207, 228
methylation 140
microbiome 36-7, 40, 45, 50, 61, 111, 141, 180
    see also gut health
mind body practices 67, 74, 125, 158, 159, 177, 178, 196

mindful eating 33, 110, 180, 225, 229
mindfulness-based cognitive therapy (MBCT) 67
mindfulness meditation 66-7, 144, 180, 196
Mirena coil 26, 121, 122
mitochondria 185, 186, 187, 190-1, 193
mobile phones 70-1, 77, 83
mobility exercises see flexibility, balance and mobility exercise
monounsaturated fats see fats, healthy
mood swings 90, 91, 93, 127, 144, 194
motherhood 2
motivation, lack of 21, 195-6
muscles 219
    building 42, 43, 49, 72-3, 172, 194, 224
    health 21, 27, 40, 90, 145
    loss 50, 72, 93, 161, 184, 194, 224
    repair 143
myrosinase 54

N

nausea 39, 60, 94
nervous system 62, 67, 145, 162
neurotransmitters 42-3, 50, 61, 118, 127, 128, 143, 145, 146, 161, 163, 180, 193, 195, 228
night sweats 91, 129
nipples, sore see breast tenderness and swelling
norepinephrine 143
nuts and seeds 43, 58-9, 102, 103, 109, 110, 123, 129, 140, 141, 144, 145, 146, 157, 159, 160, 162, 163, 164, 165, 176, 179, 190, 195, 203, 204, 208, 209, 221, 223-4, 226, 227, 228

O

oestrogen 15–16, 78, 160, 174
    detoxification 139, 140–1, 145, 156, 157–8
    endocrine disruptors 37, 80, 139, 156
    fluctuations 16–20, 25, 107, 136, 145, 154, 155, 174
    gut health 37, 50, 139, 140
    high levels/dominance 56, 119, 122, 136, 199
    causes 137–40
    diet/what to eat 140–1, 143–7
    lifestyle guidelines 141–2, 143–7
    symptoms and treatment 135–6, 143–7
    HRT 26, 28–9, 155, 189–90, 195
    joint pain 42, 163
    liver function 37–9, 138–41, 145, 157–8
    low levels/deficiency 59, 76, 80, 154–5, 195, 218
    causes 155–6
    diet/what to eat 157–8, 160–6
    lifestyle guide 158–66
    symptoms and treatment 153–4, 159–66
    phytoestrogen foods 56, 156, 157, 160
    production 21–3, 41, 99–100, 137, 154–5, 159, 172, 184, 186, 216
    seed cycling 59
    see also progesterone; testosterone
oestrogen dominance 32
olive oil 52, 53, 103, 176, 157, 191, 222, 228
omega-3 fatty acids 50, 62, 107, 109, 127, 147, 157, 160, 163, 164, 179, 204, 228
orthostatic hypotension 108
osteopenia/osteoporosis 8, 25, 92, 165

ovaries 20, 41, 99, 154, 155, 156, 173, 174, 185, 186, 187, 190, 191
overwhelmed, feeling 41, 108, 143
ovulation 16–17, 18, 21, 31, 119, 120, 137, 138, 146, 199
oxidative stress 140, 163, 176, 194, 222

P

palpitations ix, 4–5, 92, 118
pancreas 216–17, 219, 223, 224
pelvic floor exercises 193
peri grey zone 4–5
periods
    changes 5, 16, 25, 48, 90, 174
    heavy bleeding 126–7, 146, 162
    painful 47, 48, 91, 146
phosphatidylcholine 190, 228
phytoestrogen foods 37, 56, 63, 156, 160, 176, 178
Pippa Campbell Method (PCM), origins and outline 5–12, 37
pituitary gland 23, 199
plant sterols and stanols 210
plastics 37, 81, 139, 158, 192, 205, 225
PMS (pre-menstrual syndrome) x, 2, 19, 31, 32, 91, 126, 138, 144–5
    see also periods
polycystic ovarian syndrome (PCOS) 137, 173, 174
polyphenols 53, 55
poo *see* bowel movements; stools
potassium 78, 109, 130
prebiotic foods 37, 55, 63, 141
pregnenolone/'grandmother hormone' 21, 99–100, 186
probiotic foods 37, 141, 207, 208
probiotic supplements 62
processed food 60, 102, 209
progesterone 15–16, 61, 160

fluctuations 16–20, 25, 121, 144, 174
HRT 26, 121–2
liver function 37, 38
low progesterone 137, 199
diet/what to eat 122–3, 126–30
four reasons for 120–1
lifestyle guidelines 124–5, 126–30
low egg store 120
low thyroid function 120
stress 120
symptoms and treatment 90–1, 117–19, 126–30
palpitations 4–5
production 22–3, 99–100, 101, 119, 120, 122–3, 216
seed cycling 59
progestins 121–2
protein 33, 38, 40, 42, 49, 50–1, 102, 107, 108, 110, 123, 143, 161, 175, 180, 190, 194, 202, 208, 220, 221, 223, 226
HBV 221, 227
plant-based sources 51, 123
powder 51, 221, 223
puberty 17, 136, 173

R

real-life experiences
Amanda's story – oestrogen deficiency 167–70
author's experience ix–xi, 4, 69–71
Haley's story – perimenopause symptoms 84–6
Jane's story – adrenal dysfunction 112–16
Julie's story – oestrogen dominance 148–51
Nicky's story – perimenopause symptoms 31–3
Sally's story – blood sugar dysregulation 231–3
Shirley's story – low thyroid function 211–14
Yasmin's story – low progesterone 131–3
Recipes, PCM Hormone Balance 12, 235
Breakfast
chocolate orange tofu bowl 237
DIY breakfast formula 250
flaxseed bread 239–40
flaxseed porridge with apple and coconut 241
French toast 242
go-to breakfast protein shake 238
grain-free granola 243
homemade baked beans 244
protein pancakes 245
seeded red lentil rolls 246
shiitake mushrooms and spinach on toast 247
spinach and pepper egg muffins 248
stewed apples with yoghurt and almonds 249
Cakes and Puddings 303
apricot seeded flapjacks 303–4
avocado lime cheesecake 305
carrot cake muffins 306–7
chocolate and hazelnut cookies 308
chocolate and walnut brownies 309
chocolate cheesecake 310–11
lemon drizzle cake 312
millionaire shortcake 313
raspberry and blueberry almond cake 314
seed crusted banana bread 315
Dinner
beef bolognese 266–7
chargrilled pork satay salad 281–2
chicken fajitas with chickpea

tortillas and sweet pepper chilli 268–9
chicken noodle soup 270
coconut chicken noodles 271
'fakeaway' curry with coconut rice 272–3
lemon and herb chicken casserole 277
lime chicken thighs with super green cauliflower rice 278–9
mackerel and watermelon noodle salad 280
monkfish curry 275–6
pine nut crusted salmon and lentils 283–4
roasted butternut squash dhal 274
roasted cauliflower and quinoa salad with Romesco sauce 285–6
roasted vegetable pasta 287
sardine fish cakes 288–9
sea bass and samphire salad 290
turkey burgers with tzatziki 290
vegetable chilli with guacamole 292
Lunch 251
beetroot hummus 251
Caesar salad 252–3
carrot and lentil soup 254
celeriac soup with toasted walnuts and crispy sage 255–6
crispy artichoke and white bean salad 257
fajita bowls with cauliflower rice 258–9
prawn lettuce wraps 260
raw carrot salad 261
salmon and broccoli salad 262
seeded crackers 263
spiced root vegetable soup 264–5
Sauces and Dressings
everyday dressing 301
lemon gremolata 301
miso tahini dressing 302
pumpkin seed pesto 302
Side Dishes 293
balsamic braised red cabbage 297
Brussel sprout slaw 295
cayenne sauerkraut 293–4
'cheesy' cauliflower mash 296
lemon and garlic broccoli 299
sauteed kale with garlic and chilli 298
vegetable boulangère 300
Teas
acid reflux tea 318
cold remedy tea 318
liver support tea 317
Pippa's sleepy witches' brew 316
stress and anxiety support tea 317
see also Food Framework, PCM
red meat *see* meat and poultry
relationships *see* family and friends; support network, social
relaxation/rest 62, 65–6, 83, 105, 161, 162
    anti-stress toolkit 66–71, 104, 107, 124, 141, 143, 158, 177, 179, 192, 206, 224
    calming suggestions 68–9, 83
    morning and evening rituals 69–71
resistant starch, dietary 220–1
'rest or digest' mode 67, 98
restless leg syndrome 78, 227
rhodiola rosea 106, 107, 108, 145, 194
rituals, morning and evening 69–71, 128

S

sadness/tearfulness 16, 90, 122, 127
safety and HRT 25–6
saffron 127

salt balance 110
salt/salty food 90, 109, 130, 147
saunas/hot baths 81, 109, 145
saw palmetto extract 178, 179
screen time 77, 83, 104
seed cycling 58-9, 126, 129
seeds and nuts see nuts and seeds
selenium 110, 203, 206, 208, 210, 220
serotonin 42, 50, 61, 76, 127, 128, 143, 145, 161, 162, 180, 193, 195, 227
sex hormones 22-3, 41, 99-100, 102, 198
    see also oestrogen; progesterone; testosterone
sex/sex drive 21, 27, 93, 94, 172, 184-5, 188-9, 193
SHBG (sex hormone-binding globulin) 172, 174, 175, 176
short chain fatty acids 180
shortness of breath 126
skin colour and vitamin D 165-6
skin health 56, 82, 92, 93, 122, 136, 160, 172, 178
sleep 61, 65, 75-9, 82, 83, 94, 122, 141, 159, 162, 177
    adrenal dysfunction 101-2, 104-5, 111
    androgen deficiency 187, 192, 195
    blood sugar dysregulation 220, 223, 227, 230
    lack of/disturbance 2, 16, 40, 72, 91, 92, 95, 101-2, 128, 161-2, 206
    low thyroid function 206
    progesterone drops 118-19, 122, 125, 128
sleep apnoea 78-9, 206, 227
smoking 165, 225
snoring 78-9, 206, 227
social isolation 105
sodium 78, 109, 130, 147

soy products 157, 160, 161, 176, 191, 204
spearmint tea 175
spices 56, 57-8, 140, 146, 161, 164, 176, 207, 209, 222
SSRI antidepressants 162, 227
stamina 143, 145
starch, dietary 221
stimulants see caffeine; coffee; sugary foods
stools 39, 39, 94, 138
tests 5, 169
strength-training/resistance exercise 72-3, 125, 130, 144, 164, 165, 177, 194, 205, 224, 229
stress 2, 40, 42, 62, 63, 82, 90
    adrenal dysfunction 98-102, 103, 107
    androgen deficiency 184, 186-7, 195
    blood sugar dysregulation 219, 220, 224, 226
    hormones 18-19, 22, 23, 37, 41, 65, 98-9, 100-2, 119, 120, 155-6, 162, 186, 198 (see also adrenaline; cortisol)
    low progesterone 120
    low thyroid function 200, 206, 208, 210
    management 41, 56, 82, 107, 124, 125, 144, 145, 146-7, 158, 178, 226
    oestrogen deficiency 155-6, 158
    oestrogen dominance 141-2
    system 5, 22, 23, 45
sugars 129, 143, 221, 222
sugary foods 32, 40, 51, 60-1, 90, 95, 101, 102, 110, 129, 130, 144, 216, 219, 224, 229
sulforaphane 54
superficial dyspareunia 26

supplements, dietary 61–2
   adrenal dysfunction 106–11
   androgen deficiency 193–6
   and androgen dominance 178–81
   blood sugar dysregulation 226–7
   low progesterone 126–30
   low thyroid function 206–10
   and oestrogen deficiency 160–6
   and oestrogen dominance 143–7
   recommended for vegans and vegetarians 180, 193, 204
support networks, social 82, 105, 158
surgical menopause 67, 155
sweating and detox 81
sweet foods *see* sugary food
swimming 125, 205
symptom solving, perimenopause *see* adrenal dysfunction; androgen deficiency; androgen dominance; blood sugar dysregulation; low thyroid function; oestrogen deficiency; oestrogen dominance; progesterone drop

T

T3 and T4 thyroid hormones 199, 200–1, 202–3
talking therapy 82, 142
taurine 146
temperature, body 78, 94, 129, 136, 159, 207
testosterone 21, 27, 37, 38, 41, 78, 100, 154, 160, 172, 173, 174, 175, 176, 177, 180, 181, 184–6, 187–90, 191–6
therapy 82, 142, 143, 158, 193, 193
thinning hair 93, 94
thyroid-disrupting chemicals 205
thyroid function, low 23, 39, 94–5, 120, 145, 162, 198–9
   causes 200–1
   diet/what to eat 202–4, 206–10
   lifestyle guidelines 204–10
   symptoms and treatment 94–5, 197–8, 206–10
thyroid hormones 198–201, 206
tiredness 2, 33, 71–2, 89, 91, 99, 126, 206, 226
tofu and tempeh 51, 157, 165, 221
toxic relationships 82
trans fats 209
transcendental meditation 67
tribulus terrestrix 193
tryptophan 77, 127, 180, 227
TSH (thyroid stimulating hormone) 198, 199, 201
turmeric 56, 103, 109, 146, 147, 164, 176, 178, 194, 203, 206
type 2 diabetes 40, 218, 219

U

underweight, being 165, 218–19
urinary incontinence 26, 27
urinary tract infections (UTIs) 94, 160
uterine cancer 26
uterus 126, 146

V

vaginal dryness/atrophy 26, 94, 160–1, 188, 195
valerian 162
vegans and vegetarian 43, 55, 126–7, 194, 203, 204
vegetables 32, 33, 42, 53–4, 81, 102, 108, 157, 202, 207, 209, 220, 221, 228
   bitter 55, 141
   broccoli sprouts 142
   cruciferous 39, 42, 47, 54, 63, 140, 158, 176, 203

green leafy 55, 103, 126–7, 140, 143, 144, 146, 162, 163, 164, 165, 178, 123, 196, 208, 226
starchy 52
sulphur rich 54
visceral fat 179, 219, 228
vitamins and minerals 53, 103
    B-complex vitamins 36, 38, 39, 62, 77, 101, 103, 106, 107, 108, 109, 120, 123, 126, 145, 146, 158, 162, 180, 191, 192, 204, 226
    calcium 55, 165, 166
    chromium 107, 110, 130, 161, 180, 207, 220, 226, 228, 229
    iodine 203, 206
    iron 55, 126, 162, 179, 190, 204, 208
    magnesium 62, 78, 101, 109, 123, 128, 145, 146, 162, 190, 208, 226–7, 228, 229
    potassium 78, 109, 130
    selenium 110, 203, 206, 208, 210, 220
    sodium 78, 109, 130
    vitamin A 52, 200, 201, 204, 223
    vitamin C 101, 103, 110, 126–7
    vitamin D 52, 62, 77, 111, 165–6, 191, 200, 201, 203, 208
    vitamin E 52, 110, 147, 161, 176, 195, 200, 201
    vitamin K and K2 36, 52, 165, 166, 200, 201
    zinc 50, 101, 110, 120, 123, 145, 178, 190, 203, 206, 208
vitex agnus castus 126, 129

W

water consumption 49, 81, 103, 108, 111, 160, 195, 205, 222, 225
water/fluid retention 122, 147
weight/bodyweight exercises 42, 191, 194
weight gain 2, 24, 40, 90, 91, 92, 93, 95, 107, 129–30, 137, 143–4, 161, 164, 172, 179–80, 184, 186, 207, 218–19, 228–9
weight loss 202, 205, 228
weight training *see* strength-training/resistance exercise
white peony 181
whole grains 37, 52, 102, 108, 157, 162, 165, 207, 220, 226, 228
wind 49–50
womb lining 16–17, 26, 119, 121, 136

X

xenoestrogens 37, 38, 80, 138–9, 142, 158, 192

Y

yoga 67, 74, 125, 158, 159, 177, 178, 196, 205

Z

zinc 50, 101, 110, 120, 123, 145, 178, 190, 193, 203, 206, 208

Acknowledgements

First of all, I'd like to thank the thousands of incredible women I've had the privilege of working with over the years, both in my clinic and through my membership. You've taught me so much, and it's through our shared experiences that I've truly come to understand the struggles women face with their health. Without the insights gained from working closely with all of you, I wouldn't have been able to grasp the full picture of what's really going on with women's hormones, how their bodies work, and, most importantly, how to resolve these issues.

I would like to say a huge thank you to my amazing team of practitioners. Your expertise and constant support at the clinic have been absolutely essential in helping so many women improve their health and hormones, and I'm beyond grateful. Kate Leigh-Wood, Claire Dilliway and Lu Mieville – your passion and dedication are at the heart of everything we do, and honestly, I couldn't have done this without you.

A special thank you to Jo, my incredible clinic manager and right-hand woman. You keep the whole place running like clockwork, from working with our practitioners and clients to handling all the testing with the labs. Your eye for detail is what makes everything work so smoothly.

To Holly Rutter, my head of marketing – your insight and understanding of what our clients need has been invaluable. I've loved brainstorming with you, and your fresh ideas have been key to helping us grow and reach even more women. Thank you for always being so creative and on point!

I'm also super grateful to Mandy Madden, who's been brilliant as our members manager in the Female Food Club, and to Bethany Davies, our tech wizard behind the scenes. Bethany, you keep everything running without a hitch, and we'd be lost without you.

To Becca Barr, my wonderful agent, and the whole team at Bonnier – thank you for your guidance and belief in this project. A special shoutout to Brigid Moss and Dr. Christina O'Brien for your invaluable work in making this book a reality.

Of course, a huge thank you to my lovely children, Poppy and Josh, for filling my life with love and allowing me to love you back. And to my husband, thank you for always being by my side with your endless support and advice – I couldn't have done this without you. And to my wonderful parents, thank you for your constant love and encouragement. I'm so lucky to have had you supporting me from the start. My family support has enabled me to follow my passion in the world of female health.

This book wouldn't exist without the hard work and passion of so many people, and I'm truly grateful to each and every one of you.